For the Common Good

For the Common Good

Essays of Harold Lewis

Edited by

Michael Reisch

Routledge
Taylor & Francis Group
LONDON AND NEW YORK

For the Common Good

Essays of Harold Lewis

Edited by

Michael Reisch

Routledge
Taylor & Francis Group
LONDON AND NEW YORK

First published 2003 by
Brunner-Routledge

Published 2014 by Routledge
2 Park Square, Milton Park, Abingdon, Oxfordshire OX14 4RN
711 Third Avenue, New York, NY 10017

Routledge is an imprint of the Taylor & Francis Group, an informa business

First issued in paperback 2014

Library of Congress Cataloging-in-Publication Data

Lewis, Harold.
For the common good : essays of Harold Lewis / edited by Michael Reisch.
p. cm.
Includes bibliographical references and index.
ISBN 978-0-415-93549-4 (hbk)
ISBN 978-0-415-86097-0 (pbk)
1. Social service. 2. Social work education. I. Reisch, Michael, 1948–
II. Title.
HV40 .L475 2002
361 .3—dc21

2002151909

Contents

Acknowledgments

The publication of this book would not have been possible without the assistance of numerous people and organizations. The late Samuel "Buddy" Silberman, a long-time colleague and friend of Dr. Lewis, originally conceived of the project and, through the Silberman Foundation, provided an initial grant for this work. Thanks go to the entire Silberman family, particularly Dr. Jayne Silberman, and to Lori Slutsky of the New York Community Trust for their ongoing support.

Dr. Lewis's wife, Celia, helped compile his many papers and made several important suggestions about the book's structure and focus. I appreciate her graciousness and encouragement throughout this project. The staff of the Evelyn Butler Archive at the University of Pennsylvania Library helped track down several previously unpublished works. At the University of Pennsylvania School of Social Work, Dr. Ursula Bischoff was an invaluable research assistant and Laurie McAdams and Janet Heuman were indefatigable in their preparation of the first draft of the manuscript. At the University of Michigan School of Social Work, I am grateful for the technical assistance of Renee Heath, Diane Devlin, and Roxanne Loy in preparing the final manuscript. I am also grateful for the support and assistance of Emily Epstein, my editor at Brunner-Routledge, and Erin Herlihy, my production editor. All errors and deficiencies in the final manuscript are mine alone.

I had two motives in undertaking this project. One was my belief that Dr. Lewis is an original thinker whose ideas are of great potential value to current and future generations of social work practitioners and scholars. His work serves as a vital link between the social work pioneers of the early and mid-twentieth century and those of the twenty-first century. It is important for today's students to know that the issues that inspire them and the concepts that guide them have deep and strong roots in the profession. On a personal level, this book is my way of saying "thank you," and paying a small but lasting tribute to Dr. Lewis, who is and was the only mentor I have ever had.

Foreword

When I became the 10th President of Hunter College in 1980, Harold Lewis had been Dean of the School of Social Work for ten years, and the School was flourishing under his leadership. Dr. Lewis had recruited a number of new faculty, who joined that already stellar group of social workers who had come to the School from health and social service agencies and institutions, other universities, and government. In those years, he had also established himself as a leader in the College. During the summer before I took office, my predecessor as President, Jacqueline G. Wexler, generously gave me briefings about the College. She sang the praises of Dean Lewis, whom she described as one of the most brilliant, erudite, articulate, ethical, and hard-working people she had ever known. "But, my," President Wexler added, "he does talk fast!"

And later one of his colleagues who had gone to graduate school with him told me that the distinguished Professor Marian Hathway of the University of Pittsburgh School of Social Work, one of Dr. Lewis's most admired mentors, had told him when he was a second year student that he would have to learn to speak more slowly. Other people, Professor Hathway said, could not follow the rapidity of his words (or the complexity, sometimes, of his thinking), and if he were to become the intellectual leader of his profession, as Professor Hathway and others predicted, he would need to slow down and take the pace of others into consideration. Not everyone, Professor Hathway told Harold Lewis, was from Brooklyn as he was, and not everyone had a Brooklyn accent. Moreover, she added, not everyone thought and talked as fast as he did.

At Hunter, the School of Social Work, with Dr. Lewis as Dean and with the support of the philanthropist Samuel J. Silberman (Buddy to all of us who counted him as a friend), became a center of excellence in the College, the profession, New York City, the nation, and the international community. Dean Lewis encouraged faculty to do research, write, and take leadership in professional, social action, and civic organizations. The faculty was a diverse one, representing the various social work methods, fields of practice, and areas of expertise. Faculty meetings were often the forum for lively discussions of issues facing the profession, and there were consequential differences among the faculty. Never, however, in the years of my tenure as President of Hunter, did those differences become matters of personality or ideology: not with Harold Lewis, opinionated and ideological as he could be, as Dean and intellectual leader. He valued his colleagues, and he listened to what they had to say. How he loved good, substantive discussions! It was a golden time at Hunter and in the School during Dr. Lewis's twenty years as Dean.

This volume, so respectfully and intelligently edited by Professor Michael Reisch, PhD, a Hunter MSW, and now of the faculty of the University of Michigan, is a collection of Dr. Lewis's papers written between the years 1975 and 1991. Wisely, I think, Dr. Reisch organized the book by subject matter, rather than chronologically. Dr. Lewis's respect for social work practice and practitioners is manifest throughout the book, as is his lifelong preoccupation with the values and ethics that undergird the profession and inform the quotidian practice of social workers. The final section on social work education is a *must read* for classroom and field faculty in every school of social work in the nation. In particular, I recommend to the readers of this volume, "Teacher's Style and the Use of Professional Self in Social Work Education" (1991) and "Some Thoughts on My 40 Years in Social Work Education" (November, 1989).

In Chapter 2 in this volume, entitled, "The Cause in Function" (Winter, 1977), Dr. Lewis mounted an argument calling into question the formulation "Cause and Function," propounded by Porter Lee in his Presidential Address at the 1929 National Conference of Social Work. The distinction between Lewis's Cause *in* Function, and Lee's Cause *and* Function is an important one, but what interested me was Lee's belief that ". . . the dynamic leader of the cause and the efficient executive in charge of the function . . . do not often appear at their best within one temperament." And Lewis adds, "Thus, while he (Lee) saw the need for both qualities, he doubted the possibility of both being in one person." I believe Harold Lewis was himself a magnificent example of the dynamic leader of the cause and the efficient executive in charge of the function in one person. He was passionate and dedicated in his struggle for the betterment of the human condition, and at the same time he was a first-rate dean and intellectual leader.

This volume is also a fitting tribute to the memory of Buddy Silberman, the extraordinary benefactor of the Hunter College School of Social Work. Hunter was lucky to have a supporter whose sole interest was quality education and opportunity. The continuing support for quality of his widow, Lois, and daughter, Dr. Jayne Silberman, has made publication of this volume possible. Dr. Michael Reisch's editing of Dean Lewis's papers is a perfect reflection of the man. Most of all, I want to salute my friend and colleague, Harold Lewis, whose life and intellectual contributions were humane, ethical, and brilliant.

Donna E. Shalala, PhD
Professor of Political Science
and President of the University of Miami

Editor's Introduction

Harold Lewis's writings and career reveal a great deal about the changes that have occurred in the social work profession during the past half century. The distance between the post-World War II optimism that inspired Charlotte Towle's *Common Human Needs* and the devolution, privatization, and budget cutbacks that shape the field today appears enormous. To most contemporary students and practitioners, the War on Poverty of the 1960s, let alone the New Deal, is ancient history. While the profession's rhetoric regarding social justice has become more explicit, the pursuit of social justice through social policies and social activism seem like mist-shrouded memory of a distant past. In our increasingly ahistorical culture, the political and ideological forces that shaped the profession's development are rarely acknowledged.

Dr. Lewis not only wrote about these changes, he was shaped by and deeply involved in the struggles that occurred during his fifty year career. He was not a dispassionate observer but a participant-researcher in the best sense of the term.

His frequent use of the metaphor of drama in his essays is apt, because he was both actor and critic of the dramas—political and professional—of his life and times.

Like many men of his generation, Dr. Lewis did not start out to become a social worker. Upon graduation from Brooklyn College in 1941 he worked as a research analyst for the federal government. He served in U.S. Army intelligence in India during World War II, where his experiences influenced his decision to enter the field of social work. The things he saw and heard in India left an indelible impression on him throughout his career.

After working as a caseworker in New York City, he earned his MSW from the University of Pittsburgh in 1948, majoring in group work and community organization. Here he studied with distinguished social work scholars and activists such as Marion Hathway and Grace Marcus and worked on behalf of nuclear disarmament. From 1948 to 1950, he served as Research Director of United Community Services in Omaha, Nebraska before taking a position on the faculty at the University of Connecticut School of Social Work. In 1953, at the height of the McCarthy era, Lewis was forced to resign from the University because of his political activism, despite the courageous support of the School's Dean, Harleigh Trecker. He then took a position as Research Secretary of the Council of Community Services in Providence, Rhode Island.

Lewis received his DSW in 1959 from the University of Pennsylvania and, in the same year, joined the Penn faculty as Chair of its Research Sequence—a position he held for over ten years. He became Dean of Hunter College School of Social Work in 1970, where he remained until his retirement in 1990. As Dean, Lewis built Hunter into one of the premier schools of social work in the United States, while maintaining his distinguished record of scholarship and community service.

In 1969–1970, Dr. Lewis became the first social worker to be appointed a fellow at the Center for the Advanced Study of the Behavioral and Social Sciences in Palo Alto, California. Here he met the philosophers John Rawls and Amelie Rorty, whose ideas influenced his writings for the next twenty years. In the 1970s, Lewis was the first social work researcher asked to serve on proposal review panels by the National Institute of Mental Health. He also held leadership positions in virtually every major social welfare organization in the United States.

In 1979, Lewis received the Distinguished Alumni Award from both the University of Pittsburgh and the University of Pennsylvania. In 1985, he received an honorary doctorate from the University of Pennsylvania on the occasion of the 75th anniversary of the founding of the Penn School of Social Work and, in 1994, he received the Council on Social Work Education's Distinguished Lifetime Achievement Award. In 2000, he received an honorary doctorate from Hunter College of the City University of New York, which had given him the President's Medal for Excellence upon his retirement.

It is not surprising that few contemporary social worker possess a similar range of practice experience or scholarly interests. The structure of education and practice today strongly discourages a career track like the one Lewis followed. At the same time, increased academic specialization and the priority given to methodological rigor over substantive breadth in most universities preclude the development of social work intellectuals like Lewis and his teachers.

Yet, Dr. Lewis's work belies several contemporary myths about practice and scholarship. His essays are enriched, not diminished, by the breadth of his experience. The case examples he draws upon from the United States and abroad—from child welfare settings to community organization to non-profit management to social planning and research—reflect a deep understanding and appreciation of the intricacies of practice. As a trained researcher and statistician, he brought to his writing an in-depth knowledge of the significance of method, without losing sight of the importance of context. His familiarity with philosophy, contemporary research in the natural and physical sciences, mathematics, history, and the arts enabled him to discuss complex ideas in innovative ways and provide new perspectives on oft-discussed concepts. His application of scholarship from other fields demonstrates how cross-disciplinary thinking can occur in a manner that expands, rather than contracts, the horizons of social work. Dr. Lewis's ongoing commitment to and involvement in social justice causes challenges the false dichotomies that often separate academics from activism, professionals from politics. Finally, his frequent use of humor and delight in storytelling demonstrate that intellectual rigor need not be arid and that the love of ideas and the love of people are complementary sentiments.

In a career spanning over fifty years, Dr. Lewis published and presented widely in the fields of child welfare, social welfare administration, social work values and ethics, and the epistemology of social work practice. His book, *The Intellectual Base of Social Work Practice* (Haworth Press, 1982) and many of his articles are considered classics in the field and are still cited regularly in the United States and abroad, attesting to their ongoing currency. Long before the term "empowerment" was popularized in the social work literature, Dr. Lewis wrote of the "client's interest" and the "cause in function." Long before treatises on the ethical dimensions of practice were published in social work journals, he wrote about the value dilemmas of practice, research, and education. Long before the political legacy of the social work profession was "rediscovered," he was a scholar-activist who promoted the causes of peace, social justice, and human dignity, and mentored dozens of younger social work students and educators to follow a similar path. His life and work are a testimony to the most cherished characteristics of the social work profession and a vital link between the profession's past and future.

Part I

Essays on Social Work Practice and Policy

Editor's Introduction

During the last quarter of the twentieth century, social welfare and social work in the United States underwent profound transformations. Support for government intervention on behalf of vulnerable populations waned and attacks on the concept of entitlement culminated in 1996 legislation that "ended welfare as we know it." The advent of managed care jeopardized the ability of millions to access quality health and mental health services, and undermined the role of social work practitioners in both public and private agencies. Ironically, in this era of cutback, retrenchment, and devolution, social workers introduced such concepts as empowerment, multiculturalism, and a "strengths perspective" into the conceptual frameworks of their practice.

The chapters in this section, written between 1975 and 1991, confront the explicit and implicit dilemmas created by these contradictory trends. Against the backdrop of national developments (Watergate, Reaganomics, computerization) and international events (the end of the War in Southeast Asia, the Chilean coup, civil war in Central America), Lewis both anticipates and reflects many of the major theoretical and practice trends that shaped U.S. social work in the late twentieth century. These range from the influence of the Latin American conscientization movement to the impact of chaos theory and postmodernism. Constantly seeking to link past, present, and future, Lewis draws upon his rich practice experience, and his personal contacts with such social work "giants" as Bertha Reynolds, Jessie Taft, Marion Hathway, and Kenneth Pray. In a sense, therefore, his work bridges what Andrews (1993) called the social workers of "The Second Generation" with their professional grandchildren and great-grandchildren of the twenty-first century.

These chapters reflect several consistent themes. One is the importance of social workers overcoming the destructive tendency to frame issues in terms of dichotomies: for example, means/ends, cause/function, knowledge/values, individual/collective needs. A second is the importance of incorporating a social justice perspective into all aspects of practice. Having met John Rawls at the Center for the Advanced Study of the Behavioral and Social Sciences in 1969, Lewis was the first social work scholar to apply Rawls's work, *A Theory of Justice* (1971), to social work practice. A third theme, reflecting the influence of Rankian ideas about the will and Lewis's own history of political engagement, is the emphasis on action ("the doing"). A fourth is the use of analogical thinking as an essential tool of social work practice and research.

Finally, these chapters reveal not only the breadth of Lewis's vision, but also the range of influences on his thinking and his effective use of humor. He integrates concepts from mathematics, art, psychology, biology, and history with equal facility. Anticipating postmodern thinking, he makes good use of personal narratives to illustrate complex ideas. These qualities are, perhaps, best illustrated in his reformulation of practice as a "drama" rather than a problem-solving process.

Chapter 1

Social Work and the Common Good

In this essay, Lewis discusses the implications of the conflicts between self-determination and the common good, between the fear of dependency and society's failure to enable people to become independent. He concludes that social welfare is "a civilized response to the collective pursuit of . . . common goods."

How much is a person worth? Who is to judge? Do we credit self-sacrifice and debit dependency? Does self-reliance earn more brownie points than community mindedness? If we could add up each individual's worth, would the result be a measure of the value of his life?

Ask those who have to allocate a scarce resource, such as a transplantable kidney, how they choose the most worthy from among those who are waiting. Ask those who have been charged with the responsibility to cut basic life-supporting resources in a piety verging on bankruptcy how they decide which are the least essential services, and for which population. When inflation squeezes the slim budgets of the aged living on fixed incomes, and unemployment depresses the living standards of white collar and collar-less unskilled workers, which of these evils is the lesser and which is to be preferred? It might be reassuring to some to think that decisions in these matters are based on judgments of the comparable worth of persons affected. This rarely is the case.

When choices concerning the allocation of scarce resources are made, one infers that some lives are judged more precious than others. How do professions, committed to the belief that every life is precious, make choices that suggest that some lives are more precious than others? When a man condemned to death pleads to have the sentence implemented, thus exercising his right to self-determination, what about others to whom this man's life is precious? Have they no rights to be considered? The preciousness of even this tortured, criminal life is suddenly recognized through its connection with the lives of others. This man's death may, given our system of justice, hasten the death of others. Self-determination is not an unfettered right to be exercised without regard for its impact on the self-determining choices of others. Suddenly the cry "let me die" ceases to be a plea for one death and becomes a possible nail in the coffin of many. Even if this man's preferences

---

Keynote address, Minnesota State Welfare Conference, Minneapolis, March 1977.

prevailed and are given precedence over what many had decided would be for the common good, the choice is not an easy one. Clearly, we are compelled to a more critical appraisal of the meaning of the assumption that every life is precious.

Consider the juxtaposition of two goals of social policy and the alternatives they pose. The first asserts that the function of social welfare programs is to narrow the gap between the haves and have nots. While accepting the improbability of absolute equality in our present society, this view sees welfare programs as assisting the disadvantaged through reallocation of resources to achieve a standard of living closer to that of the advantaged. The second asserts that the goal of social policy is to help individuals and families achieve independence based on self-reliance, to "stand on their own two feet." This latter view sees welfare programs as serving to strengthen the capacity of those in need to meet their needs through their own efforts. Is it possible to support both these goals concurrently, and design programs congenial to their mutual achievement? Not only should such mutuality be possible, but in fact it should appear to be essential to success in meeting either goal. As a collectivity, we certainly would support a social order in which differentials that did exist did not detract from efforts to alleviate the disadvantages suffered by those in greatest need. We would expect that such an order would provide the greatest opportunity for self-reliance on the part of the membership in the collectivity, recognizing that individual self-help efforts contribute to the collective resource shared by all. But how do these two goals work out in practice?

If you seek to narrow the gap, given a finite resource, you must take from the haves and give to the have nots. Up to a point—assuring subsistence—one can get considerable agreement on this redistribution. But above the subsistence level there is little agreement on whose resources are to be reallocated, and if, in fact, such allocation is likely to promote the general welfare.

If you seek to promote self-reliance, given finite resources, you must decide on a level of assistance that enhances self-help without creating dependency. In the opinion of many, the only way to achieve self-reliance is to compel self-support for even minimal needs. Every measure taken beyond such Social Darwinian limits is viewed as bleeding-heart pampering, likely to defeat the need to promote independence.

It requires only that the reluctance to reallocate be joined to the fear of creating dependencies, to have policies proposed that would seek to achieve both goals by restricting all programs intended to do just that. We find those reluctant to reallocate and fearful of dependency justifying our doing as little as possible at a societal level to extend resources to deal with inequities and dependency needs. It is a peculiar twist of a moral stance that would achieve a social good by minimizing efforts on its behalf. The opposite view, that would use the tax structure and service allocation to narrow the gap, and that would promote self-reliance through client participation in efforts to maximize social resources for use on their own behalf, is in direct conflict with the former. As is common in value choices, the critical questions involve differences in means rather than ends, questions of ethics dealing with means rather than questions of values, dealing with ends.

It is not at all remarkable that people prefer health to illness, justice to unfair treatment, security to uncertain income, knowledge to ignorance, self-respect to indignity, aesthetic satisfaction to the unattractive. For each of us these preferences represent personal goods we would rather not do without. Because they are so central to our personal well-being, civil societies institutionalize systems to promote such goods. The health care, education, legal, economic, aesthetic, and religious institutions of our communities are intended to help each of us satisfy these basic human wants. Together they constitute a civilized response to the collective pursuit of these common goods. The scope of these collective efforts is a measure of our cultural achievement.

Difficulties arise when all persons do not have equal access to those collectively provided resources, some because of discriminatory restrictions and others because of personal limitations. Inevitably, self-help organizations develop among the deprived, to promote the availability of such resources to meet the particular needs of their members. Historically, this self-help tradition in human services has contributed to the consciousness raising efforts of have nots seeking to alter their own condition, to achieve reallocations on their own behalf. Success in such self-reliant efforts contributed to the hopes of many who would ordinarily be clients of programs to which they would have had to come as supplicants, seeking the help of others to deal with their own needs.

Obviously, self-help associations ". . . made up of persons who share a common problem and who band together to resolve the problem through their mutual efforts" combine, in an ideal way, reliance on one's own resources while seeking a more just reallocation of socially provided resources. Here, then, is an example of how both goals of social policy can exist in mutual support of each other. Such self-help associations have a long history, granting a definition that permits us to include among these associations those seeking to achieve for their members all the "common goods" through consciousness-raising, advocacy, and husbanding of personal knowledge for the collective well-being. The earliest charters of the national labor unions, the Knights of Labor, and the American Federation of Labor, reflect precisely this intention among workers joining together, seeking to deal with problems in managing personal income and family well-being. The ladies' auxiliaries associated with synagogues and churches, the fraternal associations, and related ethnic *landsman* societies, are all of this self-help variety, dating back to the earliest years in our nation's brief history. In recent times, the conscientization movement in South America viewed such consciousness-raising and self-help as central to the objectives of all educational and social service efforts. This same thrust is reflected by the press for client participation in programs intended to benefit them. In self-help efforts that seek to utilize the personal knowledge of those experiencing a common problem, be it stuttering, alcoholism, emotional upset, etc., one can recognize in areas of psychological, physical, and social functioning the same commitment to mutual support, sharing of experience, and expansion of resources as has been evident in all the self-help efforts identified.

This being the case, one would expect that those who have vociferously advocated minimal dependence on outside resources would applaud the growth of such self-help efforts. Unhappily, this is hardly our experience. In our nation's history unions have been fought, self-help associations have been starved for funds, and, in the recent takeover of Chile by the military junta, the conscientization movement in social welfare was an early target for repression. A key factor that accounts for such hostile responses is the fact that those in authority who may choose to help people in trouble, usually do not like them to make trouble about their trouble. The inevitable development of power to influence a policy and practice that accompanies self-help associations threatens the control of those who would contain the scope of reallocation efforts.

Professionals emerged within such self-help associations. They have become associated through invitation with self-help associations as experts or staff. They have joined as members to seek help in meeting a personal need. They have developed cooperative working relationships as participants in the network of community services that require interorganizational contacts and coordination. Resource allocation issues and conflicting views of what methods of helping are most effective have been sources of conflict between professionals and memberships of self-help groups. Overwhelmingly, professions seeking the same goals as such groups, find self-help efforts supportive and complementary to their own. The reason for this congeniality should be understood.

Let us consider an early period in the development of one profession—social work. In my research I found the term "social worker" first used in 1893, in the minutes of the Montefiore Ladies Auxiliary. The possibility of a professional social work service was probably first realized when workers, such as this friendly visitor, recognized the strengths residing in persons in need of help, and built service strategies on such strengths. The skill of what was to become a social work profession grew out of this understanding, although necessarily influenced by the organizational structures and administrative assignments such workers accepted as employed, bureaucratic functionaries. Promotion of self-reliance and support for the struggle to reallocate resources can evolve together as service goals in a framework that recognizes the strengths in those seeking help. These goals cannot live together where the focus is exclusively on the help-seekers' personal deficiencies and on maintaining their powerlessness to affect their own lives.

To any person in need of help, life is precious. There can be no justification in this person's view of a policy and attendant procedures that would suggest otherwise. Where he or she encounters what appears to be a challenge to this view, he or she might justifiably become suspicious. Suspicion breeds distrust, and without trust, only compulsion can sustain a helping relationship. Trust begins in mutual respect. Respect, in turn, builds on recognition of the strengths that earn it, and the life that deserves it. Focusing on deficiencies breeds disrespect and substitutes coercion in place of shared power and free choice.

When confronted with ethical dilemmas, both the professional and the self-help group must plan on their shared social purposes to arrive at mutually acceptable choices. In relation to the goals of reallocation of resources, or distributive justice, the professional and self-help group find proposals that minimize resource reallocation and sustain current inequities in conflict with their shared intentions. Moreover, they find less than convincing those calls for self-reliance, which substitute sermons on virtues and duties for increased access to the common goods. In short, in relation to both goals, people in need see such policies as unfair and those promoting them as less than trustworthy. They view the inevitable injustice of such policies as promoting the well-being of the advantaged at the expense of the disadvantaged and see this as unethical behavior. They are not mistaken. Cutbacks in service burden the poor most. Among day care eligibles, dependent and ill elderly, child care recipients, health care and education programs, inequities beget further inequities. It always seems that in our economy the poor and defenseless pay more. Clearly violated in these instances is the ethical imperative that advantages may be justified only when they raise the expectations and resources for the most disadvantaged.

But more is involved than the failure to adhere to an ethic of fairness in such inequitable decisions. These choices reflect the preferences of those in power.

These judgments suggest some lives are more precious than others. One may ask what criteria were used in arriving at these differentiating judgments. However disguised in their presentations, when such evaluations are made human lives are viewed as commodities that can be priced; and those judging have criteria that weight the social value of lives.

We come now to the critical questions faced by those who consciously must choose who shall share in the common goods when not all can. Are there virtues that can be measured, weighed, and used to select beneficiaries? Are there duties to be performed, and are some better prepared than others to perform them? Do they, who are best prepared, earn a higher priority to share in the common good? Who is to decide, and how should the decision be arrived at?

Here, I believe, the functions of the professional and that of the self-help group may differ. In making such decisions, one ought to use the best available knowledge to make the nature, scope, and likely impact of alternative choices clear. For example, if knowledge has demonstrated beyond a doubt that access cannot assure use, then access may be denied without judging the life involved as less precious.

When I arrived in India in 1944, I traveled across Bihar and Bengal by train. There was a tragic famine and cholera epidemic cutting down children and adults alike along the path of our tracks. At one station, a friend and I left our car, and approached a group of children—swollen stomachs, spindly arms and legs—obviously starving. We chose the child we thought most far gone, and sought to give her some food. The other children raised their voices in protest, causing us to seek out an English-speaking native who could translate for us. We then learned what the protest was all about. The child we sought to feed was too far gone to be fed—

she could no longer swallow. Our efforts would be wasted, whereas if we shared our food among those who still could swallow, we would be benefiting them. This happened thirty-two years ago, yet I recently recalled the experience in its full force as I considered problems in ethics and choice each of us must face.

In addition to knowing who could not use the resource, it would be important to establish who could use it, but who would cause irreparable damage to themselves and others in so doing. For example, should an atomic heart be produced before we have developed a shield that would control the damage of its radioactive byproduct? We should also seek to establish if available amounts of the goods would be insufficient to affect the need it was intended to meet. We could go further in a similar vein to suggest a first step in making a choice. Clearly, we ought to use knowledge to determine those for whom the choice would be meaningful, and those for whom it would be of no practical value, even if it gave the appearance of a fair and just procedure. When knowledge has assured us of a cohort of eligibles, all of whom could benefit from the resource, then I would concur with those who argue that none of the virtues, duties, or other idiosyncratic characteristics of members of the cohort ought to give them preference to the resource. The selection at this point should be in a random manner, approximating as closely as possible an equal probability for any to be chosen, and access then granted in the order in which selected. This procedure might have the added merit of sponsoring a widespread desire for more resources, and hopefully could press our national priorities in the direction of human service.

I would contrast this approach to equity in allocation of a scarce resource with a procedure now popular in the distribution of federal funds for welfare purposes. Perhaps a story out of the fourteenth century would illustrate this Nixon-initiated distribution mechanism. The story relates how the king of beggars, who accepted charity only when offered with respect for his dignity, was standing outside a house of worship frequented by the wealthiest members of the community. Close to a hundred hungry, crippled, ill, aged, orphaned beggars were also awaiting the end of services, when the emerging parishioners would distribute alms as they left to return home. The services ended, and the wealthiest of the wealthy was the first out. With obvious joy in what he was about, this philanthropist proceeded to draw from a large bag, handfuls of small packets of paper tied by string and threw them in all directions among the beggars.

Pandemonium broke loose, with the blind stumbling over the crippled, the aged struggling with children—cries of disappointment when a packet contained nothing—cries of joy when a gold piece was uncovered. The king of the beggars demanded of the philanthropist an explanation. What sort of charity was this that dehumanized the recipients by the manner of its distribution? How could he descend to so mean a level? The philanthropist responded in disbelief: Didn't the beggar know that this was the latest method of distributing resources? Hadn't he heard about it? It is called revenue sharing!

I would assume that more reliance for the knowledge base would be put on professional judgments than on lay judgments, although by no means would the experiential knowledge of the lay person be excluded. I would assume that more reliance for the ethical imperative to be operationalized would be placed on the professional person than on the lay person whose participation in self-help groups is based on the need for which this resource is intended. This is not primarily an argument for objectivity, because I believe those in need and those seeking to meet a need suffer differentially, but equally, from prejudices and personal preferences. Rather, this would avoid further burdening the person with the need by placing his or her own need in competition with the needs of others in like circumstances and asking that a choice be made that could involve self-denial. These role differentials, I believe, would be entirely acceptable providing a condition of trust prevailed between the professionals and self-help groups. That no such trust can be expected for those whose ethic favors distributive injustice is obvious and requires no further comment.

In summary, I have suggested that we live in times of critical need and inadequate resources. Our society, while recognizing the need for the common goods, does not assure access or allocation on a fair and just basis. Self-reliance and the collective well-being must go hand in hand as we seek to achieve an ethically sound and just distribution of these goods. Professional helpers and those engaged in self-help efforts have reason to work together to achieve this social goal because their origins are similar and their paths intertwine. They can jointly help us to a more civilized existence.

Chapter 2

The Cause in Function

This essay is the best example of Lewis's concern with ending the dualities that have plagued the social work profession since its inception. It is also one of the first essays in which he introduces the concept of analogic thinking and its application to social work practice.

Traditionally, social work literature addresses issues of purpose in practice from a narrow perspective. Purpose includes the outcomes desired from professional interventions, and the intentions that motivate the professional act. Thus, it would satisfy the practitioner to know that a goal, for example, social justice—would be realized if the intervention was to prove successful, and, concurrently, if evidence of progress toward that goal was present in specific objectives achieved as a result of particular acts. Omitted from this perspective is the reformist tradition that has always served to inspire, not merely motivate, the social vision of social work professionals. Complementing the concept of purpose, and in part compensating for the omission resulting from this narrow perspective, our literature has promoted the term "cause" as an umbrella concept under which the reform efforts of the profession and its practitioners have been subsumed.

From its earliest usage, "cause" has been linked to and contrasted with "function," in a dialectic whose contradictions are shaped by the interpretation of these polar opposites. "Cause" can include any socially significant ideal that social actions are intended to achieve. For example, adequate housing for low-income families; amendments to racial and sexual biases in the allocation of welfare resources; access to health care for all citizens; equity in access to higher education; full employment, etc., all represent causes to which, at one time or another, the profession has devoted some of its energies and financial resources. "Function," by way of contrast, refers to the sanctioned effort made by professional practitioners, to implement these hard won "causes" in the day-to-day provision of services.

Cause and function came to occupy an important niche in our professional literature when Porter Lee[1] used these concepts to argue for the view that sequenced social reform and social practice in a cyclical, recurring, and seemingly inevitable progression. Since Lee's arguments first appeared at the outset of the great depression of the 1930s, a number of authors have reviewed its assumptions

Originally published in the *Journal of the Otto Rank Association*, Winter 1977.

and modified its global claims. In the main, the inevitable in the proposed cycle, and the sequence anticipated of Cause and Function, have been modified, with the relationship of cause and function being defined as one of parallel development, with no assurance of "Cause" being realized through "Function." In the discussion that follows, a more critical view of the relationship of cause and function is proposed, the essence of which is captured in the phrase Cause *In* Function. This break with past formulations is deemed crucial to an appreciation of the ethical component in every act of practice, and the inseparability of means and ends. It is through such an integration of Cause *In* Function that a more encompassing view of purpose in practice can be realized.

Porter Lee, initially, described what he viewed as a normal social process, the move from a cause sought and won to a function that realized in practice the intentions contained in the cause. He contrasted the zeal that inspired a cause with the intellect that assured the success of the function. Nevertheless, his analysis of his own hypothesis compelled him to conclude that the time had come when the cause must be incorporated into the function. In those threatening days of 1929, he believed the profession must not respond to the challenges confronted it by going back to a day when social work was exclusively or predominantly a cause. He argued that we must meet (the challenge) with the sober recognition that it is and must be both cause and function. Finally, he noted his belief that "the dynamic leader of the cause and the efficient executive in charge of the function . . . do not often appear at their best within one temperament." Thus, while he saw the need for both qualities, he doubted the possibility of both being in one person.

There are several assumptions contained in this view that have not been substantiated by experience. The sequencing as suggested in the hypothesis "from cause to function" and the separation as suggested by "cause and function," obviously did not satisfy Lee either, hence his seeking biological and personality justifications for the social processes he sought to explain.

In a provocative recent essay, Robert Rosen,[2] a leading theoretical biologist, sought to answer a question which most of us accept as fact. Do we really need ends to justify the means? He contends . . . "that in some important sense we *need* to engage in these kinds of activities (i.e., politics, education, planning, economics, etc.) quite apart from attaining the goals we frame to justify them; and that we will go even more seriously astray if we do not recognize the real roots of our indulgence in these activities." Man, he believes ". . . has a biologically-rooted need to engage in complex activities, . . . and it is the activities themselves which are needful, not the ends which are supposed to be attained by them; these needs are the inessentialities and the byproducts." Finally, he concludes, "We need to extend this lesson to the whole of our experience; namely, that our happiness—in a real sense, the quality of our lives—lies in the doing and not in the done; in the doing is where our real goals lie. And these goals need require no rationalized ends to justify them."

While I am hardly equipped to affirm or deny Rosen's thesis, nor to accept the biological imperative it implies, it seems reasonable to assume that human activity is purposeful, and that experiencing the activity is one of its more significant purposes. There would appear to be ample evidence that thoughtful persons engage in intentional activities and are concerned to evolve satisfying procedures for achieving their ends. One need not attribute to purpose a motivating function, nor deny this function to a biological urge, to observe, as Rosen does, that much of the quality of life lies in the doing and not in the done.

Turning to the experience provided by our profession, one cannot help but wonder how ends and means, intentions and procedures, get expressed in professional helping activities. It is my contention that the Porter Lee hypothesis did not anticipate the Rosen hypothesis. It failed to appreciate the ends in means, the social purpose in individualized helping, and the cause embedded in function. But what is more disconcerting is the experience of the past decade during which divisive formulations that dichotomized the profession, such as practice versus social action, social versus individual change, etc., purchased the same inadequate understanding of the means–ends issue, freezing the cause–function dichotomy into curriculum and separating faculties into ideologically nonproductive contending camps. Far from contributing to responsible social change, failure to understand the unified character of action has permitted socially irresponsible perspectives on practice to survive.

The helper is the focus of my concern, and his or her experience in activating both cause and function in his or her practice will be explored for what it may add to our understanding. I am not here interested in the nature of the problem being addressed by the helper, whether it be a social policy issue, a troubled personality, or a financial deprivation. I believe that whatever the problem it is in the helper's activity that he or she confronts the issues posed by the Porter Lee hypothesis. It is in the activity that the evidence of cause in function will appear.

Reforms generally are won through struggle on the part of their beneficiaries, who engage in direct conflict with those who must yield some privilege to pay for the costs involved. Reforms, resulting as they must from contending interests, are never given for all time. They must constantly be renegotiated, they can never cease to be a cause for those who benefit from the resources they make available. I'm reminded of the Director of Catholic Charities in a city in the Midwest, who was presenting his agency's budget to the United Fund Budget Committee.[3] When asked if he has any useful measures whereby the effectiveness of his services might be evaluated, he listed some of those commonly cited, but hastened to add, that as a Catholic, he would deem his agency's services successful if they helped his community to a more Christian, caring, sharing way of life. Thus, for him, the offer of the resource was itself a major measure of success. As I understood his remarks, he argued that his church believed that the reformation of the human spirit, through charitable effort, was an ongoing cause, which his agency's services made possible. He could no more separate his cause from the agency function than Rank[4] could separate the will from the creative act.

The helper is always engaged in a political, economic, aesthetic, scientific, and self-realizing activity when he or she cooperates with a client in creating a service. When he or she arranges his or her own inner resources, as well as those provided by his or her agency, in some priority order, and allocates them on the basis of his or her preferences, he or she is engaging in a political act with serious implications for distributive justice. When he or she seeks the most efficient and effective utilization of these husbanded resources, he or she is engaging in a productive act with serious economic implications; when he or she disciplines his or her activity to reflect agency, professional and personal style, he or she is influencing the aesthetic quality of his or her service and the environment in which it occurs. When he or she informs his or her activity with what is known and understood, he or she both utilizes and provides information for improving on the science of human relationships, and when he or she engages his or her whole self in these activities, as Rosen would suggest, he or she more fully realizes this self, and enhances the possibilities available to him or her to achieve personal happiness. In brief, the helper imparts to his or her helping relationship a culturally enriched dimension that marks his or her activity as civilized. It is for this reason one can speak of our helping profession as a civilizing profession, because its practitioners cannot help but act in a civilizing manner if their efforts are to prove truly helpful.

The view of the helper as a civilizing agent is hardly justified if in fact his or her activities by plan or oversight fail to address each of these dimensions of a civilized culture. Whether, as Rosen argues, each of us engage in all these activities because of our biological needs, or as others may contend, we do so because we are urged on by intentions that we freely and willfully formulate, when we fail to see the wholeness of the act we ought not construe such failure as proof that it lacks such wholeness. When Porter Lee sequences cause and function, or separates them as cause and function, he in effect destroys the wholeness of the act in order to analyze it. This requires, as a minimum, that we consider not only propositions of the "if this . . . then that" variety, but also propositions that allow for time and place to be included in derived generalizations. These take the propositional form "from this through time to that," a form frequently employed by process-oriented theoreticians. I would add the need to consider propositions of the form "this is to this as that is to that," reasoning by analogy, if we are to manage meaningful units of action in our understanding of practice. Reasoning by analogy is the manner in which imagination enters practice, and is the most frequent source of creativity in practice.

I propose we recognize the *cause in function*, the *ends in means*, the unity of action. Further, that we recognize service as that which is created by the helping process, and the only real measure of the actualization of program and resource for social welfare purposes. That service be viewed in a dialectical fashion, as the evolving form and substance of the unity and conflict of cause in function, necessitates the constant addressing of both sides of this conflict if positive social change is to be achieved. I have argued that if the helper fulfills his or her civilizing function, he or she must approach his or her activity with an awareness of all its dimensions lest he or she fault his or her contribution through oversight and misunderstanding.

Chapter Notes

1. Porter Lee, Director of the New York School of Social Work (now Columbia University School of Social Work) was President of the National Conference of Social Work in 1929. This essay refers to his presidential address.

2. Robert Rosen (1970). *Dynamical system theory in biology.* New York: Wiley-Interscience.

3. Lewis is referring here to his experiences in Omaha, Nebraska, in the late 1940s.

4. Otto Rank's ideas strongly influenced the development of the Functional School at the University of Pennsylvania.

Chapter 3

The Client's Interest

Unlike most works that focus on issues of power in social work practice, this essay addresses often overlooked conflicts of interest inherent in the complexity of practice and the professionalization process themselves.

The revised NASW *Code of Ethics* asserts the primacy of the client's interests and states that the social worker's primary responsibility is to clients. Basing this guideline on clients' interests, rather than clients' rights or worth, is helpful because interests are more likely to reflect competing claims influenced by societal as well as personal needs and desires. But clients' interests may conflict with those of workers, agencies, and the community, and choices among interests are inevitable. Clearly, while responsibilities may be allocated to promote interests, not all interests can be satisfied, and there may be circumstances that would commend attending to workers' or agencies' interests, in order to better discharge responsibilities to clients' interests.

Clients' interests are often difficult to identify. It is not always clear who is the client, particularly in social work practice that is not treatment focused. Nor is it a simple matter to decide, in relation to practice involving families, groups, and intergroups, which of the differing interests evidenced by participants in the helping situation are to be considered central and which peripheral. This essay suggests the need for a guiding principle to determine clients' interests, if adherence to the Code's ethical imperative is to be managed in everyday practice. It also suggests a possible approach to the adjudication of this and other imperatives included in the Code. The Code provides guidance for worker attitudes and behavior in seeking to adhere to the primacy of the clients' interests, noting what is to be encouraged or avoided in providing services to the client. It provides no guidance for determining what constitutes clients' interests.

WHAT CONSTITUTES AN INTEREST?

In their normal state, persons seeking help do not differ markedly from the general population in the personal interests they wish to satisfy. While individuals

Invitational lecture to Ethics Committee, New York University School of Medicine, January 31, 1980.

may differ in their ordering and intensity of interests, they do not differ in their desire to experience security, health, justice, knowledge, self-fulfillment, and aesthetic satisfactions. If, by the clients' interests, we mean these fundamental human needs and desires, it is obvious that any help offered clients is likely to be related to the advancement of one or more of these interests. Nor would it be remarkable if we were to find that clients themselves indicate their priority choices among those interests for which they seek help. In the usual situation, the choice of agency or the choice of program or the request for a particular service will, to a large degree, designate such clients' preferences.

The difficulty one has with this global formulation of clients' interests is that it clarifies very little of what constitutes the core problem for a worker seeking to act in a manner that gives primacy to such interests. The worker, too, shares these interests in common with the client. The agency and community usually have similar interests in mind in sponsoring the services they offer. Such a general perspective on interests does not clarify the difficulties the worker encounters in seeking to act in the clients' behalf. The need for a code provision based on the client's interests stem from the possibility that conflicting interests can arise, and that choices will have to be made in favor of one or another of the client's interests or the interests of others.

WHEN CLIENT AND WORKER PERCEPTIONS DIFFER

For example, the client's perception of the problem to be worked on, for which help is sought, may focus on a basic interest that the worker does not judge to be the central interest to be served. Confronted with this difference, workers may opt to accept the client's perception as the first order of business, on the grounds of the practice principle that commends the worker to "start where the client is." If they follow this option, the client's interests are, in fact, defined by the client and, in accepting them as a priority, workers would be giving primacy to them. But this may be a false positive if, in fact, workers have a different, more accurate, view of the client's needs more likely to further the client's interests.

Should workers choose to give primacy to their own definition of clients' needs, they must contend with another stumbling block to an objective appraisal of alternatives. Workers normally practice in relation to preconceived frameworks that are assumed to provide accurate and relevant guidelines for appraising clients' needs. Models of practice, with their peculiar theoretical underpinnings, direct the worker, telling him or her where to look, and what to look for. Inevitably, such directives screen in some observations and omit others. More important, they provide workers with preferred explanations of what they are observing, and give acceptable meanings to otherwise disparate events. The worker's definition of clients' needs thus must inevitably reflect the worker's preferences as well. In these circumstances it is difficult to determine whose preferences, the worker's or the client's, are being given primacy. Add to this problematic situation the concurrent influence of agency and community interests that often determine whether service will be rendered, and it is obvious that without some guiding principle for determining clients' interests the first requisite for acting on this ethical imperative will be absent.

INTERESTS DETERMINED IN PROCESS

In the service transaction, clients' interests are always in flux, as the clients' needs and desires change. For this reason, sound practice requires the continuous exploration of a client's interests for the duration of the worker–client contact. This characteristic feature of the helping process provides the most reliable alternative for determining clients' interests. Clients' interests are most accurately identified through the mutual efforts of worker and client, as both seek to establish the objectives and goals their relationship aims to accomplish. Clients' interests, in other words, are the negotiated identification of clients' needs and desires, and are not a given, to be stated by clients or determined by workers. Through a process of helpful exchange, wherein clients' needs and desires and available resource are considered, both parties, clients and workers, reach a practical and meaningful definition of clients' interests.

As noted earlier, this process starts with the initial request for service by clients and ends with the termination of the service transaction. Because the process entails judgments about needs, desires, and resources, it is likely to be complex, involve differences of perceptions, and will be influenced by agency requirements that condition the availability of service. It is in relation to these interacting factors that ethical dilemmas are likely to arise for workers seeking to adhere to the principle that gives primacy to clients' interests.

Granting a negotiated definition of clients' interests, the following principle is proposed as likely to minimize violations of the Code prescription. The worker must give primacy to those clients' interests that: (a) jointly encompass the futures the worker and those whose professional judgment he or she respects deem likely to satisfy client needs and desires; and (b) if realized, would be acceptable to both the worker and the client.

RESPONSIBILITIES: CONFLICTING INTERESTS AND OBLIGATIONS

When the Code declares that the worker's primary responsibility is to clients, it gives tacit recognition to the fact that the worker has other responsibilities as well. These can be roughly categorized as responsibilities to colleagues, to the agency, to the wider community, and him- or herself. The Code does not rank these responsibilities, but merely gives precedence to clients' interests over these others. Nor does the Code anticipate a situation arising wherein a combination of responsibilities in these other areas might displace clients' interests as primary.

Obviously, situations do arise where the need of many have to be given precedence over the needs of a few, where all may be clients. Faced with clients whose interests are in conflict, which clients are to be given preference in commanding the worker's attention and the program's resources? On this the Code remains silent, but we need not.

In situations where different clients have interests that can not be fully satisfied, the choice is likely to be made on the basis of interests held by one or more of the other categories of persons having a stake in service transactions. Thus, the benefits to the agency and/or the community may be cited to justify the choice of one set of clients' interests over another. Similarly, the self-interest of the worker and/or colleagues may determine the choice. Thus, inevitably, we are led to make choices among other interests than those of the client's in situations where all clients' interests cannot be satisfied. Given the usual service situation where resources are insufficient to meet identified needs and desires, this Code requirement will, with rare exception, call for priority judgments not provided for in the guidance it offers.

Nevertheless, these competing interests cannot be ignored, especially as one considers the duties and obligations this Code requirement imparts to the various parties in the service transaction. A social worker's responsibility to a client can hardly be met without the client's accepting and acting on the obligations incurred in the client's role. Thus, the client who refuses to keep appointments as scheduled, refuses to provide documentation legally required to establish eligibility for a service, or in other ways, for a variety of reasons, knowingly chooses not to participate in an appropriate manner in the service transaction, can hardly expect the worker to fulfill this ethical imperative on that client's behalf. Nor can a worker be expected to carry this responsibility where physical threat to his or her well-being creates excessive risk. Client obligations, and those of the agency as well, thus influence the opportunities workers have to fulfill the duties assigned to them by the Code requirement.

OTHER INFLUENCES ON WORKERS' ACTIONS

In judging a worker's adherence to the prescribed behavior, we must inevitably judge not only the opportunities to follow the Code, but the worker's willingness and ability to do so. For example, consider the differential power relationships that characterize worker–client transactions, and how these influence willingness to adhere to the directive that clients' interests have primacy. In the typical casework situations, the worker's control of resources, and the nature of client needs and desires, places the worker in an ordinate position to exercise control over the helping process. In the typical group work situation, the control exercised by the worker is mitigated by the extent to which the group itself, as a resource, is subject to the control of its members. In community organization, research, and administration service situations, and in client-controlled agencies, such as unions, the worker may find the client in control of decisions affecting his or her advancement and continued employment. While these helping processes share common elements, they are sufficiently different in their power relationships to strongly suggest a difference in worker influence and control. Obviously, motivation to pursue a process that puts clients' interests first will not be immune to the fact that failure to do so leads to different consequences for workers in different power relationships.

But let us grant a well-motivated worker having ample opportunity to act on the Code's prescription, what about ability to act, where situations of need determination and elaboration of desires vary in the skill required to negotiate an acceptable definition?

It is a generally accepted imperative that the worker should not undertake to do what he or she is not equipped to do, that is, that he or she act within the limits of competence prescribed by his or her knowledge. Necessarily, workers differ in what they know, and such differences are recognized. The social work profession now classifies different levels of educational preparation as professional. We assume differences at each level in what is known, and in the nature of competence that flows from different preparations. How, then, do we determine what is an appropriate consideration of clients' interests, when there is a differential in workers' abilities to arrive at definitions of interest, an assumption implicit in the levels of preparation of the worker? Are BSW, MSW, and DSW social workers to be equally expected to act in the client's interests, when they differ in their trained abilities to determine such interests?

The answer to both these questions is not to be found in an analysis of worker performance, but in worker function, as determined by an accepted, enforced, certifying procedure. Agencies and the profession are expected to provide the public and likely consumers of their services with some assurance that workers will not act in situations where they lack the knowledge to act appropriately. Thus, agencies will by design differentiate in assignment of functions on the basis of worker educational preparation, previous experience, or demonstrated competence. The profession will seek differential classification through licensing, certification, educational credentials, etc. The result sought in these gatekeeping functions is the appropriate fit of workers into slots for which they are judged to have the skills necessary to practice. In brief, these screening devices would resolve the dilemma posed by levels of professional practice by locating each level where it can be expected to do an acceptable job, and in such circumstance can be legitimately held to the Code requirement.

Unhappily, in reality the assignments of workers to tasks can be and often are determined by other considerations, such as available funds, levels of demand for agency services, legislative mandated policies, etc. If the profession depends solely on the screening process described, it will inevitably have to face the fact that precisely in those situations where the screening does not work, violations of the Code will be likely. In part, the profession recognizes this possibility when elsewhere in the Code it encourages workers to avoid acting in situations where they lack the knowledge to act. When the worker chooses to follow this directive on the grounds of clients' interests, he or she may find him- or herself in conflict with agency interests. Choosing not to act in a situation requiring action, even when justified on the grounds of inadequate knowledge, can constitute a serious breach of responsibility to client and agency. Because one would assume that the less adequately prepared worker may be less likely to recognize when the knowledge he or she has is deficient, this Code safeguard is a weak one at best.

JUDGING A VIOLATION

Given the concerns and problems associated with an effort to determine clients' interests, and the duties, obligations, and responsibilities of the parties involved in a service transaction, how ought one evaluate a situation where the worker's adherence to the Code is questioned? The prior discussion provides us with basic guidelines.

We must assume that, within acceptable boundaries, workers will maintain some running record of the client's interests being pursued. The absence of such a record is usually an indication of inadequate performance, suggesting termination of the worker in the particular assignment, rather than a breach in ethical behavior. We must also assume that gross violations of this Code item, such as physical or psychological abuse or misuse of the client; exploiting the client for personal gain; subjecting the client to unusual and uncalled for stress to further the worker's or organization's ends, etc. will surface in a form and manner that permits relatively clear identification of questionable behavior, with the worker having to disprove, rather than the challenging parties establish, possible violation of the client's interests.

Of far greater significance for the profession are the ordinary situations that arise in practice for the average practitioner, where question is raised in the mind of the worker him- or herself, or others, as to the possibility that a violation of this ethical imperative is occurring in the ongoing practice. It is in relation to the deviations in normal practice, more than in unusual and bizarre occurrences, that one should judge the ethical stance of a profession. For this reason, the following steps are proposed as most useful in making a judgment about one's own or other's practices.

1. The opportunity to violate the Code must be evident. Lacking an opportunity, there can be no question of violation, even if there is willingness and ability to do so.
2. There must be evidence of personal, organizational, or other pressure that would motivate the worker to violate the Code, and concurrent evidence of the worker's

responding to such pressures in a manner that suggest willingness to violate the Code. Lacking evidence of motivation and willingness to violate the Code should lend caution to a judgment of unethical behavior, but by itself would not exclude the possibility of such behavior.

3. Granted both the opportunity and willingness to violate the Code, there must be evidence of ability to do so. Lacking such ability, there can be question whether the appearance of unethical behavior reflects a premeditated, deliberate, or realistic choice on the part of the worker. Temporary states of confusion, loss of control attributable to physical and mental dysfunction, assignment to tasks about which profound ignorance as to their implications is evident in the awareness of the worker involved, and other such circumstances may not excuse, but may mitigate the attribution of an ethical lapse on the part of a worker.

If a review of evidence concerning opportunity, willingness, and ability all point to the likelihood of an ethical breach, the worker or those judging his or her performance should seriously monitor the behavior in question, audit the activities incumbent upon the worker in the tasks assigned to his or her function, and seek from all concerned with and likely to be affected by the worker's actions, their judgments relevant to a breach of the Code requirement. Where the issue of a possible breach is self-addressed—i.e., has not surfaced for others, but has come into the awareness of the worker him- or herself, he or she should seek some form of peer review to assist in sorting out the troublesome behaviors that prompt the concern, so that a more objective appraisal is possible.

No procedure can be error-free or infallible. Self-criticism, as Kenneth Burke once observed, is the most unfair of all, because there are no holds barred. The worker who consciously seeks to monitor his or her own behavior is least likely to violate the Code by engaging in actions of which he or she disapproves. In the final analysis, it must be in the culture of the profession, in the culture of the employing agency, and in the accepted provisions set up by the community to hold professionals responsible for their behavior with clients, that one must seek the societal safeguards that those professionals who are not self-aware fail to invoke in ethically ambiguous situations.

This discussion does not address large areas of activity that are relevant to its central theme. For example, what are the obligations and duties of the agency to both worker and client? What factors must be considered in authoritative settings where societal and clients' interest may in fact conflict? What is the profession's responsibilities to its members to assist them in difficult situations where adherence to the ethical Code may require considerable or even intolerable personal sacrifice? I believe responses to each of these similar questions require the same analyses of meanings that are considered in this essay, and that the guidelines and principles suggested take us one step forward in facilitating the type of analyses required.

Chapter 4

The Helping Process

Lewis uses the metaphor of drama in this essay to discuss the implications of deficiency in knowledge-based theory on social workers' comprehension of their practice. Reflecting on the effects of social service cuts, he discusses the role of "trust" in the development of both social policies and models of social work practice.

Over forty years ago, when I entered social work as a social investigator for the New York City Department of Welfare, much heat was being expended in the debate between the "functional school," with its preference for the "helping process" formulation of practice, and the "diagnostic school," which favored a "treatment" formulation. As a novice, whose primary interest was research, I found the debate enlightening, but also disturbing. I assumed these two views reflected more than semantic differences; that they involved differing perspectives on the human condition, different explanations of how such conditions developed, and consequently, different perceptions of how one provided services.

I soon learned that these differences were more significant for academics than for line practitioners. My research pointed to the trying circumstances of the recipients of social services and suggested that differences in approaches were insignificant in shaping day-by-day practice in comparison to the needs of clients. In short, that in social work practice, the act overwhelmed the theories proposed to govern and explain it.

After two score years during which I have been exposed to both these approaches, and then some, I must agree with my earlier impressions. My agreement is largely based on what I have learned since then, buttressed by my belief that professional helping is a far more complicated effort than some assume. There is now general agreement, I believe, that our profession lacks adequate knowledge-based theory to fully comprehend its practice.

In my brief presentation, I will argue for a broad perspective, one that locates the helping process in a societal context, involving more than the relationship between worker and client. I will cite the influence of economic, political, and cultural factors on the milieu in which help is given, and on the choice of methods to be used in its rendition. I will then touch on ethical issues that the milieu of

Presentation at St. Luke's-Roosevelt Hospital, March 23, 1988.

practice and the assumptions of method pose, and why they defy resolution. I'll conclude with some additional comments on Maimonides's observation made centuries back—that the highest step on the ladder of charity is to help in such a way as to do away with the need for help.

WHAT IS HELPING?

According to Webster's *International Dictionary*, to help is to furnish with strength or means for the successful performance of any action or the attainment of any object to do what is needed on behalf of (one or oneself). Thus, helpful actions furnish relief from pain, disease, distress, provide assistance to remedy flawed situations, or to change them for the better. Help places emphasis on that which or one who furnishes relief or support, in contrast to aid, which implies more strongly cooperation on the part of the one relieved. Unhelpful acts hinder, hamper, weaken, or aggravate a situation, circumstance, or person. Obviously, if this is what professional helping intended, one can benefit from schooling to learn how to be an effective helper.

In my conceptualization, the profession's helping drama is analogous to an impromptu performance. This drama involves actors (the worker and client); action (what occurs in their relationship); agency (the sanctioning entity); scene (the political, economic, cultural context); and mission (the end to be achieved). What complicates this drama is the fact that the actors do not always agree on a script; the action is often responding to pressures generated by context rather than the need to be met; the agency largely determines what resources are available and for what purpose they will be used; and the scene dictates the assumptions about need and person that limit what practice can attempt.

Helping people to help themselves, by informing them and working with them to advocate for their own needs, is the central mission intended by all the professional actors in the service drama. Some believe this objective is best achieved by maximizing the service provider's role, and others would maximize the client's. Where one locates a practice model along this continuum serves to identify the model's ideological preferences. It is my thesis that the scene—economic, political, cultural—usually favors one location on the continuum over others.

Thus, in times of radical change, in the 1960s, for example, client participation was a critical element in this scene, and program innovations reflected the ideology of consumer control of the helping process. In the 1970s, as our society shifted to a more conservative view, the scene stressed a problem-oriented view of need. Agencies moved to set restraints on service provisions, expecting client participation, but emphasizing doing-for rather than doing-with. Currently, we are under the influence of the radical right with the emphasis on doing-to, rather than doing-for or doing-with the client. The current tendency to blame the victim, directs our attention to the "sick" side of the service recipient, discounting the possible useful contribution one can hope to derive from client participation. In this period, emphasis on process directs professional attention to practice methods rather than programs and problems. Agencies are struggling to survive cutbacks in federal funding, and the increasingly demanding unmet needs of service recipients.

Consider, for illustrative purposes, the impact of the Reagan years on social services in general, and the drama of practice in particular. Reagan—accepting market norms, values, and processes—translated the concept of helping as far as the government was concerned, into a means for achieving the sovereignty of the individual consumer. He argued that government intervention was not helpful; it deprived consumers of freedom of choice in the market, promoted dependency, and had a dampening effect on the economy. By limiting government interventions through decentralization, deregulation and privatization, the informed individual consumer was freed to make choices in his or her own best interests, thus increasing the possibility of maximization of individual welfare or utility.

In this view, consumers become active participants in the processes through which the market meets human needs, and the role of intruding professional helpers in this process is minimized. The call for client participation thus is met through the normal functioning of the market. If we are to believe the data that report the results of this helping model on social welfare programs, it has come close to generating a series of social catastrophes. The neediest consumers are not informed; have few choices, and no resources to take advantage of those available. Wherever one looks for the results, it is clear that the disadvantaged have been further disadvantaged by this helping process—the rich have gotten richer, and the poor, poorer. And those we most often seek to serve have borne the brunt of a misinformed, callous, social policy. They have had it done *to* them, by our market economy.

Moving from the scene to the agency dimension of our drama, we observe a contraction of resources in the non-profit sector, with a shift to for-profit programs as a precondition for survival. Public programs seeking to control costs are opting for purchase of service alternatives, and helping to promote competition between for-profit and non-profit private agencies. The result has been a creaming of less financially demanding cases by the private sector, with the residual, most costly cases ending up on public caseloads. If this trend continues, we will have a two-tier system of social services, with the have nots occupying the lower tier.

The Reagan years have also hobbled the actors in the helping process. Clients have had to endure further stigmatization when applying for service. Concrete services and short-term services shape the kind of relationships workers and clients experience. Concurrently, the shrinkage of available resources has resulted in more and more clients with basic needs that cannot be met adequately, if at all, by the very programs set up to assist them. Workers have been emotionally and physically drained by escalating service demands. They are experiencing a battering that contributes, along with inadequate salaries, to a departure of trained practitioners from voluntary and public agencies. Staff turnover has reached intolerable levels, as the recent study of the non-profit sector has confirmed.

The relationship of worker and recipient has prompted a crisis management approach to practice, in situations that ought never take on this flavor. Housing needs translate into homelessness; marital difficulties more frequently appear as spouse abuse; child neglect disintegrates into physical and sexual abuse; school learning problems are evidenced in massive dropout rates; the list goes on. In short, the "action" produced by the actors in the drama, resembles a fire-fighting scenario. It is analogous to open heart surgery, where the effort is made to keep the patient alive, while seeking to repair the damage that threatens his or her survival.

Finally, in this drama, the mission—of helping the client achieve that state where he or she can help themselves—is lost sight of. Instead, the aim is to simply stem the deterioration that accompanies stressful, depressing, overwhelming unmet needs.

Clearly, the Reagan years have contributed to the *hard work* involved in trying to be helpful. But a more fundamental, if less tangible element, has surfaced during these years that truly burdens the helping drama: *distrust*. More and more of the population have come to distrust public officials and the policies they advocate; agencies and the conditions they set for access to their services; workers and the manner in which they use their authority to compel client participation; and the long-term purposes of the system supposedly established to help them.

TRUST

We know that a fundamental requisite for a helping relationship is trust. In the earlier discussion of the Reagan era, I have suggested the manner in which societal factors have served to undermine trust in agencies and service providers. The doubts created by this lack of trust include doubts on the part of recipients as to the motives of helpers, and the extent to which helpers respect clients' autonomy and dignity. In turn, this doubt promotes resistance to the helper's expectations that the client will respect this expertise and recognize his or her authority, based on competence. In short, when clients do not trust the helper's motives, a relationship that delegates authority degenerates into one that is authoritarian. When this happens, it is likely that the helper will rely more on doing *for* clients, than doing *with* them.

When agencies entertain doubts as to the motives of funding sources and are directed to attend to the cost:benefit equation with the stress on cost, they also experience the polluting effects of distrust. It is a fact, one that should not be ignored, that effectiveness of service is positively correlated with availability of resource to provide it. As budgets are cut, or needs increase and resources do not, agencies are called upon to make do with less, and the most likely responses will inevitably burden the relationship through which help is to be rendered. It is not only the client and worker, but the administrator as well, who must face up to the implications of these developments. The resulting distrust of the intent of the whole system, sets fires in the minds and stomachs of those still capable of burnout. This distrust also poisons interagency relationships—witness the complaint of public agencies, that the privates are creaming the client pool, and dumping the most difficult, costly and dependent recipients onto the public's caseloads.

Accompanying distrust, is a renewed contention by all concerned, that rights are being violated. If there is little respect for a person's needs, can one assume respect for his or her rights? Will privacy be sacrificed in order to obtain funding? Will new technologies substitute electronic circuitry for a human interface? Will a caring relationship become a rarity? What about rights to access? What about the right to know? Is it any wonder that increasingly, in the social services, as well as the legal and medical systems, violation of ethical principles has surfaced as a major source of contention between clients, workers, agencies, and funding sources?

As a profession, we remain uninformed in two crucial areas for lack of systematic research on which to base our practice. We do not know the extent and nature of the impact of organizations on the delivery of social services, having to depend on anecdotal reports or descriptive surveys that do not probe deeply into the dynamics involved. We remain equally uninformed as to the impact of our technology on the delivery of service. In relation to technology, we have shown far more creativity in imagining new models of practice than in systematically evaluating their effects and effectiveness. The Alice-in-Wonderland principle that "if you don't know where you're going, almost any road will take you there," seems to apply to this proliferation of means, in foggy formulations of ends. Thus, in respect to organizational and technological influences, we are not clear as to what form and location of helping is more or less burdened by auspices and method.

As an organization-based profession, we are also assisted and burdened by the bureaucratic supports and hindrances that I need not detail, because they are all too familiar to those who work in socialized professions. But solo operators, those who have opted for private practice, also are subject to bureaucratic demands, if they wish to comply with third-party payment requirements; tax and insurance requirements; referral procedures that meet professional standards; basic supervisory controls; the expectations that accompany high standards of consultation, etc. As a Dean, in one of the largest educational bureaucracies in the Western world, I am particularly sensitive to the burdens bureaucracies lay upon professionals in return for sanctioning and financing their practice. On the other hand, I can appreciate the enormously important and helpful function of bureaucratic rules and procedures in protecting the rights of persons, and assuring continuity of service where the agency, not the actors, provides stability.

True, hindering routines and horrendous recordkeeping tasks dampen enthusiasm generated by other aspects of the helping process. Yet, the experience of those in whose footsteps we tread is best conveyed by rules and principles. We know that the novice is in need of the guidance such rules and principles provide. The application of these guidelines work to limit false starts; protect clients from unwelcome paternalism; allow for critical appraisal of the idiosyncratic in individual styles; assures some level of distributive justice in the expenditure of limited resources, etc. In most cases, the bureaucracy has served these purposes, yet our frustrations incline us to belittle the positives.

Those who would off-handedly recommend an end to such organizations remind me of a Sholom Aleichem story about the people of Chelm. After many injuries caused by Chelmites falling off a dangerous precipice, the town built a tall fence around it. Some years passed and the townspeople noted that no deaths were occurring at the precipice, so they removed the fence. The point is to improve on the way these bureaucracies work; in so doing, their limitations will prove less burdensome. And in those instances where the organization is functioning relatively well, don't be in a hurry to fix it.

If lack of trust burdens efforts to establish professional relationships, the lack of knowledge burdens efforts to make such relationships meaningful. Lack of knowledge affects both actors in the service transaction. Knowing how to access; to intervene; to pace the interaction; to measure results; etc. is crucial to action, even more than knowledge of what and what for. Confronted by complex and deep-seated conditions that clients bring to the service transaction, workers, in practice, tend to be eclectic in their choice of method of intervention. The client, in turn, often does not know how best to formulate the request for service; how best to convey its meaning and urgency to the worker; what help the agency is prepared to offer; and what obligations are to be assumed if the request is to be honored. Both parties may be unable to assess entitlement programs or influence the response of other service providers. In short, what one doesn't know *can* hurt and often does. This audience certainly needs no elaboration on this point.

However, the past eight years of deregulation, decentralization, and privatization have produced a chaotic service arena. If the new hard science theories about organized chaos, or planned randomness needs illustrative cases, the social service arena can provide rich soil for testing relevant hypotheses. A byproduct of organizational chaos, in which the client and worker both have lost faith in the possibility that agencies can coordinate services is the rush to develop case management as a viable approach to service provision. What organizations can't do, hopefully, the individual worker working with client may be able to do. Whether bypassing the chaos will succeed depends on what resources are available. If access will continue to depend on who you know, not what you know, then we may experience another instance where the most disadvantaged are further disadvantaged by the service system.

Another dimension of all current models of intervention is an elaboration on "opportunity–choice" theory. Ideally, where a client simply requires the transfer of resource, the transaction should not be burdened by any other intervention. In simple terms, if the client is hungry, feed him; if he is freezing, clothe him; if he is homeless, shelter him. If life is to be valued, then basic needs should not go unmet for other, paternalistic reasons. But, as we all know, opportunity to access such resources are not equally distributed among various sectors of the population. Thus, it is argued that lack of opportunity, for many of our clients, more than lack of motivation or capacity, results in some being disadvantaged. Effort to provide opportunities, in this view, is a commendable objective for service programs intended to help. Now, I would like to take this concern a step further and deal with its more general application: the role of choice in assuring a client's moral right to participate in decisions affecting him or her. Specifically, what factors enhance the helping process?

Efforts to empower the client have received considerable attention as a helping modality. By focusing on means that enhance the dignity of the client, and by educating the client to an understanding of the situation that contributes to his or her needs not being met, including personal as well as system failures, the client is empowered—that is, is made aware of alternative options open to him or her—and, in short, enhances his or her choices. Obviously, different variations of systems, ecological, and other practice formulations that encompass the larger environment in the problem definition, share many of the attributes of an empowerment approach. Along with the current interest in client advocacy, these approaches share common assumptions about systems access as a critical tool in assuring successful helping.

Others emphasize a cognitive approach to problem solving. The stress in this instance is on the cognitive activity of worker and helper, which can reasonably be expected to provide alternatives for clients not thought of by him or her. Various educational approaches to helping, including problem-solving, rational, and behavioral approaches, share much in common with these cognitive emphases.

The empowerment approach puts heavy stress on the emotive, the being of the client; the cognitive approach, in contrast, stresses the intellectual. Both, however, seek a major objective: to expand choices available to the client.

There are also approaches that stress the doing, in contrast to the knowing and being, as useful in promoting choices. This school of thought builds on a tradition of participatory democracy as prevalent in service efforts sponsored by mutual aid groups, neighborhood associations, community development programs, and self-help societies. Here again, generating opportunities for choice is a central objective. From the preceding, it is possible to identify a principle that a wide range of approaches to helping share in common—one they all judge helpful.

Increasing the range of choices available to the client, and promoting opportunities to exercise them, should be a primary objective in any mode of intervention.

The natural byproduct of the exercise of this principle is the empowerment of the client, and the increased advocacy function of the worker. A second principle that builds on the power inherent in knowledge, also can serve to unburden the helping relationship:

Respecting the client's right to know so that his or her choices are informed and exercised freely should be a primary objective in any mode of intervention.

The natural byproduct of the exercise of this principle is an enhanced awareness on the part of the client—a consciousness raising—and a concurrent expectation that the worker is informed and able to transmit accurately and appropriately what the client has a right to know.

In their specific applications, in the rules they generate in practice, adherence to these two principles can go a long way toward overcoming the burdens to the helping process noted earlier. Nevertheless, I'm sorry to note, helping will still require "hard work," and an unsupportive environment will continue to breed distrust.

Chapter 5

Reasoning in Practice

Beginning with a discussion rooted in the philosophy of science and mathematics, this essay reflects Lewis's long-standing emphasis on the importance of the intellectual aspect of practice. He introduces a recurrent theme in his work—the use of analogic—as a tool to link past, present, and future, and to underscore a central point that "social work—as work—is intended to achieve change."

In one of his essays on science, Poincaré identifies two styles of creative effort in mathematics: the logicians who prefer to treat their problems by analysis, and the intuitives, who prefer the geometric method. For Poincaré, logic alone could give certainty and was, therefore, the instrument of demonstration; intuition, the instrument of discovery. More recently, Polyani, in viewing the role of the scientist in proof and discovery, calls attention to the difference in investment of the self and commitment in personal knowledge, in fulfilling either role. All scientific effort necessarily involves the scientist in a feeling, personal way. Discovery, biased in favor of the intuitive, leans more heavily on the commitment of the total self, whereas proof, directed as it must be primarily by logical prerequisites, leans more heavily on the rational. The individual style of a scientist may incline him more to one than the other area of scientific endeavor, but there is apparently no intrinsic reason for assuming that any particular scientist could not potentially contribute in either area. Certainly, few scientists writing about their practice deny a role for the intuitive as well as the logical in their work.

The elegance of scientific proof and the mysteries of scientific intuition have long attracted the interest of scientists and students of science. The study of scientific thought processes has in recent years itself become a science. Imagination, too, is thought to play a critical role in both proof and discovery, witnessed by the self-report of scientists. No scientist who has addressed the creative process in science has suggested segregating the imaginative scientists having an interest in discovering rather than proof.

From the vantage point of science, Blenkner's division of function in the social work profession based on the intellectual inclinations of the practitioner is certainly a narrow view. She argued that scientific effort in social work stressed

Originally published in *Smith College Studies in Social Work 46*(1), July 1975.

the logical and rational while the imaginative and committed are identified primarily with casework practice.

> Probably two of the most important characteristics of the good case worker are an intuitive, imaginative mind and a capacity for deep identification with others of the sort Murray terms 'critical empathy,' coupled with a strong drive to succor the person in distress. The good scientific worker, on the other hand, must have traits of a different order: a conceptual analytical approach to the phenomena and a drive to arrive at conclusions through rational induction or objective deduction form explicit principles. While the traits of a good caseworker and the good scientific worker are not mutually exclusive, to find them in good measure in one and the same person is rare, and may, indeed, be a source of blocking and confusion in their otherwise fortunate possessor. Other things being equal, the temperament of the person will to a large extent determine whether his choice of profession will throw him into a primarily helping or a primarily investigative role; that is, there is a libidinal satisfaction and investment in the particular type of person (Blenkner, 1950, 99).

Assuming that all human beings add to what they conceive as their own personal knowledge by intuitive insights, as well as by logical analysis, it is understandable that Blenkner did not argue for a mutually exclusive characterization of these traits. Nevertheless, her position appears to treat these humanly inseparable traits as practically incompatible. While it is doubtful that most practicing scientists would accept an explanation, such as Blenkner's, that limits satisfactions and investment in their work to the logical and analytic, it appears that social workers are more accepting. For some time, the intellectual demands of practice have been dismissed as incidental to "critical empathy" by those who purchase the view that locates the "head" of social work in the research function, and the "heart" in the service relationship. It would appear that Blenkner's assumptions have had wide support in the profession. For almost a quarter of a century since her position was elaborated in a major casework journal, no challenge to it has appeared in print. Nevertheless, her assumptions should be challenged lest they continue to justify research efforts often typified by their dreary lack of innovative method and a mystical practice characterized by idiosyncratic styles. As a first step in initiating such a challenge let us consider whether, in fact, casework practice excludes "a conceptual analytical approach to the phenomena and a drive to arrive at conclusions through rational induction or objective deduction . . . "

REASONING IN PRACTICE: ASSUMPTIONS

In order to practice effectively, it is necessary for workers to relate themselves to what is true, rather than to what they may wish to be true. It is also essential to the performance of tasks that realistic appraisal provides the basis for action. In practice workers do not discount self-imposed and socially sanctioned distortions; they appreciate them as aspects of the view of the world around them, and use them in arriving at a judgment of what they accept as true.

In professional practice, knowledge is intended to have consequences, and this intention imparts to knowledge a value component. Social work—as work—is intended to achieve change, and this intention is best realized when it is guided by what is the case, rather than by what one wishes were the case. To work well, the social worker ought to know; to achieve change, he or she ought to consider consequences and be guided by values. These assumptions seem to me to be essential to an understanding of social work as work, involving signification rational components. While I recognize that work encompasses physical, intellectual, and emotional effort and that these are inseparable in action (Babcock, 1953), for our purposes I will focus only on the intellectual work involved in practice. What I consider to be the case, therefore, may prove otherwise were I to view all elements as a whole in the discussion that follows.

ANTICIPATION

The social worker, intent on affecting a process and contributing to the shape of the future, is constantly involved in anticipating events. Three types of anticipation involving intellectual effort seem to me essential to our discussion. The client, to be properly understood, must be related in some way to previously stored categories, or assigned to a class of clients with whom he or she shares common characteristics. Classification and analogy here serve as modes of anticipation, for they suggest attributes for the specific case that might not be immediately apparent but, because of other evident indicators, appear probable. The worker also anticipates the nature of the client's past experiences in order to construct for him- or herself some explanation of how what is has come to be. Finally, the worker anticipates the possible consequences of his or her interventions, and in so doing invests the present with the influences of a probable future. I will elaborate on these types of anticipation, for they encompass significant intellectual work, involving reasoning of a complex, challenging future.

CLASSIFICATION AND ANALOGY

Attaching a meaning to attributes of the client for the purpose of representation is a necessary aid in identification, and a worker's ability to do this appropriately is one measure of his or her skill. Each meaning is associated with a class of attributes from which other not previously identified attributes may be inferred. This intellectual work provides the worker with a basis for describing the client in a language that communicates to him- or herself, and to colleagues who use a similar language, the form or structure of the service situation. While classification is a necessary condition, it is not sufficient to develop the meaning of a situation and what is important in it. In addition, analogy is essential. Thus, classification and reasoning by analogy are necessary elements in arriving at an appropriate anticipation of the client's manifest condition. The former describes the facts, whereas the latter preserves the form of the relation among them.

CLASSIFICATION

In assigning attributes to categories we are often arranging them in some order, reflecting the relationships of classes to one another. The degree to which our knowledge of attributes provides accurate and precise measurements influences our ability to achieve more or less sophisticated ordering of relationships among classes. The sounder our knowledge, the more accurate our descriptions of the phenomena we observe, the more probable our reasoned anticipations are of being fulfilled.

Two characteristics of social work classification processes appear to influence the reasoning about classification in professional work. The process whereby identification and description are achieved, in theory at least, is initiated in the beginning of the professional contact and ends in the termination of service, not before. During the full service encounter there is a potential for new observations and, therefore, better informed assignment to categories. This potential may not be realized because of psychological influences, such as the phenomenon of closure, and by confusions resulting from an oversaturation with indigestible data. Nevertheless, the process of service provides a constant check of classification assumptions, sometimes altering earlier anticipations derived from them. Further, in the specific situation, the attributes that are used to assign the case to a class becomes increasingly less significant as the characteristics that identify the case with a subclass are recognized. In the common parlance of the profession, the latter development is viewed as "individualizing" each client and his or her situation. A class calculus, when applied to classification in social work practice, should be understood in light of these processes whereby assignments are made to categories.

ANALOGY

The integrating character of action, as it puts together in his or her own distinctive ways what the worker knows and values is often discussed, but not fully understood. The reasoning process whereby this wholeness is achieved in performance is typically analogical. Scott Buchanan's observation of the function of analogy in law and medicine suggests the possibility that this form of reasoning is shared by many professions:

> The whole system of case precedents starts with an initial sort of archetypal case, and the cases are lined up after this. The law grows through analogy. You

> never get an abstraction out of this. Lawyers don't like to. Of course, it has something to do with the very difficult intellectual process that goes on in a courtroom—making a general law apply to a specific case with all its special circumstances and details. The law is general and as you start the reasoning, you're not sure it's going to apply, but you make it apply through a series of analogies, or precedents. The same thing came up when I was doing philosophy of medicine. This is the way diagnosis works, too. You identify disease through a syndrome of patterns, analogous with each other (Quoted in Wofford, Jr., 1970, 33–34).

Social workers rely primarily on compositions of current experiences for storage in memory and for recovery from memory of those principles and rules for action associated with previously stored analogous compositions. In practice, social workers, not unlike lawyers or doctors, must make their generalized principles and rules apply to specific cases, with all their special circumstances and details. They necessarily will use all the tools of reason to achieve this goal. Such tools serve an orienting function, helping workers locate themselves and the client in the unique life space within which their service roles are enacted and point the direction in which change ought to move them. The peculiar attribute of analogical reasoning, however, is its capacity for encompassing in one composition the special circumstances and details of the individual case, including much that may be appreciated and understood, but not established as known.

Analogy has the virtue and involves the risk of accepting as true much that in fact remains to be established. It allows for a loose association of similar types, freeing the worker from a range of uncertainties and doubts that would inhibit action. Reasoning by analogy draws on the worker's imagination, thereby enriching his or her repertoire of professional activities by capitalizing on the wide range of analogous stored compositions unique to his or her style and experience. It encourages creativity and originality in practice, without having to jettison previously learned principles and rules (Rapaport, 1968).

The risks entailed in reasoning by analogy are many. Practice often yields similar-appearing phenomena, which later prove to be essentially different. The attractions of certainties in an action situation may encourage a worker to rely on resemblances of past and present experiences, even in circumstances where the context has so radically changed as to alter the meaning of the same event, even for the same client.

As is true of any tool, reasoning by analogy may serve as a crutch rendering support for a weakness in skill while, in the process of use, promoting a dependency that stymies further development of professional competence. Social work education makes considerable use of social learning procedures. Modeling practice after experienced mentors, the novice may evidence a dogmatic adherence to inappropriate analogs, justified by faulty theory, promoting a mechanical approach to practice. These risks in the use of reasoning by analogy require that caution be exercised in order to avoid its uncritical application. Nevertheless, in situations requiring action in which unanticipated consequences play an important role, choice and decision are necessary while recognizing the unavoidable uncertainties inherent in work intended to shape the future.

I know of no models of practice discussed in social work literature that are straightforward replicas of the activities modeled. It seems more appropriate to view such models as analogs. This suggests another caution. Arguments that are valid in connection with logical models of formal systems, should not be uncritically applied to analogs advocated primarily for heuristic purposes in practice (Hesse, 1967).

Social work analogs have differed in what they have chosen to model from practice. "Problem-solving" that achieved a certain degree of popularity in the last decade, focused on the rational, cognitive processes, stressing the applicability of the formal elements of scientific procedures as these appear to operate in the service encounter. The "helping" model, on the other hand, focused on the roles of the actors and the influence of setting in the service situation, suggesting that the impromptu drama had heuristic value as a replica of the practice performance. More recently, systems theory and social contract theory have furnished some social workers with models of practice. Whether, for the reason cited, or for convenience, we choose to catalogue all nonformal models as analogs, or we accept the interchangeable use of these terms as is common in social work literature, their intended functions are similar; they are expected to provide some meaning and order to the attributes that constitute the basic elements of descriptions and classifications.

THE PAST

When workers look to the past, they are concerned to learn of origins and to develop explanations. These are not their only concerns in using the past in practice, but I will consider other uses later. Ideally, workers are aware of the limits of recall, and are suspect of facile assumptions of causality. They seek facts that meet the criteria of authenticity associated with retrospective inquiries. They recognize that knowledge of origins may suggest explanations, but not achieve them. For the social worker, explanations are most useful when they account for all the known facts and suggest others that have not been previously identified.

Explanations in social work must be applicable to the specific case. Thus, explanations of how social injustices may have contributed to the client's problem–condition cannot stop with broad generalizations. Evident truths—e.g., the pressures of a slum upbringing, poverty, discrimination because of ethnic, racial, or religious origin, etc.—must explain how this client in his or her life experience was victimized by these social injustices, and what his or her response to them did or did not achieve in his or her natural thrust toward health, security, and pleasure. In the absence of lawlike statements (Weingartner, 1967) that justify conclusions for specific cases from statistically probable outcomes, the social worker must locate those elements of client strength evident in past survival efforts which can be promoted in assisting the client to a more successful self-realization through his or her own self-determining efforts in the future. This may require of the worker, with or without the client's full involvement, direct engagement in efforts to alter circumstances that appear to preserve and perpetuate the injustices judged by the worker to be currently causally related to the client's condition, and that sometimes serve to undo and defeat efforts at improvement of this condition by service intervention. The worker seeks explanations of an etiological nature through systematic inquiry, utilizing established "knowns" to summarize his or her ex post facto observations, and to test hypotheses that give meaning to these observations.

However well-developed the knowledge of the etiology of the condition observed, there exists a need to establish this specific client's unique responses to the factors contributing to his or her condition. This need is inevitable since one pervasive function of the social worker is to assist the client in maximizing his or her use of service resources whatever his or her condition, its origin and causes, expecting that the client's efforts (to the degree to which he or she is capable) will contribute to the achievement of the service goal.

The worker, in looking back, may seek initially to trace from their origins subsequent events that link the past to the present or may attempt to unravel a stored past, recovered from the client's recall and corroborated by collateral evidence. In either case, the worker has the option of viewing his or her own role as an observing participant, serving as agent rather than spectator, whose procedures for observing are themselves ingredients in the service relationship. In this view procedures become important work tools. They have definable impact, are subject to calculated implementation, and they assist in the accomplishment of a desired end. Accepting the past as currently unalterable, but nevertheless influential, suggests the variety of uses to which the past may be put for service purposes, in addition to determining origins and conjectures that explain. In the role of agent, workers usually have some control over the circumstance under which the past is included in the service encounter. They can influence the scope and character of what will be recovered them, when it will be recovered, and the form in which it will be recovered. Their capacity to use their judgment in choosing from among the possibilities open to them is undoubtedly an important ingredient in any measure of their competence.

The uses of the past in the present, and the uses of classification and analog, are directed toward the third type of anticipation, without which practice remains devoid of rational purpose; that is, prediction. In deciding on modes of intervention, workers must consider their probable outcomes if purpose is to guide their choice of action. In this sense, the future as anticipated consequence enters to shape their work in the present.

PREDICTION

How do social workers decide on what is to be taken as true, as known? Consequence of action, in our view, includes past as well as anticipated outcomes. Outcomes on which particular truths lay claim for support are those that have resisted violation and remain yet to be exhausted in practice (Goodman, 1965). While the outcome of a worker's activity may be independent of what has happened in similar circumstances in the past, the past need not be ignored. As a matter of professional practice, moreover, it is unlikely that it would be. Granted that in their daily service activity workers will be most influenced in anticipating consequences by what is occurring in front of them, with *this* client in *this* circumstance, and that different workers may perceive these complicated occurrences differently, there should be noted those traditional influences that act on a worker's understanding of the events he or she is experiencing. On the one hand, the worker will entertain the possibility that certain outcomes cannot be known (Emmet, 1966; Scriven, 1965). This cautions him or her against an inflexible determinism where human choice acts as an intervening variable. On the other hand, there will be some reliance on projections from past experiences, past regularities analogous to mental compositions arising out of his or her current experience. Such resemblances serve to confirm previously identified consistencies and support his or her propositional formulations as explanations of evident events and anticipated outcomes.

The worker's view of reality must include the uncertainty that accompanies the evaluation of the action in which he or she is involved. The uncertainty experienced may stem from the complexity of the task, its difficulty, its lack of familiarity, and will be tolerated by the worker to the degree that he or she is able to risk action without assurance as to possible consequence. Truth and reality in the worker's personal inner-directed perception of his or her task thus have unusual significance for the work he or she will perform.

Prediction, for the social worker, takes on means not ordinarily associated with its use as a criterion for asserting the truth of a law-like generalization. The social worker predicts, in Daniel Bell's words ". . . as much to 'halt' a future as to help it come into being" (Bell, 1968, 873). The social worker in practice knows that what has already happened to a client need not determine what will happen to him or her, otherwise the worker would see no reason for intervening in the situation for which his or her services are sought. Since prediction pertains to what has yet to happen, the worker is as often concerned to prevent a likely occurrence as to promote preferred events. This meaning associated with prediction in practice attaches to "principles," a crucial function in the profession's practice science.

By combining propositional statements and commendations in a single formulation, principles serve as predictive tools that can guide action while increasing the range of choices open to the actors. In turn, the activities of the worker and client actualize the prediction in work. A principle-determined prediction proposes what potentially can happen but ought to be avoided, and what is possible and should be sought.

The limitations of such principle-sponsored predictions deserve some consideration. If looking back yields no explanation of assorted events for which projections have evolved, it is unlikely that formulations will facilitate practice. Whose concerns should be dealt with? How should they be defined? What resources are to be allocated to their mitigation? What results are intended? In what form are these results to be evidenced? These questions inevitably attach themselves to the definition of the professional task.

The unique characteristics of a client situation that assist the worker in individualizing each unit of service have their counterparts in the unique pattern of decisions the worker takes in arriving at a definition of his or her role in the provision of service. The worker is aware of significant parameters that shape his or her activities and the need to characterize the particular service encounter within the framework of these parameters.

Thus, the worker assumes that in any social service activity the problem to be dealt with may be formulated differently by him- or herself and the client. Workers must seek to reconcile this difference in order to enter into and sustain a meaningful dialogue with clients. They recognize that problems to be worked on carry the imprint of societal, as well as personal influence. They must appropriately evaluate these influences in the particular case if their efforts is to be directed at significant targets. They know that both they and their clients have relevant roles in the service process, and that each role has a distinct impact on the process. How control of the process is to be distributed between them is a persistent concern during the service contact. The goals to be sought as seen by agency, client, worker, and community may be complementary or contradictory. If focus in service is to be maintained, some reconciliation of these goals is imperative. Finally, it is essential that the encounter be subject to constant surveillance, lest inappropriate and damaging interventions go undetected, and helpful ones go unrecognized. The process of evaluation should provide an opportunity for client, agency, and community to observe the encounter and feedback corrective judgments that workers can weigh in their own evaluations of achievements and failure.

Parameters are sometimes posed as polarities, whose interpretations and contradictions provide the stimulus for change in the service encounter. The worker–client relationship is, in this view, characterized by tensions stemming from the worker's and client's differing perceptions of the problem to be worked on, its definition, goals, control of the process, and appraisal of the service encounter. Where dialogue on these differences can be initiated, service is possible. Where no differences obtain, the direct transfer of agency resource to meet client need may be preferred to one involving professional social work intervention. Where a dialogue is terminated, social work service ends.

As a first step, this discussion suggests no small need for conceptual acumen and an analytical skill on the part of the caseworker. At every turn he or she is driven to arrive at conclusions based on formal, dialectical, and analogical reasoning. If Blenkner had argued that such reasoning was necessary in casework, but that the evidence shows that such reasoning by caseworkers typically does not occur, such empirical support for her position might pose an entirely different set of hypotheses than those suggested by her dichotomizing assumptions. For example, as in scientific work, so in casework practice, there may be those who incline to the analytic as contrasted with others who favor the intuitive. The former might focus on refining the techniques of practice and proving their effectiveness. The latter, being more concerned with innovations in practice, might focus on the discovery of new techniques and developing their application. If the evidence confirms Blenkner's statement that intuitives are more frequent than analytics in casework and the reverse is true for research workers, then we will need to consider what social conditions and societal preferences affecting our profession channel these "types" into their respective careers in social work while inhibiting the entry of others. Such inhibiting factors could be targeted for change, and not rationalized as seeming unalterable, inherent, personality-selecting attributes of the different practices involved.

BIBLIOGRAPHY

Babcock, C. G. (1953). Social work as work. *Social Casework 59,* 415–422.

Bell, D. (1968). Twelve modes of prediction: A preliminary sorting of approaches in the social sciences. *Daedalus* 93, 873.

Blenkner, M. (1950). Obstacles to evaluative research in casework. *Social Casework 31*(3), 97–105.

Buchanan, S. (1938). *The doctrine of signatures: A defense of theory in medicine.* London: Kegan, Paul, Trench, Trubner & Co., Ltd.

Emmet, D. (1966). *Rules, roles and relations.* New York: St. Martin's Press.

Goodman, N. (1965). *Fact, fiction and forecast,* 2nd ed. Indianapolis: The Bobbs-Merrill Co.

Hesse, M. (1967). Models and analogy in science. *Encyclopedia of Philosophy 5,* 354–359.

Rapaport, L. (1968). Creativity in social work. *Smith College Studies in Social Work 38* (3), 139–161.

Scriven, M. (1965). Unpredictability in human behavior. In B. B. Woman (Ed.), *Scientific Psychology* (pp. 412–424). New York: Basic Books.

Weingartner, R. H. (1967). Historical explanation. *The Encyclopedia of Philosophy 4,* 7–12.

Wofford, H. J., ed. (1970). *Embers of the world: Conversations with Scott Buchanan.* Santa Barbara, California: Center for the Study of Democratic Institutions.

Chapter 6

The Problem with the Problem-Solving Paradigm

Using diverse sources—from cultural criticism, the philosophy of history, mathematics, and chess—and applying the metaphor of a drama, Lewis provides an alternative to the problem-solving paradigm that dominates social work practice theory. He cautions "When people are mistaken for the problems they evidence, there is a danger that one may view them as a problem to be solved."

For several decades a problem-solving paradigm has served social work practitioners, administrators, and researchers well, helping to organize, partialize, implement, and assess a variety of social work functions. Throughout this period, however, expressions of dissatisfaction with the results produced when employing the problem-solving paradigm have surfaced in the critical literature. The doubters have pointed to limits in its theoretical base, and the confused meaning of its key terms, while others have sought to compensate for the constraints inherent in the assumptions of rationality that underpin the paradigm. The criticism and doubts suggest more deep-seated limitations in the paradigm, of which these disturbing outcroppings are merely symptomatic.

Rather than pursue the critical paths of the doubters, I will assume that the problem-solving paradigm has much merit, serves us well, but does generate the many difficulties correctly identified by its critics. The point of departure of this paper, accepting those givens, is a challenge of a different order. Focusing on the direct practice of social work, it will argue that its practitioners are not primarily engaged in problem-solving activities. Moreover, while social work practitioners deal with problems, they do not necessarily aim to solve them. If solving problems, as a concept, makes sense at all in a human service context, it is likely to be the recipient of the service, not the person rendering it, who solves or resolves his or her problem.

One can analog the practitioner's contribution to the service problem-solving effort to the mathematician who does not solve problems, but merely moves the problem from one side of the equation to the other. Mathematicians *deal* with

Paper presented at the New York State Conference of Social Work Educators, Albany, November 1984.

problems and, at best, recast them into formulations more amenable to their resolution. In an analogous fashion, social work practitioners help clients exchange one formulation of their problems, that they cannot manage, for another that they can.

The problem-solving paradigm in social work practice builds on a cognitive, rational view of the helping process. It assumes clarity about many things, including the condition to be altered, the means likely to bring the desired change about, and the goal to be realized as a result of this cognitive, rational intervention. There is a heavy reliance on techniques that are expected to educate the recipients so that they may depart from the professional encounter more able than before to anticipate, recognize, avoid, or deal with problems should they again appear in their life space.[1]

Of course, most who favor the problem-solving paradigm do not ignore shortcomings in the crucial knowledge areas that limit what currently can be achieved. They recognize that all approaches to practice share these shortcomings, but expect better results in the short run, and improved applications in the future, if their formulations are adhered to. It is in relation to their expectations that serious doubts arise. The reality of practice does not resemble a cognitive rational process, yet their formulation requires one to assume that it does. The reasoning required to find such a resemblance evidences all the elements of a dogmatic fallacy. The error consists in the belief that with the problem solving paradigm it is possible to produce notions about the helping transaction that are adequately defined in respect to the complexity of relationship required for their actualization in the real world. Since it can be demonstrated that such a notion is beyond our ken at this point in time, imposing it on the real world of practice is constricting rather than freeing, distorting rather than clarifying.

WHAT IS MEANT BY "PROBLEM-SOLVING" WHEN EMPLOYED TO DESCRIBE SOCIAL WORK PRACTICE?

Most often problem-solving is perceived as an intervention that clears up, explains, resolves, or works out to result or conclusion a matter involving difficulty in setting or handling. It is not intended where the reference is to the difficulties the client generates for the practitioner, focusing instead on the problem such persons present in their own life space when seeking or referred for professional assistance. Nor does social work problem solving include solutions that describe anything that is required of a hidden series of moves that constitute a solution in a problem, as in chess. Most often steps in an intellectual process (i.e., problem identification and assessment; question formulation; design for data observations, collection, and interpretation; intervention, and evaluation of results) constitute the elements to be addressed. Efforts to evolve an approach to practice that incorporate these elements have been described in our literature. Some advocates of this paradigm argue that a practice that builds on these elements will evidence many attributes associated with the scientific method and conclude from the resemblances that such a practice is more scientific than others. This claim suggests more about the claimant's misunderstanding of scientific methods and their applications, than the scientific nature of their approach to social work practice.

If, as I contend, the practice of social work is not primarily a problem-solving practice, then the use of the problem-solving paradigm necessarily promotes certain unavoidable difficulties. I'll first attempt to demonstrate the lack of fit of the paradigm and the practice. I will use a thought experiment for this purpose. I will then suggest an alternate paradigm, explore its attributes, and depict a preliminary application of this alternate paradigm to an understanding of practice. Because this intention is an ambitious one, it will be approached with caution, first exploring some background.

THE HELPING TRANSACTION

In the normal course of social work practice, consumers of social work services identify or help a worker identify many problematic situations that are troubling them. The worker recognizes the episodic character of some problems, the chronic character of others. The degree to which the client and worker attribute the source of the problem to psychological and social factors can vary. Still, some agreement is necessary if a helping relationship is to develop and be sustained. For the worker, the presenting problems, however defined, are instances of a more general pattern that defines the client's social situation and personality, and how both are manifest in the client's behavior, attitudes, and values. For the client, each problem is the reality that must be confronted and dealt with, if well-being is to be achieved. For the worker, the client's problems are partializations, instances of a more general pattern. These problems are the particulars to be dealt with; incremental steps that in the aggregate achieve significant changes in their more general manifestations. For the worker, the problem-solving paradigm offers a promise of control, a sense of order, a rational depiction of cause and effect—in short, an intellectual tool that overcomes the lack of these elements in more traditional interventive modalities.

But what will be acceptable as a resolution of a problem is largely incorporated in its formulation. The parameters that are relevant to the problem as stated, the who, what, when, where, and how elements of the problem as formulated, will determine the who, what, when, where, and how of acceptable solutions. When the client formulates the problem or when the worker does, issues to be dealt with are being considered. Thus, in practice, a problem, far from setting the agenda to be worked on, in fact reflects an agenda already enacted.

This attribute of problems encountered in practice is rarely appreciated by the "problem-solving" worker, for understandable reasons. The process whereby the problem is formulated does not follow a problem-solving paradigm. It entails creative exchanges of an unpredictable nature, the use of analogical reasoning, the appreciation of emotional as well as intellectual investments in the substantive content being worked on, and it ultimately comes to some closure on the combination of these elements, summarized by the "problem" as formulated. One can elaborate on each so-called step in the problem-solving process and find a similar exchange. The characteristics of a growth process appears to hold the helping relationship intact and is associated with each phase of the problem-solving process. This growth process, however, is not adequately contained within the problem-solving paradigm.

Consider, for example, the distinction between a condition and a problem. Lack of shelter describes a condition experienced by many homeless people, or by community residents who observe this condition. The condition becomes defined as a problem when someone conceives of it as such, out of a sense of concern, social well-being, personal discomfort, or for other self-serving or other-serving reasons. There may be reason to believe that altering the condition will concurrently resolve the problem because where the condition—the reality—is lacking, conceiving of the problem is unlikely.

Thus, it would seem in this instance that problem-solving involves the concrete act of providing shelter and the solution is not located in the mind of the problem formulator, but in a change in the circumstance of the client. The fortuitous renovation of a property that cannot be rented may generate a shelter in which the homeless person may choose to camp out with no intervention at all on the part of any service provider, who may conceive of the condition as a problem. This illustrates a rather common experience, when a would-be social service problem is resolved without the aid of a professional problem solver.

But consider further the possibility that the homeless person does not wish to utilize the available shelter. We now have a condition called "unmotivated client"—shorthand for a client who refuses a preferred solution to the client's problem—which the client may not or does not consider a problem. The client may in fact prefer the "homeless" condition to those circumstances that would result should he or she enter the shelter. If the "problem" is now defined as a lack of motivation, as well as a lack of adequate shelter, it is conceivable that additional problems attendant on the condition and efforts to rectify it, will be generated. Should the client elect to enter the shelter, do the chain of "problems" that the original condition generated suddenly vanish? Hardly, because clients carry aspects of such other problems with them into the shelter.

Thus, the condition that generated the "problem" may cease to exist, but certain associated "problems" remain, no longer dependent on the condition that generated them, but now perceived as resulting from more deep-seated personal and social shortcomings experienced by the client. Putting aside the important influence of class, culture, race, and social status on what one conceives as a problem, the effort to persuade a client that he or she has personal problems that the worker believes need attention may be even more difficult a task than that of providing shelter. At the very least, the worker will have to engage the client in a "relationship," however defined, so that some instruction can occur, helping both the worker and the client to reach a mutually acceptable definition of whatever problem is thought to exist.

Normally, a practice designing such an exchange in the context of a professional relationship may require considerable skill. The exchange will reflect the worker's and client's strengths and limits. The worker, moreover, may be more preoccupied with his or her problems in designing and sustaining the relationship, than with the "conditions" in the client's person that he or she believes, and wants the client to believe, are problematical.

Let us assume all goes well, by which I mean the worker and client are both able to use their interaction to good purpose, whether or not such purpose is shared in common. The client, for example, may be motivated to accept the shelter and participate in a group that will help him or her manage his or her other basic needs more effectively for his or her own well-being. The worker, too, has succeeded in providing a protective service to a resistant client, concurrently developing greater skill in this type of service, and greater awareness of the impact of homelessness and inadequate shelter on the general condition of the community. We would still have to ask what problem, if any, has the worker solved? And, more important, how did the process of working with the client compare with the problem-solving process as an interventive procedure for achieving desired changes?

It is apparent from the preceding discussion that the exchange between worker and client can be sustained so long as there is agreement that a problematic condition exists, and that the expenditure of effort may affect the condition for the better. It is also evident that what constitutes the problem associated with the condition may be differently perceived by both parties to the transaction. For the worker, the relationship that seeks to rectify a personal attribute that generates difficulties for the client, such as lack of motivation, is likely to prove more helpful if the presenting condition serves as an instance of the more general, motivational, personal problem. Nevertheless, unless the worker deals with the condition that prompted the service, there is little reason for the client to trust the intention implied in the worker's reformulation of the client's problem.

Evidently, not only can a condition exist with no problem associated with it, but a condition can generate a problem that is not viewed as such by the person thought to have the problem. A problem, in turn, can be generated by a condition and persist even after the condition is altered. Such problems generally are abstracted from specific instances and located within a perspective informed by practice theory, intended to guide intervention.

Returning now to the observation that there is creative activity involved in this so-called problem-solving exchange, how account for its influence in this homeless client service? The creative process focuses on what develops, what grows, what is newly manifest in the situation. In contrast to the intellectual work that seeks an inventive resolution to a problem, the aim of the creative process is discovery. Causal reasoning are more comfortable for problem solving. It offers more control, reaching into the past to learn the etiology of the present. Analogical and dialectical reasoning are more comfortable for the creative process, in unraveling development over time and tolerating ambiguity in uncertain situations. The problem-solving paradigm makes heavy but not exclusive demands on the analytical skills of the worker, whereas the creative process emphasizes the gestalt, the pattern, the imagery that enlightens one's understanding. In the instance of the homeless client, it is obvious that both the analytical and the gestalt skills are needed and will be utilized. It is also obvious that neither is likely to encompass in its reasoning model, the whole of the other. If this holds true for this instance, it challenges any claim that would contradict this example, including the claim that social work practice in reality is fully addressed by the problem-solving paradigm.

Is there an alternative paradigm that would come closer to mirroring what occurs in direct practice? Would such an alternative encompass what is now included in the problem-solving paradigm and, in addition, capture the creative in such practice? I would answer in the affirmative to the first question, but with far less certainty, a conditional yes, for the second. In the remainder of this paper, I'll present such an alternative noting its limitations that account for the conditional yes in my answer to the second question.

From Kenneth Burke's work (1945), I will borrow his conceptualization of the elements of the drama and their philosophical implications. From Paul Schrecker (1971), I'll borrow his conceptualization of "work in history," and from Lippett and Pearlman (1958), I'll borrow the practice framework within which their conceptions of problem solving are elaborated. To each, I express my appreciation for their thoughts, while freeing them of any responsibility for the uses to which their formulations will be put.

Burke identifies five elements of the drama: the actors, action, scene, agency, and goal. He suggests that each provides a different perspective on the drama. From the perspective of the actors, one derives an idealist view; the action yields a realistic view; the scene suggests a materialistic outlook; the agency a pragmatic one, and the goal a mystical view. The drama is impromptu, with all elements coming into being and achieving their identities as their interaction spells out the story line.

When seen as a form of human work, located in time and place, seeking to improve the well-being of its participants, the social work practice drama provides an alternate paradigm, describing any helping process that depends on relationships among people. In an impromptu drama, participants at times engage in problem-solving activity, and in the practice of social work such activity necessarily has its place. But, at most, it is only part of what transacts in a relationship that creates its own script. The emotions, attitudes, commitments, trusts, and beliefs of the actors; the expended energies, feelings, and confusions of the action; the press of the context; the historical moment of the surrounding; the functions assumed or assigned as obligations or duties by participants that, acted on, define their roles; the clarification and modification of purpose as the deepening relationship alters objectives. All these are critical to an understanding of the drama, yet most are made subordinate or go unattended in a purely problem-solving paradigm of direct practice.

It is useful to consider how much more fully the drama paradigm accounts for the many facets of the practice experience. It is not by chance that both Lippett and Helen Harris Perlman (1957), in their analysis of problem-solving as a tool for influencing change, use the broader framework of the worker, the client, the agency, the problem, the intervention, and the result. If we review the thought experiment involving the homeless client, in light of this alternate paradigm, the enrichment of the depiction that results is startling.

Consider, for example, the nature of facts in a helping relationship. Herbert Aptekar (1970) explores this issue as follows:

> What was "true" at the beginning of a case, from the standpoint of both client and worker, is often no longer true at the middle phase or ending. I refer here not just to the beliefs of both client and worker but to changing external circumstances. Our "truth" will not stand still, so to speak, but changes even from interview to interview. The parent who hits his child for running in front of a car yesterday, may be ashamed of his action today. The "fact" that the child ran in front of the car is uncontrovertible and the fact is and remains that the parent hit the child. What we are faced with, however, is the difference between the way the parent felt yesterday and today—it is in a way, an eternally elusive truth—a truth constantly to be sought. No sooner do we have it pinned down than it is no longer the truth, the whole truth, and nothing but the truth. In our case, truth seems to be in a constant state of being created and that is what makes it so elusive. I think we must pursue it, but we must be conscious of the fact that it is always a step ahead of us, so to say.

Applying Aptekar's reasoning to the condition of the homeless person, we confront the conflict in perception of the fact as regards the client/worker view of a shelter. To the client, it may not be viewed as a home, with all the warmth and supportive surrounding the term "home" suggests. It may not even be viewed as a haven, because it often may be more threatening to the homeless person than the isolation and intemperate weather on the street. Yet, the client's perception of the shelter may change even as the fact, shelter, remains intact.

The worker, in turn, may see the shelter as precisely that—a place of refuge from bad weather, a support service for the client in need of a bathing facility, delousing of clothes, possibly some medical attention, etc. In discussion with the client, this worker's view may change, too. What is finally the meaning of shelter that both will accept will emerge in their enactment of the service drama, and will, as Aptekar observed, "be in a constant state of being created."

Obviously, the clarification of meaning of shelter is not a problem to be solved, it is one to be dealt with, to be pursued. As part of the drama of practice, we are forced to view the actors in light of the problems they have in dealing with the "problem" of meaning of shelter. Likewise, we have to account for the activities that both engaged in trying to clarify meaning. Recognizing the different parts to be enacted (the action), we are pressed to understand the function of each (the agency) in clarifying meaning and the roles they employ in carrying their parts appropriately. Nor can we ignore the scene—the power relationship of the resource provider and the user; the press of community norms versus the norms of the recipient; the limits of care that can be provided; and the nature of the unmet need that is inherent in the condition. Not the least is the requirement that attention be given to the differing and changing goals of worker and client, resulting from altered objectives as they develop a helping relationship. While one can identify problems in each perspective of the drama that can be addressed in the helping relationship, the gestalt that encompasses all perspectives and brings them collectively into focus in each transaction is the critical requirement. Unless the gestalt provided by the drama paradigm is appreciated, the person may be lost sight of, sacrificed to the problems identified and in need of solution.

When people are mistaken for the problems they evidence, there is a danger that one may view them as problems to be solved. As the Japanese learned in the late 1930s and early 1940s, they misjudged reality when they identified a "Chinese problem" and sought to "solve" it. Much to their dismay, the arrogance of the problem solver proved costly, as the Chinese successfully demonstrated they were a people, not a problem. Following on a decade of effort to reduce social work services to a cost:benefit issue, as a way of monitoring its efficiency and effectiveness, the focus on practice turned to the "accountability" problem. More recently, "case management" has been promoted as an approach that would assure efficient and effective practice that was accountable, as well. It is not surprising that this "case-management" approach has raised questions such as the following: Is the effort intended to "manage" cases (i.e., clients)? Is it to be a people-processing approach that seeks the termination of relationships rather than promoting them? Certainly, managing people is not the same as serving them. If the drama paradigm, rather than a problem-solving framework, is applied to case management, questions concerning goals, scene, and agency take on added significance. The gestalt of elements of the drama sharpens the worker's awareness of his or her role—as change agent, mediator, counselor, helper, enabler, as well as problem solver.

Thus, in summary, the "shelter" problem in actual practice becomes a process issue, to be dealt with, and never completely resolved. As meanings change, the issues around shelter are altered, and a new problem that is more susceptible to influence arises out of the worker/client effort to reach agreement on its meaning, and how to address the issues it poses. When all the elements of the drama are brought together in the service transaction, the "problems" serve as instances of the more general concern that holds the helping relationship intact. Finally, by accepting the creative potential of each helping transaction, the worker and client alike work on problems only so long as the client needs the worker's support in reformulating them in such a way as to make them amenable to the client's problem-solving capacities.

One final observation: I have chosen to engage in this critique of the problem-solving paradigm because I believe it does not do justice to our practice and lends itself too readily to the questionable ends of those who see people in need as "problems" to be solved, rather than as persons to be served. An ideologically neutral problem formulation does not exist in a profession that depends on relationships between people when providing its services. The impromptu drama paradigm recognizes this fact, not so the problem-solving paradigm, and possibly more than any other of its attributes, makes the former alternative more attractive as an intellectual tool for understanding our practice.

Chapter Notes

1. Perlman (1957, 16), for example, describes as a major function of the worker to "help people enhance and effectively utilize their own problem-solving and coping capacities."

BIBLIOGRAPHY

Aptekar, H. (1970, February 20). Personal communication.

Bell, D. (1965). *The end of ideology*, rev. ed. New York: The Free Press.

Burke, K. (1945). *A grammar of motives*. Berkeley: University of California Press.

Burns, E. M. (1958). Social welfare is our commitment. In E. Winston, E. Berlatsky, G. Hamilton, and J. Hoffer (Eds.), *The social welfare forum* (pp. 3–19). New York: Columbia University Press.

Dewey, J. (1933). *How we think*. Boston: D.C. Heath & Co.

Hamilton, G. (1951). *Theory and practice of social casework*, 2nd ed. New York: Columbia University Press.

Kraus, H. (1948). The future of social work. *Social Work Journal 29*(1), 3–9.

Lehrman, L. J. (1954). The scientific nature of the social caseworker's professional process. In E. E. Cockerill (Ed.), *Social work practice in the field of tuberculosis*. Pittsburgh: University of Pittsburgh School of Social Work.

Levy, C. (1967). The problem in the social work problem-solving process. *Journal of Jewish Communal Service 43*, 304–311.

Lippett, R. et al. (1958). *The dynamics of planned change*. New York: Harcourt-Brace.

Lourie, H. L. (1954). The responsibility of a socially oriented program. In C. Kasius (Ed.), *New directions in social work* (pp. 31–53). New York: Harper.

Perlman, H. H. (1957). *Social casework: A problem-solving process*. Chicago: University of Chicago Press.

Pincus, A., and Minahan, A. (1973). *Social work practice*. Itasca, IL: F.E. Peacock.

Schrecker, P. (1971). *Work and history: An essay on the structure of civilization*. New York: Thomas Crowell Co.

Siegel, D. H. (1984, July–August). Defining empirically based practice. *Social Work, 29*(1).

Siporin, M. (1975). *Introduction to social work practice*. New York: Macmillan.

Smalley, R. S. (1967). *Theory for social work practice*. New York: Columbia University Press.

Whitehead, A. N. (1955). *Adventures of ideas*. New York: Morton Books, New World Library.

Chapter 7

The Battered Helper

Lewis employs a classic social work strategy in this essay and reframes the issue of worker "burnout" as one of "battering." From an analysis of the sources of this battering, he expands his discussion to the ethical issue of balancing concerns of "good" versus "right." Lewis concludes "Ordinarily, in a situation free of conflicting valuations of good and right, right ought to take precedence over good."

Caught between the fists of the economy-minded altruists and the grasping hands of desperate clientele, the social work helper is punched and pulled whichever way he or she turns. Contracting resources and escalating needs squeeze the worker, whose functions and roles ask him or her to mediate the impossible. The same economic forces that reduce what money will buy affect what can be provided and what is required. It is not surprising that a disturbing syndrome that once shaped the behavior of an occasional helper now threatens to become a prevalent disease.

What heat is to fire, anger is to the battered helper. Anger, fueled by no-win circumstances in which he or she finds him- or herself, burns him or her up till the helper burns out. Even the balm of client satisfaction and personal reward that in the past helped rationalize the failed cases and unhappy details of service is rarely available to the helper in these inflation-ridden times.

The burnout is manifest in many ways. Irritability, exhaustion, desperate measures to deal with routine problems, impatience and distrust, resignation, and withdrawal—all contribute to a cool, defensive facade in an unfeeling presentation of self. To the client, even an automatic phone-answering service can seem more human than the burned-out worker confronted by a pressing request for help. There is much more to this syndrome than can be measured by absentee rates, worker error, and cost-efficiency figures. Recent research suggests high burnout rates occur:

1. Among younger, inexperienced workers with little supervisory responsibility
2. In large caseloads and more formal organizational structures
3. Where leadership-provided structure and support are lacking

---

First published in *Child Welfare 59*(4), April 1980.

4. When workers do not know what is expected of them, and communication of rules and regulations is unclear
5. In work environments with little autonomy, opportunity for innovation, and low staff support

EMPLOYMENT REWARDS

Yet turnover rates for burned-out workers do not follow an expected separation pattern. This is a disturbing finding, because it could indicate that lacking other job opportunities, burned-out workers may remain on a job when in heart and spirit they have already gone elsewhere. A variety of studies indicate that persons seeking employment in the helping professions do so for nonmaterial as well as material reasons. If one is seeking wealth and status, employment in the helping profession is counterproductive. The nonmaterial rewards are more likely to be realized. Thus, human service workers seek to satisfy personal beliefs about caring for others; they wish to lead socially useful lives, want to use their talents in human relationships to achieve social justice and promote individual, group, and community well-being. They seek out health, education and welfare programs that profess similar intentions. They are encouraged by those who recruit them to believe that if they perform their assigned functions well, not only will their clients benefit, but they will derive considerable satisfaction in their work.

Evidence also suggests that workers quickly discover how far reality departs from these expectations. The process workers experience as they are forced to shed one illusion after another when confronted with impossible assignments has been likened to the stages Kübler-Ross identifies for the terminal patient: shock, denial, anger, bargaining, depression, and acceptance. In my research on parental neglect, these sequential reactions also appeared to describe the reactions of parents confronted with charges of neglect of their children. If the underlying fear of loss of control that is present in the dying and in neglect situations reflects a similar fear in the burned-out worker, the process experienced suggests a helper in need of help, not one available to provide it for others. It is not too useful to learn that some workers manage to avoid the syndrome. These appear to be workers who escape to supervisory slots, who ferret out and utilize strong agency support networks, who manage to gain a differential caseload giving them relief from certain persistent stresses, who are eligible for sabbaticals, vacations, special leaves, and other rest times that can be strategically spaced, etc. For most workers, these options are not available, and when available are of such limited scope that they fail to stem the burnout process.

This discussion does not pursue the line of inquiry suggested by current research and autobiographical reports on burnout. Instead, it focuses on a more encompassing concern inherent in a broader category, the battered helper, of which the burned-out worker is but one byproduct.

THE MORAL DILEMMA

In the usual practice situation requiring worker judgments, the worker must reconcile means and ends in choosing what is right and good for the client. This choice is the most difficult one the worker has to make. In those situations where clear and controlling rules govern the range and manner in which alternative actions can be considered, less choice is available, or not at all. Of course, where choice is eliminated and judgment unnecessary, there is no need for the worker.

For our purposes, it is assumed that helping situations involve complex judgments, where there is need for a human interface that can be provided only through worker–client interactions. In recruiting persons to carry out these interpersonal assignments, the importance of motivation and skill is recognized, but equally important are attributes such as physical stamina, psychic resiliency, and emotional maturity. What kind of worker her or she will be is clearly as important as what he or she will know and do. Unhappily, where work assignments allow for little use of what he or she knows and limits what he or she can do, they syphon off motivation and diminish opportunity to improve skill. These obvious byproducts of inappropriate employment of professional helpers are not the central concern in this discussion, although they are relevant to it. What is central is the damage done to the worker's physical health and psychic well-being when constantly confronted with moral dilemmas in his or her effort to be helpful. It is the emotional and intellectually draining confrontation resulting from the mediating role the helper is expected to play that produces the battering.

An extreme instance of worker burnout, one unrelated to social service provision, can place in stark relief the moral dilemmas inherent in problems addressed here. It is generally recognized that demanding work, physical or mental, burns up energy and depletes a worker's resources. Where the depletion exceeds replenishment, burnout will occur. The most flagrant example in recent history of a system deliberately designed to exploit worker burnout occurred under the Nazi government in Germany. An analysis of the shortened work-life span, increased rate of illness, etc., documents this pattern in the employment of German workers in heavy industry during that period. Its ultimate expression was achieved during World War II, when Polish, Russian, Yugoslavian, and other laborers were worked to complete exhaustion under German-controlled management.

PERTINENT ASSUMPTIONS

From the experience under the Nazi regime it is possible to abstract assumptions that helped justify the policies followed:

1. The products produced by the labor involved could meet necessary standards.
2. The labor supply was expendable and could be replaced at lower cost than would be required to sustain the same labor pool at nonburnout standards.

3. The welfare of the laborers themselves was not a critical consideration in view of higher priorities in the allocation of resources.
4. The work force could be coerced and controlled so that protest and outright revolt could be suppressed at acceptable cost.

If these four assumptions are applied to the current situation in the human services manpower pool, the moral dilemma is sharply defined.

1. The product in the human services is the condition of life of people, particularly children, the aged, dependent, and handicapped. Standards of acceptability for their condition of life define what the worker would consider "good" for these clients.
2. The labor supply consists of persons engaged in helping services who are usually better situated than their clients, but not so distant in standards that they cannot identify with and appreciate what would be the impact of standards set so low as to seriously threaten the health and well-being of their clients.
3. The welfare of these human services workers is a concern, but not a critical consideration in terms of national priorities. Their right to higher priority ranking as judged by resources allocated for their support and training suggests a relatively low status in the national, regional, state and city labor market.
4. To the degree that these workers have the right to organize and can be organized to pressure on their own behalf, to that extent will their own efforts determine the degree of control they will have over their conditions of employment. Acceptable costs will be determined by political and economic negotiations based on the utilization of this right.

"GOOD" VERSUS "RIGHT"

Items 1 and 2 make clear that what is "good" for the client may be judged differently by the worker, the client, the agency employing the worker, and funding sources. Items 3 and 4, on the other hand, specify rights and determine priorities in resource allocations that affect the scope and quality of labor employed and services rendered. Thus, in situations where the helper must use judgment in choosing among alternatives to achieve what is right and good for the client, it is almost certain he or she will face conflicting views about what is good and right for him- or herself as well. Ordinarily, in a situation free of conflicting valuations of good and right, right ought to take precedence over good. Where what is judged good for the client and worker is to be given precedence over what is right for them, provision should be made to assure that rights that may be sacrificed are yielded because such sacrifice is clearly in the worker's and the client's interests. Conflicting variations are inherent in such a situation, and such conflicts are central to worker performance. This leads to a moral dilemma in practice—one that batters the helper, keeps him or her awake nights, anxious and tense while on the job, and preoccupied with ethical doubts that kill job satisfaction and produce chronic depression.

Clients reveal by word, deed, and condition when the defined good falls far short of humane treatment. An inadequate level of help offered promotes serious distrust on the client's part, in that he or she sees his or her worth valued at less than minimal conditions of life. When clients protest, individually and in organized groups, the worker knows only too well how real is the basis for their protest. If the agency's resources dictate such deficient definitions of "good," the worker must in practice support a standard he or she considers inadequate. Such dilemmas produce intolerable internalized conflicts and inner-directed anger. Add to this that the worker's salary often appears to be in competition with the client's needs, since both are included in the same program budget, which is always short of what is needed to cover adequate standards for either client or worker.

If this ethical dilemma were the only pressure on workers' psyches, it would be damaging enough, but to this is added the equally draining ethical dilemma affecting their "rights." Although prompted to enter the helping profession by expectations of a high order, and expecting to exercise a benign influence on those who seek their agency's help, they quickly discover that their methods are not so powerful as they thought, nor can they apply them as need dictates because program resources are deficient. They then learn that their work is not highly valued in the circles that distribute resources; that their efforts are demeaned, as are the clients they serve. In short, what they assume to be their rights in prior allocation are not seen as rights by crucial others. Further, should they seek to organize and exercise pressure in order to realize these rights, the right to organize is also placed in question. As with salary, so with organization; their efforts in their own behalf are purported to be unprofessional and self-aggrandizing, at the cost of services to clients. Thus, as was true with the judging of what is good, determining what is right serves to turn workers' doubts inward, deepening the self-critical anxiety and producing uncertainties that deny the body rest.

WORKER ORGANIZATION IS NOT ENOUGH

What has to be done if this battering is to be ended? As a rule, the author accepts the premise contained in the old adage: God helps those who help themselves. The battered helper must find ways to assert his or her right to organize in his or her own behalf, and to use such organization to press for the other right—the right to a higher priority in the distribution of shares. Such organization may take many forms and all needs to be explored.

But such organization will in the long run not significantly alter the pressures on the helper unless the help he or she renders is more highly valued. This requires that clients organize in their own behalf to press for a quality standard of "good" that the worker can also accept as humane. Given the interrelationship of resources to support workers and their well-being and resources to meet client need, unless the good of both advance together they are not likely to advance for either.

Although agencies can influence the battering somewhat by seeking more funds, reducing caseloads, arranging variations in assignments, providing other support services, etc., so long as their budgets are determined by unacceptable definitions of good all such measures can provide only temporary relief. Moreover, agency administrators will frequently be put in the situation of having to defend an inadequate definition of good, and participate in a denial of what are here described as rights.

A change in the long run can only occur with a broader change in national priorities, and in the self-image of workers that often is shaped by the status given their efforts in such priority rankings. Unless a change occurs in the current inflationary economy, one could add to worker burnout the demise of programs and an undermining of trust in the economy as a whole. What must be fought for is removal of food, housing, energy and health care from the impact of inflation, coupled with a publicly supported supplement to assure minimally adequate standards for the most disadvantaged. Seeking this goal, the battered helper would find a constructive outlet for the anger generated by these moral dilemmas.

BIBLIOGRAPHY

Kübler Ross, E. (1969). *On death and dying*. New York: Macmillan.

Lee, D. S. (1979, Spring). Staying alive in child protective services: Survival skills for worker and supervisor: Part 1 — A preliminary examination of worker trauma. *Arete, 5*(4).

Schneiger, F. (1978, November 1). The worker burnout phenomenon: Implications of current research for the child protective system. New York: Community Council of Greater New York, Newsletter supplement.

Chapter 8

Management in the Nonprofit Social Service Organization

In this essay, Lewis applies a Rawlsian social justice framework to the administration of non-profit agencies. He also challenges the tendency to apply concepts and methods derived from the for-profit sector to the evaluation of the work of non-profit organizations: "In our field, where need—our definition of demand—far exceeds allocated resources, a certain amount of selected inefficiency appears essential for survival."

The late 1950s and early 1960s in social service organizations were bullish years for innovators. The mid-1960s to the end of the decade saw "problem solvers" come into their own. Today, as resources contract and demand expands, the call is out for managers. Is it only by chance that this cycle, often repeated in social welfare history, appears to coincide with periods of major social unrest, liberalization, and reaction? Coincidence or not, the fact is that managers now enter center stage, as economic distress and political reaction threaten social services in all fields. In the eyes of professionals who must deliver the service, talk of budget cuts, personnel freezes, program retrenchment, and organizational rigidity linked to demands for accountability, is managerial talk. Managers in such trying circumstances find themselves speaking of efficiency, when the professionals—in daily practice—speak of insufficiency. Managers had best be strong and wise people, for theirs is an unenviable lot.

The need for intelligent and concerned management of non-profit social service organizations has never been greater. There are more of these organizations. They are involved in increasingly complex and costly operations. They now influence the lives and livelihoods of millions. But greater need does not necessarily attract better or greater resources. Administrators have always been there, minding the store in social service agencies. But apparently in the eyes of managers who can judge, these administrators are not very good managers.

Originally presented at the Seminar on Education for Management of Social Sciences, at the University of Pennsylvania, January 5, 1975, sponsored by the U.S. Department of Health, Education, and Welfare. Lewis acknowledged his debt to Albert O. Hirschman, author of *Exit, voice and loyalty: Responses to decline in firms, organizations and states* (Cambridge, MA: Harvard University Press, 1970) for a number of analogs used.

Among social service administrators, there are many who accept this evaluation, readily expressing their own feelings of inadequacy. The upsurge in management courses and concentrations in schools of social work, the experiments in joint programs with schools of business administration and public administration, and seminars on management, all testify to a degree of agreement between the outside evaluators and those evaluated. On the assumptions that such agreement exists and that it is the social work managers who seek to learn more about management from the business school managers, and not the other way around, this discussion takes the perspective of a client seeking the service of managerial specialists.

DIFFERENT CULTURES

It is important to clarify the situation of social service administrators; what it is we want help with, and what factors in our circumstances condition the use we can make of help that may be provided. We come from a culture very different from that of the business manager. We operate non-profit organizations and can, with little effort, spend for good purposes more than we have, thereby incurring a deficit, but no loss in profit. When our consumers no longer need our services, an optimistic interpretation is that success has been achieved; this is hardly the case in business when customers stop buying a firm's product. In the social service organization concern for fairness often takes precedence over efficiency. The service ethic considers unequal advantage justified only if it raises the expectations of the least advantaged. Because the most disadvantaged are also more likely to experience difficulty in making appropriate use of opportunities, special and costly effort may be required to reach out to them. This, despite the fact that other claimants who do not need this special effort are sufficient in number to absorb totally the available resources. What business would spend resources to attract the most difficult to serve and usually most deprived customer when there are more than enough cooperative and affluent customers prepared to buy all it has to sell?

In business, when competition doesn't bring efficiency, adversity will. In social service, rarely does competition compel efficiency, and adversity is not likely to be the result of clients taking their business elsewhere. Given our lack of resources, selective inefficiency may be a necessity for organizational survival. In one city I know well, if the society to protect children from neglect and abuse systematically and efficiently reached out and informed the total community of its charge and the services it was expected to provide, not only would it be overwhelmed with needy cases, but its overload would swamp the courts, public assistance agencies, and children's institutions. In our field, where need—our definition of demand—far exceeds allocated resources, a certain amount of selected inefficiency appears essential for survival. Non-profits' organizational cultures differ in important respects from that of business, and unless we understand these differences, it may be difficult to play an appropriate service role.

DIFFICULT DAYS AHEAD

The clamor for our services that will increase with rising unemployment and inflation is not, of course, evidence of a healthy demand. Success measured in terms of basic human needs met and social problems overcome is increasingly unlikely in these difficult times. We have more than once experienced times when our clients increased in number as the means for meeting their needs declined. We on the firing line know our consumers are restless. They take seriously the promise of justice and fairness. They will not accept an efficient operation that leaves their needs unattended. We may be devoted to our tasks, but we are also human. Managerial help, to be useful, should provide supplements to our courage and convictions, to prepare us to suffer the anger and distrust that will be heaped on our heads not for our failings, although they be many, but for the failing of our profit-oriented political and economic institutions.

An important characteristic of social service organizations is their monopoly over the type of resource they offer their clientele. Usually, as noted, there are no competitive services that offer the consumer options. Moreover, since the cost is rarely carried by consumer payments, the threat of nonpayment or withdrawal by individual recipients may be irritating but rarely fatal. Unlike the private monopoly that public policies regulate to protect the consumer from exploitation and profiteering, the non-profit social service organization can hardly be accused of exercising these negative options for its own gain. The critic of these organizations must look elsewhere to find fault, and this leads to the traditional charges that have always hounded the managers of social service programs: laxity, antiquated methods, and ineffective and inefficient operations. What ill serves the consumer, our critics assume, must be because of mismanagement, since motives seem to be absent. How the agency offers service, the service offered, and the lack of responsiveness of the program to changing conditions are the key targets.

Another characteristic of social service organizations is the use of unit service cost, in the absence of profit, as a measure of efficiency. When goals are displaced as functions, this also serves as one measure of success. Those who recall the Ormsby-Hill Family Agency cost studies and their follow-ups will remember how cost measures were used in these ways. Thus, while the non-profit organization and the profit organization both want to maximize client–consumer satisfaction and minimize client–consumer ill will, the former would achieve this purpose at the minimum cost per unit service, while the latter would achieve it without threatening maximum profits. That the social service organization can incur deficits without a loss of profit suggests the role of service costs as an equivalent to profit as an indicator of managerial achievement.

PROMOTING TRUST

Client satisfaction in the non-profit social service agency is in part dependent on the quality of service and in part on the quality of the processes and procedures through which the service is provided. Since most of the service entails intimate human contact between the worker and client, these two elements—what is being provided and how it is being provided—are not readily separable. For close helping relationships to serve successfully as vehicles for service, mutual trust is crucial. Trust is evident in the ability, willingness, and opportunity to share one's self with another. A client seeking social service help more often than not chooses an agency, not a particular worker. Thus, trusting the agency is a major requisite for instilling trust in the worker–client relationship. Good management should, therefore, embody in the agency's organization work those elements that promote trust. Developing trust must have a high priority in any procedure instituted to assure accountability.

Returning to the unit cost and satisfaction functions, it is apparent that good management should seek an appropriate mix of both, normally somewhere between the minimum of the former and the maximum of the latter. An effective manager would provide guidance in approaching this ideal blend. An unwise manager would focus on one element to the exclusion of the other. What social service managers need help with is the body of established principles of practice in approaching this blend.

Costs per unit in the condition of excessive demand and fixed income that typically confronts the social service organization can be altered by changing worker productivity, operational efficiency, quality of service, and characteristics of clients. The options to increase the price and extend the market are not usually available. Managers, then, face limited internal choices in seeking to lower unit costs without courting client ill will. They can hire less costly staff, require more productivity of staff, limit waste, give less to each client, and choose only the clients who need less. If none of these options works, the manager can control intake in order to manage with available resources, but this would not necessarily control unit costs.

PRIVACY AND ANONYMITY

A third characteristic of the social service organization is that it must respect the privacy of the client, while distinguishing privacy from anonymity. To develop trust, opportunity must be provided to demonstrate its presence. Both the client and worker must have something they are free to share with the other. Where there is no privacy, there can be no free choice to share, and trust is hardly likely to infuse the relationship. Privacy, therefore, requires sufficient personal contact to permit recognition of differences and idiosyncratic attributes. It requires a feeling and knowing human interface between client and agency. Anonymity masks client differences and seeks to assure uniform treatment. It minimizes worker judgments. The destructive result of failure to appreciate the difference between privacy and anonymity has been amply demonstrated in the New York City experience with the separation of income maintenance and service in the Department of Social Services. The clientele of this agency lost trust in the agency's program.

EFFECT AND EFFECTIVENESS

Two popular terms in the language of managers, "effect" and "effectiveness," should not be confused with issues of efficiency and accountability. Effectiveness measures are based on criterion variables intended to judge achievement of goals associated with terminal values. Effect, on the other hand, is measured in relation to criteria derived from purposes associate with instrumental values. The former helps in judging a program's success; the latter provides the basis for judging the achievements of a practice. Those who base managerial decisions solely on effect measures risk the tyranny of small decisions. On the other hand, those who base managerial decisions solely on effectiveness measures risk remaining in doubt as to what, in fact, did or did not help. An appropriate mix of both types of outcome measures provides a basis for choices to be informed by functional and goal achievements. For example, at the functional level it is important in a child neglect situation to determine if the help given did provide supervision previously absent. This is a measure of effect. On the other hand, it is important to know that as a result of such improved supervision, the child attended school regularly, experienced less interruption in expected routines because of illness, imprisonment, etc. The latter measure shows whether the social purpose of the program was achieved. With the foregoing discussion as background, it is possible to address specific issues of efficiency and accountability, areas in which those who manage non-profit social service organizations need most assistance.

EFFICIENCY

Consider the following not uncommon experience in social service agency personnel management. The agency proposes to upgrade the educational preparation of its staff to improve the quality and efficiency of its services. In addition to setting up an in-service training program, it proposes to underwrite, by released time or scholarship, the costs of employees attending graduate programs in areas useful to the agency. It selects the best candidates available on its staff; they attend the program, return after graduation for an obligated period, and leave the agency.

The worker who received the education has increased his or her economic options. The new competence brings a wider range of job choices, and greater maneuverability. The worker seeks out the best agency, not necessarily the one that invested in the worker. But the agency may still want to pursue this policy. It can be rationalized as preparing personnel for the profession, thus assuring the presence of competent practitioners in other programs to which this agency often must turn for help with its clients. Theoretically, if all agencies followed the same route, the general level of practice would improve, and the market would ultimately distribute appropriately the various talents needed. However, there may be another reason for maintaining this policy.

Suppose the agency, as much as the talented worker, recognizes the low level of its practice, but has a locked-in senior staff, with little likelihood of turnover. Also assume the agency has a relative monopoly on employment opportunities for a particular skill. In these circumstances staff at the lower level in the agency program have no place to go, in the agency or elsewhere. Discontent is inevitable, and the politics of organizational practice can be brutal. The more talented, frustrated employees may use their ability to highlight, for client and community alike, the limitations of the quality of service, and may organize the staff to "Fanshen" (turn over)—as the Chinese say. Faced with this possibility, the organization's leadership can opt for education as an effective tool to defuse the powderkeg, decapitating the potential leadership through a process that provides the more able with the options to go elsewhere.

This hypothetical case points up to the need to examine both the political and economic factors that influence managerial decisions. Failure to do so may be the major inefficiency in social service organizations. Discussions of technology, rational decision mechanisms based on up-to-date information retrieval, sound management of fiscal resources, control and planning systems, quality control or organizational statesmanship, personnel administration, or goal-directed practice—all make for interesting and useful dialogues, but still one encounters the cases of the Pennsylvania Railroad, Lockheed, and the Pan Am syndrome. In social service organizations with access to the more sophisticated technological hardware and software—such as large public welfare departments—the same syndrome is evident. Obviously, help is needed in formulating principles of managerial practice to guide political and economic judgments. Such principles will at least promote a principled practice, using the best available technologies to achieve goals and purposes.

ACCOUNTABILITY

The issue most in need of attention in relation to accountability is posed by the question: Accountability to whom? Lacking the choice to go elsewhere, social service consumers form a natural base for a political pressure group with considerable sustaining energies.

But there is also accountability to the funding source, community, profession, one's superior and, last but not least, oneself. Which of all these accountabilities deserves the highest priority? Mechanisms and techniques for assuring accountability differ in accordance with the interests of those for whom the results are intended. Obviously, groups that can exercise the major influence will demand and get the major attention. If the funding source threatens to cut off payment, its interest will be attended to, and soon. In a review of the clout likely to be available to the different populations to whom one can be accountable, the weakest group may well be the least organized. A unionized staff or an organized profession can make a more telling demand than individual persons. A board, a single or major funding source, or collaborating funding sources can speak in a more commanding voice when united than when disagreements produce no clear message. Weakest of all is the unorganized client whose problems bring him or her to the agency, and whose personal inability to manage seriously limits his or her energies and other resources needed to command accountability. The major help social service managers need with the problem of accountability is a set of guiding principles to inform the use of technologies in a manner that would assure a just and fair, not merely a convenient, response to request for accountability. This may require, at times, that we assist in organizing future troublemakers. In the short run, it is unlikely that managers will promote a source of power that can be used to restrict their choices. In the long run, failure to do so may not only restrict choices, but eliminate choice entirely.

THE PRACTICE SCIENCE OF MANAGEMENT

I agree with those management experts who recognize a distinction between theoretical science and practice science. Although we need the former to tell us where to look and what to look for, the latter provides us with the "how." Practice science is formulated in terms of principles and rules, not laws. And because practice sciences intend consequences, they are never value-free. This paper was intended to emphasize the linkage of knowledge and value in professional managerial practice.

CONCLUSION

I have noted the following areas where assistance would serve both our immediate and long-term concerns. We need to know principles of management that will do the following:

1. Communicate in the organizational work of the agency those elements that promote trust and concurrently respect privacy
2. Help us approach an appropriate mix of unit cost and client satisfaction functions
3. Provide a basis of choosing an appropriate mix of effect and effectiveness measures to inform managerial decisions
4. Guide us in making appropriate political and economic judgments
5. Inform our use of technologies in a manner that will assist us in assuring a just and fair, not merely a convenient, response to requests for accountability.

Chapter 9

An Historical Perspective on Helping People in Times of Rapid Change

Lewis reflects on some of the major events and individuals who influenced his views of social work practice, in particular the ideas of Bertha Reynolds. In so doing, he finds the similarities in issues and interventions that span a career lasting over half a century.

In 1937, I participated in the Hunger March in Washington, DC. The slogan that appeared most often on the placards carried by the marchers was "Chamber of Commerce—where are the jobs?" The question was addressed to the Chamber—the voice of big business—in response to newspaper headlines that quoted the Chamber as claiming there were plenty of jobs to be had if people wanted to work. The marchers faulted the economy for their plight; the Chamber faulted the marchers. Other slogans displayed by the marchers touched on deficiencies in financial relief, housing, and educational programs, reflecting the interests of the different sponsors of the demonstration.

In August 1991, some quarter of a million marchers assembled in Washington, DC on Solidarity Day to demonstrate their concern that troubles here at home were not being attended to. Placards carried slogans protesting lacks in health care coverage, inadequate unemployment benefits, the absence of housing for thousands of homeless people. President Bush, who expressed his belief that the recession was ending, decided not to act on the permission granted him by Congress to extend unemployment benefits. He also noted that billions were being spent on AIDS research as reason to reject the charge that not enough was being done to help the victims of that health catastrophe. Besides, he noted, the spread of AIDS could be controlled if individuals exercised good judgment and restraint.

I cite these two demonstrations, over half a century apart, to highlight the persistence of similar concerns about the functioning of our economy and the allocation of its resources and the different perceptions as to its problems and their causes.

In 1989, Helen Perlman wrote:

Unpublished paper, written in October 1991.

> From the perspective of more than a half century, I believe that there has, in the main, been great forward movement in the quest to humanize our society and enrich its individual human lives and that social work has taken its vital part in that quest. When I entered social work there was no federal system of public assistance, no Medicare and Medicaid, no supported system of mental health services, no unemployment compensation, no social insurance, no social security, no public support for special, or higher education.[1]

Obviously much has changed in the past fifty years in the societal context of social work practice, but much has not changed enough. I'll elaborate on this historical encapsulation, briefly, from an economic, political, and social perspective.

In the 1930s and 1940s the profession extended its practice domain into a number of fields, developing specialties based on unique skills required in each field. In the early 1950s these specialties merged into one association—NASW—committing the profession to a generic, as well as specific, skill base in practice. At the same time, graduate and undergraduate programs of social work education merged to form the Council of Social Work Education. These two mergers paved the way for a rapid expansion in graduate and undergraduate professional degree programs.

In a recent work, two social work scholars reviewed the history of these developments—treating social services as a commodity subject to a market economy. They argue that our profession's development is best understood as an occupational entrepreneurial effort to attain a monopolistic control over a specialized competence. The authors conclude that the strains within the ranks of social workers—between those who emphasize "social treatment" and those who stress "social justice"—can, to a large extent, be attributed to the pressure to establish occupational control over a particular sphere of "helping activities." In their view, the economic factor operates to affect every level of practice, influencing all helping activities.[2]

Extending this economic perspective to encompass the goals of the profession confronts us with the significant failings of a market economy. The spread between the haves and have nots widens, even as the social services seek to narrow the gap. Efforts to achieve equality of opportunity fail because inequality of condition prevails.

During the past half century, a number of practice paradigms evolved and served practitioners, administrators, researchers, and faculties well. These paradigms helped to organize, partialize, implement, and assess a variety of social work functions. One such paradigm, a problem-solving model, will serve to illustrate how the context of practice influences its choice of methods. I assume that this paradigm has much merit, serves us well, but generates many difficulties identified by its critics. In seeking to examine this influence, we must consider that the techniques of the profession are not empty schemata; they are comprised of functional culture-bound, value-laden skills.

How can we explain the rapid rise and dissemination of the problem-solving paradigm in social work after World War II? In the postwar period that witnessed a widespread acceptance of this model within the profession, the in-house polarization of practice theoreticians into two warring camps reached an uncompromising stalemate. The diagnostic school contended for a treatment model, and the functional school for an educational frame of reference. As Perlman demonstrated in her very insightful text, by using a problem-solving paradigm, one could capitalize on the strengths of both approaches for the benefit of practice.[3]

In the wider arena of intellectual contention, the problem-solving paradigm fitted the demand for a further intellectualization of the profession, as it moved to become a more integrated academic discipline within the university. Moreover, in the postwar period, an end to ideology was proclaimed as the path of the future.[4] The value-free problem-solving paradigm gained in popularity in the political and economic spheres; it was expected to relieve our nation of unnecessary moral baggage that could only hinder efforts to fulfill the "savior" role.

In social work, a number of liberal thinkers, intellectually gifted and experienced in program design and development, saw an opportunity to expand the narrow interest of the profession in direct service into the broader arena of social welfare policy. Donald Howard, Philip Klein, Kenneth Pray, Lester Granger, Hertha Kraus, Evelyn Burns, Benjamin Youngdahl, Marion Hathway, Harry Lourie, to name some of the better known spokespersons for this view, called for social welfare statesmen-planners, administrators, and policy specialists, who would help shape the welfare programs of our nation, contributing to a more just society. In their view, social work had largely consisted of casework, fulfilling a residual function. Social work focused on the failures of the system and individuals in it. Unstated, but implicit in their view, was a concern that the intellectual leadership of social work practice in the postwar period—Gordon Hamilton, Charlotte Towle, Jessie Taft, Virginia Robinson, Bertha Reynolds, Gertrude Wilson, Ruth Smalley, etc.—had survived the war, but had not digested its significance for the future role of the profession. Some appeared to believe that direct practice, particularly services that depended on relationship skills, were likely to diminish in significance for the profession. The full employment they anticipated was expected to prevent the more prevalent problems direct services sought to address.

In the postwar period a new breed of scientifically oriented social scientist/social worker surfaced in the profession. New faith in technology inspired by the war, the mastery of the atom, Sputnik, and the electronic computer revolution in communications, affected the profession. The profession turned to this new breed of researchers with high expectations. Their problem-solving capacities would provide the theoretical grounding for the statesmanship role and concurrently strengthen the knowledge base of direct practice. This expectation proved illusory. Very quickly the policy scene was shaped by far more significant forces in the nation—the economist-led war on poverty, the civil rights struggle for social justice, the awakening of women's political action groups, and the student-led antiwar movements. After some preliminary efforts at description and classification, these research problem solvers moved into evaluation efforts. They focused on determining whether social work helped those who were recipients of its services. The stress was on accountability.

The post-World War II euphoria reached its peak by the end of the Korean War. McCarthyism labeled the welfare reformers as dangerous. As the nation drifted into the Vietnam War, the savior complex was dissipated. Our country's world leadership role suffered considerable deflation. As new coalitions of Third World nations evolved, our nation's economic and political policies abroad were found wanting. The United States' version of welfare was seen as deficient at home, and not likely to be more effective when exported elsewhere. Our social work practice theory was first sought after and then seen as parochial. Its adaptability was experienced as limited. The profession's attraction for the best intellectual problem solvers declined, as more promising career opportunities were opened in other fields. If, as proved to be the case, this era did not turn out to be the "American Half Century," it also did not turn out to be the half century of problem solvers in general, and social work problem solvers in particular. In fact, the problem solvers within the profession proved more adept at identifying problems than solving them.

Our profession responds to changing societal conditions by innovating programs; reformulating problems and concepts; and altering, combining, and inventing methods of intervention. New programs capitalize on community changes affecting common human needs. Program innovations provide us with evidence of risks entailed when requisites for program innovation are not in place. On the other hand, innovative programs have been built on considerable prior experimentation, with some apparent success. Altering problem formulations are less risky, and tend to produce incremental changes.

Changes in the processes of intervention by combining methods as generalist theorists have done, or by substituting one method for another, need not alter the principal assumptions of methods, but may provide more opportunities to adjust the delivery of service to fit the need of recipients. A more fundamental change in processes occurs when new knowledge alters practice theory, for example, when psychodynamics directed practice to focus on the client's psyche as the target of intervention. As Bertha Reynolds observed, the focus on the psychological helped to individualize clients, but in the process to isolate them as well. Basic assumptions changed in the 1930s and 1940s. By the mid-1950s, the focus shifted to the client's social functioning. In response, educational, problem-solving, and systems approaches evolved. It may be helpful at this point to provide an example of how changes in the social context of practice had an impact on an approach to intervention.

Soon after the onset of the Great Depression, voluntary sector agencies exhausted their funds for financial assistance. Community Chests could not raise the monies needed for this purpose. As cities and states assumed this function, they too ran out of funds and turned to the federal government for relief. The need to feed, clothe, and shelter the escalating numbers of dependent, countrywide, provided the political support for a federal takeover of financial assistance programs. With the relinquishing of their relief functions, the voluntary sector also experienced an exodus of professional staff, joining public welfare programs as supervisors and executives. Schools of social work increased field work placements for students in public relief agencies. The faculties of schools sought to explore the changing role of social work practice in public welfare settings.

In 1937, Jessie Taft advised social workers to respect the limits of their methods of intervention.[5] She cautioned them to trust their common sense: when people are hungry, feed them; when they are homeless, provide them with shelter; when they are threadbare, clothe them. Then attend to their psyches. In 1968, Irene Olson, a welfare commissioner, demonstrated in her doctoral dissertation that ADC families whose basic survival needs are being met, are able to make good use of casework services; those whose conditions are more precarious cannot. In 1988, Helen Perlman concluded her analysis of the Chumung County Experiment with the observation that the casework method fails when those it seeks to serve lack the basics in health care, income support, shelter, and nutrition.

Thus, in the half century of societal changes separating Taft's caution and Perlman's conclusion, evidence supported the belief that:

1. Casework interventions fail if basic survival needs are not being met, and
2. Casework interventions alone do not meet survival needs; therefore,
3. Meeting survival needs must precede or accompany casework interventions if they are to succeed.

Based on systematic observations that have stood the test of time, item 3 incorporates the impact of practice experience in many settings. It suggests a strategy for planning and implementing services.

Finding that the strategy works is a necessary, but not sufficient justification for acting on it. In addition, one must decide whether it ought to be acted on. The "ought" judgment differs from the "can" judgment. The "ought" is informed by an ethical commendation that is consistent with the value frame of the profession.

In this example, concern for distributive justice is a central value to be implemented by the proposed action. If a fair, as well as sound, allocation of service is to obtain, equals must be treated equally and unequals unequally. If justice is to prevail, then the most disadvantaged, i.e., those who basic survival needs are not being met, ought to anticipate increased benefits from the manner in which benefits are distributed. If it can be shown that this ethical outcome would be realized if item 3 is acted on, then "can" is complemented by "ought," the knowledge claim and the ethical claim are joined, providing support for the directive and command inherent in a practice principle.

This example illustrates the process whereby practice principles may come to be accepted as guidelines for practice. These principles, and the rules they generate, inform and justify our professional acts. If societal changes do impact on our practice, this impact should be manifest in our store of practice principles. The impact of efforts to implement the suggested principle stimulated a reexamination of casework practice. To help clients achieve a survival standard, social workers needed to broaden their practice skill, aiming at mastery of techniques that promote resource development. Seeking to rally community support for measures that expand the availability of health care, housing, income supports, etc., the worker is challenged to assume an advocacy role and to enrich his or her practice with group and community work skills. On the other hand, the worker must be conscious that the application of the casework method largely to those clients who evidence the potential for success in the helping relationship, will often exclude the most disadvantaged from receiving the services they need.

We are familiar with the charge that our profession's family agencies separated themselves from the poor when they relinquished the relief function. The shift in function ultimately contributed to the separation of services from financial assistance, and in public income maintenance programs separated the recipients from services as well. We also know from experience that many workers resolved the dilemma by moving into private practice where clients can make good use of their services and afford them as well.

Let us consider in more depth the relationship of social reforms to the functions that implement them. If you will grant, for the present, that social work practice is a form of social action, then it should not be difficult to accept the premise that the practitioners of social work constitute the profession's largest pool of social activists. When these practitioners join with others to advocate changes in programs and policies, legislation and regulations, their actions contribute to social change. Judging from our literature, it is more common to contrast practice and social action than to see them as part of a continuum.

In 1929, Porter Lee described what he viewed as a normal social process—the move from a cause sought and won to a function that realized in practice the intentions contained in the cause. He contrasted the zeal that inspired a cause with the intellect that assured the success of the function. Nevertheless, his analysis of his own hypothesis compelled him to conclude that the time had come when the cause must be incorporated into the function. In those threatening, predepression days, he believed the profession must not respond to the challenges confronting it by going back to a day when social work was exclusively, or predominantly, a cause. He argued that we must meet (these challenges) with the sober recognition that the profession is and must be both cause and function. Finally, he noted his belief that the dynamic leader of the cause and efficient executive in charge of the function do not often appear at their best within one temperament. Thus, while he saw the need for both qualities, he doubted the possibility of both being present in one person.

There are several assumptions contained in this view that have not been substantiated by experience. The sequencing, as suggested in the hypotheses "from cause to function" and the separation, as suggested by "cause *and* function" obviously did not satisfy Lee either; hence, his search for biological and personality justifications for the social processes he sought to explain. My presentation dissents from both the hypotheses and the rationale used by Lee to justify it. In my view, the cause in function and the dialectic of their interaction in the service transaction make for a principled practice. Only when reforms are manifest in the intervention of the worker do they become part of the history of the profession.

This is more likely to happen when the worker's actions are guided by practice principles. The failure to see the unity of cause and function in action has led to a separation of means and ends in the rendering of service.

I do not believe one can demonstrate a cyclical development of economic, social, and political forces in our nation. Nor do I believe we can demonstrate a cyclical developmental pattern in our profession. In a study of one school's curriculum over a fifty year period, I did find a relationship between societal changes and curriculum emphasis. It appeared that in times of conservative economic and political dominance, the profession focused on its helping processes and occupational status. The school's curriculum in financially threatening and status-challenging times stressed methods. In periods of liberal economic and political policies, new resources were made available and power centers shifted to attract new constituencies. The school curriculum emphasized a problem focus. Finally, in periods of crises associated with radical changes in the economy and in the political arena, previously dormant constituencies exercise their economic and political muscle, demanding additional resources. These periods stimulated the development of new programs and the radical modification of old ones. In the school of social work, curriculum innovations responded to the requirements for personnel to staff new community programs.

It may be that the relationship I found between dominant societal trends and social work educational curriculum is unique to the school studied. We do know that programmatic changes entail conflicts in ideology, and tend to be radical in their implications. Problem reformulations are stimulated by the promise of new resources. Process formulations focus on skill in the application of methods and aim to secure the turf claims of the profession. The unequal emphasis on process, problem and program makes possible a variety of educational programs. Different patterns, therefore, may exist concurrently.

CONCLUSION

The choice of economic, political, and social perspectives was based on my personal experience in the profession. Necessarily, this choice hardly attends to the cultural, class, ethnic, gender, and racial perspectives that would provide a more rounded history of the period. Nevertheless, the following observations abstracted from my analysis may be useful for your deliberations.

1. *Avoid the deep slumber of decided opinion.* My analysis warns against imagined certainties. The historical record highlight unresolved dilemmas and nonrational choices. Even when taken separately, these perspectives resist simplistic interpretations.
2. *All things change, regardless of pace, giving each moment a distinctive face.* Small changes in complex systems may make waves. Large changes in simple systems may hardly sustain a ripple.

3. *Thought is born of failure*. The greater the failure, the more searching is the kind of thought necessary. Given the history of our failures, there is much need for deep thought in our profession.
4. *Challenge the whole, while sustaining the part.* If a system is sick, one may not detect it from inside the system. If you buy into the system uncritically, you may justifiably be accused of selling out to it.
5. *Avoid false dichotomies.* In the short run they promote unproductive conflict. In the long run they confuse and deceive.
6. *Know your own history and avoid an identity crisis.* Alienation from one's product starts with ignorance of forces that separate you from your own creations.
7. *Keep focused on the Cause in Function.* Keep means and ends in view, and balance the need for organizational efficiency with an awareness of both the effectiveness of one's programs and the effect these programs have on the clients and communities they serve.

Chapter Notes

1. Helen Harris Perlman (1989). *The dancing clock and other childhood memories.* Chicago: Academy Chicago Publishers.

2. Stanley Wenocur and Michael Reisch (1989). *From charity to enterprise: The development of American social work in a market economy.* Urbana, IL: University of Illinois Press.

3. Helen Harris Perlman (1957). *Social casework: A problem-solving process.* Chicago: University of Chicago Press.

4. See Daniel Bell (1965). *The end of ideology*, rev. ed. New York: The Free Press.

5. Jessie Taft (1937). *The dynamics of therapy in a controlled relationship.* New York: Macmillan.

Part II

Essays on Social Work Values and Ethics

Editor's Introduction

Other than Frederic Reamer and Charles Levy, no social work scholar in the past thirty years has devoted as much attention to the ethical issues involved in social work practice as Lewis. His essays on ethics span the range of practice interventions from clinical practice (see "Ethical Assessment") to administration, policy development and implementation, and teaching. Although he is concerned with the development of an ethical framework to help resolve persistent practice dilemmas, Lewis never hesitates to display (and justify) his own value preferences (e.g., for social justice, self-realization, mutuality, and freedom of trust; against racism). He consistently links his discussion of social work ethics to contemporary political and social issues, using them as both examples and metaphors. Therefore, ethical discourse for Lewis, is never an abstract exercise; it is always a central component of social work practice.

Three themes are particularly striking in the essays that follow (and in other essays on ethics Lewis wrote that were not included in this volume). One is the use of images to convey ideas about ethics that are similar to those employed to illustrate general practice principles. The metaphor of the drama is a particularly striking example; another is the emphasis on the integration of opposites (value and knowledge; knowing and doing; charity and justice). This demonstrates how Lewis followed his own advice about the use of analogical thinking. It also subtly conveys the inextricable linkage between discussions of practice and discussions of ethical practice. For Lewis, the two discourses are inseparable.

A second theme is the imperative of taking action on behalf of one's values and beliefs. This is equally true if one is engaged in agency-based practice or social work education. Using the NASW *Code of Ethics* as a model for teachers,

Lewis asserts that it is an ethical responsibility of educators "to advocate for the goals and objectives of the profession. This requires partisan activity . . . and engage[ment] in social action, with all its consequences."

A third theme—or perhaps a characteristic of these essays—is their remarkable prescience. This is best illustrated by quoting from the last essay in this section, "Morality and the Politics of Practice," written thirty years ago—before the Watergate scandal had broken, before Reaganomics, before Iran-Contra, before "welfare reform":

> In a society where social practice and policies evidence a lack of regard for distributive justice and privacy, trust is the earliest victim. . . . If this destruction of trust is allowed to continue, it will, in time no longer be possible to engage in an ethical social work practice. Instead, a dehumanized welfare service, void of a caring human interface, will take its place. . . . [Trust] will be undermined where racial, class, cultural, and ethnic differences deny equal and fair access to available resources.

Chapter 10

The Ethical Component in Practice

In this essay, Lewis outlines several central ethical principles for social workers that go beyond those articulated in the NASW Code of Ethics, *linking these principles with the concept of empowerment. He recognizes, however, that "one cannot legislate an inner-directed adherence to an ethic or truth, but one can promote a context that encourages such adherence."*

If we are to systematically develop useful ethical imperatives to guide the work of practitioners, then we need to clarify what we mean by practice principles. When professionals lack practice principles in their work, they risk an uninformed practice and, in all likelihood, an unethical one as well.

Social work ideologists have long been committed to right two evils that have accompanied the development of social systems: gross class inequities in the possession of means and the enjoyment of ends, and the terrible costs in human suffering associated with the vagaries of a profit-motivated market and a competitive, individualistic political economy. There have always been those in the profession who have favored cooperation and mutual aid over competition, equality in access over privilege, and the planned utilization of socially provided resources over laissez-faire. Some have argued that it is possible within the existing political economy to enhance self-esteem through useful work and education; promote individual dignity through creative self-expression in combination with others; and provide necessary social supports to right the injustices of the system, even compensate for the inequities that stem from natural deficiencies and unequal statuses that disadvantage many at birth. Others despair of this possibility, believing that more fundamental changes in our political economy and much deeper understanding of the human condition are necessary prerequisites. This disagreement, of course, reflects conflicting views in the wider community as to how the good life for the greatest number is to be achieved. For our purposes, we assume that these different perspectives on means will persist.

It is possible to focus attention on agreed-upon ends rather than means thus maintaining some degree of inner professional harmony. In the past this has permitted the profession to speak with one voice on a number of crucial issues. But is

Originally written in April 1987 for an unpublished manuscript entitled *Ethical practice in troubled times: Papers, 1955–1985.*

it possible to specify ends to which all social workers can subscribe? I think so. One such arrangement of ends is exemplified in the conceptualization by Charlotte Towle of common human needs.[1] This formulation starts with a set of personal desires, deriving from these desires the range of human needs to be satisfied. It provides one possible acceptable representation of the good life our profession seeks for all people. It assumes that all people would benefit from physical and psychological well-being, justice, security, self-realization and salvation, knowledge, and beauty. There is evidence that all civilized societies seek to provide these goods by creating salutary political, economic, religious, scientific, and aesthetic arrangements that organize communal resources and provide social support to help individuals and groups satisfy the needs they serve. When social workers pursue their profession in health-related programs, legal and protective service organizations, income support and work-world settings, public and voluntary personal service agencies, and formal and informal educational programs, they contribute their skills to the processes whereby the community assists individuals and collectivities to meet these common human needs. For our profession, the utility of this and similar formulations is their capacity to bridge differences that an initial focus on means inevitably exacerbates. Moreover, such formulations may focus on ends that would be sought in any political/economic arrangement, whatever our state of knowledge.

Consider further the nature of common human needs. A condition can achieve the status of a substantive human need only when some means can be identified for altering the condition in a preferred direction and some resource allocated toward that end. Many significant human conditions do not achieve the status of a need because they are viewed as unchangeable or, if changeable, not subject to improvement, or not amenable to any available means for bringing the change about. Living with the knowledge of the transient nature of life; accepting the effects that come with the passage of time; and recognizing the differences gender, race, and ethnic origins make in one's situation in life are all aspects of the human condition. They do not represent needs, but may influence the desires that generate needs. Means that promise to alter human conditions toward preferred ends are essentially what we describe when we define professional work. Practice principles inform and commend such means, providing the justifications for their use. Thus, the formulation based on common human needs incorporates within it conditions to be altered, goals to be achieved, and principles of practice that inform and commend the activities that will assist in meeting these needs. In this formulation, it is possible to develop means and ends that are more than congenial, that in fact are inseparable in action.

As a normative profession we have long been concerned with philosophical issues touching on values and ethics. Labels we have earned in the past, such as friendly visitor or do-gooder, despite their less-flattering connotations, correctly perceive the intentions that inspire our efforts. We would not want to be seen as unfriendly; we would not want to do evil. Those who have pursued our roots back to earlier religious and secular origins and social reform movements, and have traced our branching out into many human service arenas, have noted a consistent commitment to mission. Concurrently, as we have sought to improve on our practice skills we have been sensitive to the need for competence, that is, knowing when and where to use these skills. Turn to any page in the National Conference publication series, from the 1870s to the present; peruse any test written especially for our own practitioners; audit classes in our Schools of Social Work as Pumphrey did,[2] and you will find a pervasive interest in value issues and the dilemmas they generate. In striking contrast, such inquiry will also reveal a dearth of material pertaining to ethics. Even when we attempt empirical analyses of our students', faculties', and practitioners' moral preferences, the focus of such studies and the measurements obtained stress terminal and instrumental values, largely ignoring ethical imperatives.

There are two exceptions that make this silence on matters ethical more penetrating. Considerable tumult is periodically generated around efforts to formulate and reformulate our profession's *Code of Ethics*, and less frequently and somewhat muted, around instances when charges have been made that the Code has been violated. The second exception relates to certain selected subjects that persist in attracting much attention because the problems they pose are prevalent in practice, constantly reappear in new forms, and cannot be resolved by current empirical methods of problem solving. Among such subjects are included: confidentiality; paternalism; equity in access to services; the client's right to know; the right to withhold or deny services; the role of the client in policy and service activities. Allowing for such exceptions, our literature and curricula have practically nothing useful to say about methods for developing ethical imperatives. Ignoring actual formulations of such imperatives, they rarely report on the utility, the strengths and limitations of imperatives, in specific applications. The relatively recent interest, therefore, in the possible application of ethical theory to social work situations suffers from the same difficulties as are experienced in attempts to apply generalizations from the theoretical sciences to social work. In both instances, the formulations serve an orienting function, telling us where to look and what to look for, but do not add to our understanding of the "how."

The importance of the "how" should not be underestimated. Consider the vague directives incorporated in our *Code of Ethics*. For example, we are admonished to act in the client's interest. Try to make clear what constitutes the client's interest, and how one might act so as to advance such interest. Then formulate a set of ethical imperatives that would assure a principled practice in this regard. You will quickly discover that the exercise is far from simple. To help practitioners follow the *Code of Ethics* and to evaluate practice adherence to this Code item, we first need to clarify the ethical directives that are intended to guide such practice.

Whether we are concerned with virtues, obligations, or common-good issues, we must pursue their elements analytically. We must master the hard evidence that is relevant to the consequences that flow from unprincipled behavior. We must hazard the formulation of those necessary behaviors and attitudes through which ethical imperatives are implemented. Our failure to do so has hampered our efforts to assure adherence to our *Code of Ethics*.

It would represent a giant step forward in the quality of social work education, for example, if all course work were targeted to elaborate on the ethical component in practice principles. If this elaboration were to occur and faculty and students were required to pursue the value as well as the knowledge justification for such principles, ethical concerns would not go unattended. If this much were achieved, the separate courses focusing on the methods employed in developing ethical imperatives to guide practice, with special application to pressing dilemmas confronting practice, could be justified as in-depth elective offerings.

We recognize the uncertain nature of much of our practice, and the difficulty we face in efforts to demonstrate a causal relationship between our intervention and ultimate outcomes. For this reason, we are best advised to view our practice as highly experimental in nature. The protection of the human subjects included in these experiments must be a central concern. True, the weakness of our interventive techniques lessens the danger of harm to those experimented upon, but this hardly compensates for failures in this area.

Ethical imperatives prescribe the behavior required to achieve a moral practice consistent with claimed values. Thus, when a practice principle commands a practitioner to carry out some action, this command contains moral authority because it is endorsed by an ethical imperative. In effect, the practice principle states that if you do as I say, you can expect to achieve what I predict, and you *should do* what I say because what I advise is both true and right.

For example, in the previously noted illustration a practice principle might state: "Clients shall participate in decisions that affect them." Confronted with a need to choose among alternatives in a service encounter, a worker can draw on this principle for guidance. The principle informs the worker that if clients participate in decisions that affect them they are more likely to act on those decisions than they would be if they did not participate. The "shall" element links the principle to its ethical justification.

This mental process has implications for all practice. If it accurately reflects what happens when a worker faces ethical choices, he or she cannot operate on the basis of practice principles and concurrently engage in unethical practice. Moreover, because professional interventions are intentional and their consequences are expected to achieve preferred ends, they are never free of moral choices. The ethical dimension, not the theory that informs the actions, provides assurance to the worker that what can be done *ought* to be done.

These moral choices are always embedded in conditions and circumstances that facilitate or hinder their selection. In practice, reasoning from consequences or from imperatives rarely suffices to arrive at a prudent action. Even when both approaches are utilized, having to reconcile their different conclusions is frequently necessary. To avoid an opportunistic resolution of differences, while maintaining a prudent perspective, rules for compromise and reconciliation are essential. Whether it is possible to develop rules for prudence is another matter.

Finally, it must be noted that only a small fraction of practice encounters is likely to surface ethical dilemmas. The tendency to focus on dilemmas contributes to the problem-solving perspective by casting such dilemmas in the "problem" frame, and hence directing attention to the problem solving view of how they can be resolved. The absence of conflictual ethical choices is far more prevalent in practice. For such choices no problem is entailed. There is no need for the problem-solver skills. Characteristically, such choices call for judgments that promote behavioral and attitudinal outcomes consistent with the wider value frame of professional practice. This wider frame locates ethical choices in the dual social function attributes of social work practice, assuring social justice and concurrently contributing to social control.

PRINCIPLES FOR A JUST PRACTICE

Clients of social service programs are among the most disadvantaged persons in our society. Social workers employed in these programs normally serve such disadvantaged clients directly, or work with persons interested in promoting services for them. The principal moral justification for professional social work practice is, therefore, to be found in the dedication of the practitioner to the improvement of the circumstance and expectations of these clients. We should base whatever strategic principles we propose for a helping profession in a morality that inspires a just order, or risk encouraging a practice that promotes an unjust one.

Distributive justice, although by no means the whole of a just order, seems to me a particular concern of a helping profession serving the disadvantaged. In whatever other respects a society may be judged just, if, in its distribution of awards and punishments, it penalizes the least advantaged, the society must inevitably contribute to the defeat of piecemeal professional efforts intended to aid them. For this reason we assume as necessary conditions for a practice science in social work certain ethical imperatives that promise to direct professional activities toward the achievement of distributive justice.

Social institutions incorporate into their practice those established patterns of behavior that they are charged to maintain in the society that supports them. While they may differ in their functions in relation to the *status quo*—some primarily concerned with control or maintenance, others with the restoration of restructuring of social relationships among competing groups—all are directly involved in activities or events which inevitably advantage some, and may disadvantage others (Eckland, 1968).

Perhaps the most extensive deprivations of our society are associated with racial discrimination. Widespread and deep-seated patterns of behavior that disadvantage racial minorities do in fact deny to many that fair equality of opportunity that we assume is an essential prerequisite for achieving a social order in which distributive justice prevails. Other bases of discrimination resulting in unjust deprivations are known to exist. Given the knowledge we have of the role of social institutions in any society, and the ethical imperative earlier enunciated for achieving distributive justice, the following principles should inform the work of social workers:

1. The profession and its associated institutions must, in the work and attitudes of their constituents, combat unfair discriminatory practices or be judged as perpetrating the disadvantages such discrimination entails.
2. In choosing program goals and purpose, it should be assumed that ability and motivation among the disadvantaged are more widespread than opportunity.
3. Institutional restrictions that limit opportunities, as well as the personal shortcomings of the client that may curtail his or her options, are legitimate targets for change.
4. Opportunities to participate in the development of programs, in the formulation of policies and procedures, as well as in the practice decisions directly affecting their lives must be afforded the disadvantaged as a minimal expectation of organizations and practices intended to help them.

These principles may be generalized to cover a variety of discriminatory practices we know to be prevalent in our society, including denial of fair opportunity to racial and religious minorities, women, handicapped persons, the aged, the poor; etc. For the purposes of this discussion, racially based discrimination will serve as illustrative.

The propositional elements that inform these principles are derived from known facts about social institutions and their functions in any society, racial discrimination and its impact on all groups, institutions and services in our society, and changes that are required if evident inequities in opportunity are to be eliminated. The commendations that inform these principles are derived from the ethical imperative accepted as essential for the achievement of distributive justice. Together, these proposititional and value statements justify the principles proposed. The experiences of social workers also serve to justify them in a way that encourages their acceptance in practice.

Social workers, in their professional and nonprofessional experience, have the opportunity to observe and evaluate the unjust practices of the communities in which they live and work. They compose for storage in memory these perceptions of prevalent social inequalities and recover them when they seek to understand events and circumstances new to their experience. Certainly, life experiences differ among social workers and such differences extend to the social context and circumstances of their encounters with racial discrimination. There are workers who have been the victims of unfair behavior and others who have practiced such behavior without a conscious awareness of its implications. There are undoubtedly some who have rationalized the injustices they have observed, attributing evident inequities to the influences of fate, faith, or fundamental biological differences. Whereas some workers would find support for the suggested practice principles in their total life experience, others would view these principles as contradictory to what nonprofessional and even certain professional experience would suggest.

Workers who would accept these principles for professional practice but deny their applicability to their behavior when not involved in professional work, would have to manage serious inner-directed conflict. One may suppose that the mental compartmentalization of behavioral norms that must accompany such contradictory directives is likely to be successfully maintained when reinforced by external influences. Social structures, community norms, and institutions appear to facilitate and reinforce mental compartmentalization of behavioral rules by supporting differential role expectations in different settings. It may be that increased dependence on such external structures to sustain mental compartmentalizations would ultimately deprive the worker of considerable freedom to respond imaginatively to client need situations, reinforcing a more rigid, habituated rule-dominated practice. This is a heavy price to pay, but probably unavoidable, if inner-directed conflict is to be controlled.

Experience teaches us to accept as a matter of fact the ability of most persons to engage in inconsistent behavior, and we accept this as normal, so long as contradictory behaviors are not simultaneously evident in the same social context. A helping profession (and its associated institutions) that promotes such inconsistencies, however, cannot expect to compartmentalize them so readily. Policies and procedures are never entirely private in an institution; the tensions generated by contradictory policies are communicated to the practitioner and his or her clients and are not likely to be fully absorbed in intraorganizational stresses and strains. The profession can hardly afford to be inconsistent in its principled behavior, lest it be judged dishonest to the degree that its rules subvert professed intentions. If, for the individual, inconsistent behavior in professional and personal activities can be depleting of energy and resource, for the profession it can be calamitous.

There is a process, not clearly understood, whereby principled behavior is achieved. For the individual worker, there is the need to determine for him- or herself that the propositions and commendations of the principles to be followed are true and right, and this normally requires that he or she experience in practice the positive consequences that follow upon their application. He or she may, in relation to the set of principles proposed, find personal and social reasons for supporting their directives, recognizing that they are intended to increase the choices open to a client. As he or she works with clients and discovers for him- or herself how personal and social factors contribute to the conditions he or she seeks to change, he or she will compose for storage in memory the self-confirming proofs that develop and sustain convictions, and will be more willing to act on them.

One cannot legislate an inner-directed adherence to an ethic or truth, but one can promote a context that encourages such adherence. A practice environment that is increasingly intolerant of workers who profess ideals but fail to evidence conviction about them in their work, is likely to inspire principled behavior. This is sensed by workers who seek employment in agencies that practice what they profess, assuming that in such agencies they will be encouraged to do likewise.

The social work profession attaches considerable importance to its code of ethics and similarly seeks a community environment that is sympathetic, that encourages the profession to act on the basis of its convictions. While the profession is aware of its limited capacities and deficiencies in skill, there is much evidence of community restraints and deprivation that disadvantage programs employing social workers, severely limiting their opportunities to achieve at the level of their known capacities.

A measure of a practitioner's skills is his or her ability to take into him- or herself both the client situation and worker situation and to develop a balanced perspective that frees him or her to act on the basis of the practice principles they inform. Unlike the rational process whereby suggested principles are derived, the processes that the practitioner experiences in developing and sustaining a conviction to act on these principles must include work and the opportunity to observe its consequences. The assumption long held by social work educators that methods are mastered in their application—rests in part on this necessity *to do* in order to know what acting on a principle really means.

Patterns of worker activity provide the vehicles through which guiding principles are actualized. "By their deeds ye shall know them" accurately describes the role of action in the appraisal of professional intentions. The first principle proposed includes in its formulation an appreciation of this characteristic of practice when it denies the possibility of a neutral stance toward racism. This principle assumes that one cannot enter the stream of community life and remain dry, nor avoid some deflection of its flow. Either the worker imparts a principle in his or her practice, or departs from it, and his or her actions provide the evidence by which his or her adherence to principle can be judged.

The third principle carries with it the implicit expectation that the worker will be knowledgeable in actions intended to change institutional structures as well as actions intended to structure personal and interpersonal change. It does not assume that these need be separate or qualitatively distinctive actions. The principle further recognizes that institutional arrangements in troubled communities must not model professional and organizational goals, but serve them. If the profession is to act in accordance with its commitment to distributive justice it must be prepared to transform itself and other community institutional structures and agencies employing social workers.

This third principle visualizes a societal and personal component in every service encounter. In seeking to maximize the client's utilization of resources, the worker's casual interests direct him or her to focus on personal social restraints, which determine the current opportunities available to the client. This would be the case whatever the nature of the client's problems, whatever their etiologies. Utilization of service appears in practice as action and, in the context of the helping process, is an important form of *social* action. It is not likely to be enhanced where opportunities available for improved utilization are so limited as to deny notice.

In fulfilling his or her function, the worker may abstract from the service encounter indicators that suggest compositions of personal deficiencies and limited abilities. He or she may also identify societal deprivations. He or she will have to decide on their relative importance to the client's utilization problems and act on the basis of his or her evaluation. Unfortunately, given the compartmentalization of knowledge in the various disciplines—psychological and sociological—workers are likely to be programmed to store and recover compositions accordingly. The need is apparent for constructs that can bridge the artificial barriers created by compartmentalized formulations and that can encourage compositions that do not decompose the wholeness of the social–individual meaning of the service activity. Much of the polemical literature that has characterized professional discussion of micro/macro change, of individual/social causation, would be irrelevant had we the knowledge that freed us to represent the wholeness of practice in our conceptualizations.

There may be other reasons for maintaining a compartmentalized view of practice. If the worker perceives the problem to be primarily societal in origin, he or she can attribute failures in service to socially produced deprivations. If he or she perceives the problem as personal in origin, failure in service can be attributed to limited capabilities and abilities in the client. In either case, the failure will not be primarily the worker's. Thinking about the condition to be changed in the compartmentalized fashion can soften self-criticism. It also may encourage the worker to view him- or herself as a neutral element in the causal chain that disadvantages the client. Pressured by inadequate funding, program and skill deficiencies, and the emotional stresses that accompany helping processes, this rationalization could fulfill an important soothing purpose.

The price paid for such mental chicanery is continued failure to achieve the goals of service. It makes no sense whatsoever to conceive of the social worker as a change agent, a term currently popular in the profession, yet attribute to his or her work no immediate and significant responsibility for outcomes of service. It makes even less sense to see individuals and institutions as beneficiaries of service, while denying them a central role in its development. The fourth principle, therefore, requires organizations and professionals intent upon helping people, to include those for whom their services are intended and resources are organized and distributed to meet these needs (Warren, 1971). The knowledge basis for the propositional element in this principle has received extensive documentation in the literature of social work, particularly as a result of the experiences of antipoverty, community mental health, and client self-help programs.

This principle does not require that those who are intended to benefit directly from the program have control of it, but does not exclude this possibility. There is increasing evidence that many client groups favor such control, and experience may prove that it is an essential ingredient for sound practice. Conceivably, client control may provide one of the more important opportunities that traditionally have been denied to the disadvantaged in our country.

The profession of social work, in a society where distributive justice is known not to prevail, will never be free of threats to its goals and programs. It will need the active support of all persons committed to its goals, particularly those who stand to benefit directly from its services. Such support will likely be forthcoming from persons who have a stake in all phases of the social processes whereby services are developed and provided. It is to be expected that those who reject the ethical imperative that justifies this principle will find fault with its application. On the other hand, it is probable that those who identify with the ethic will not treat kindly the organizations and individuals who stand aside and remain silent when the goals and programs intended to achieve it are threatened. Adherence to the fourth principle can serve as an important safeguard against the irresponsibility of acquiescence.

Chapter Notes

1. Charlotte Towle (1945). *Common human needs.* Washington, DC: Federal Security Agency, Social Security Board, Bureau of Public Assistance.
2. Ralph Pumphrey, coauthor of *The heritage of American social work.* New York: Columbia University Press, 1961.

BIBLIOGRAPHY

Eckland, B. K. (1968, Spring). Retrieving mobile cases in longitudinal surveys. *The Public Opinion Quarterly 32*(1), 51–64.

Pumphrey, R. E., and Pumphrey, M. W. (Eds.). (1961). *The heritage of American social work: Readings in its philosophical and institutional development.* New York: Columbia University Press.

Towle, C. (1945). *Common human needs: An interpretation for staff in public assistance agencies.* Washington, DC: Federal Security Agency, Social Security Board, Bureau of Public Assistance.

Warren, R. (1971). *The community in America.* Chicago: Rand McNally.

Chapter 11

Ethical Assessment

This essay examines the well-known process of assessment through an ethical lens. It explores the question of how to balance a client's interests with the goal of furthering the community of interests. It also links the problem of ethical ambiguities in an interesting way to the expansion of social workers' knowledge.

An ethical assessment is an evaluative process, similar to other assessments conducted by practitioners. It is intended to help the practitioner determine if an ethical issue is present, what it entails for practice, and how one reasons about such issues, granted the provisional conclusions that result from an assessment process. The assessment determines the nature and scope of the issue and suggests interventions that would be ethical. This essay defines certain key terms employed in all ethical analyses and provides clues to how one can recognize an ethical issue. The content of an ethical assessment is described, and the application of the two most prevalent approaches guiding the reasoning about ethical issues is discussed. Finally, a procedure is proposed to help the practitioner arrive at decisions affecting ethical issues.

DEFINITIONS

Terms such as "good" and "right" are normally used to express moral judgments. In this analysis, they are to be understood as terms of moral appraisal in relation to which an action is to be judged. For our purposes, certain goals or considerations that all people and societies aspire to—such as knowledge, security, justice, well-being, salvation, aesthetic satisfaction—are goods or are grounds for rights. Most often, a need to choose between competing goods and competing rights underlie ethical dilemmas.

Two great traditions in normative or applied ethics are encompassed in various forms of utilitarianism and formalism. Utilitarianism bases moral judgments on the consequences of an act if it were to be performed; formalism, on some formal feature of the ethical imperative (a principle of conduct) under which the act is performed. For example, the utilitarian may evaluate a lie on the basis of the

Originally published in *Social Casework, 65*(4), April 1984.

amount of pleasure and pain what would result and decide to lie if the consequences favored pleasure over pain. The formalist, on the other hand, having adopted a principle to which he or she is committed—that it is wrong to lie—would hold to it whatever the consequences in all situations to which this imperative applies. The formalist's reasoning is often referred to as deontological; the utilitarian, as teleological. In this essay, the term *consequentialist* will refer to a teleological approach to ethical issues and *formalist* to a deontological approach.

In social work practice, values are seen as affecting the choice of objectives and goals. Values surface for consideration where purpose is addressed. The tradition speaks of the profession as value-laden, but sees the ethical "oughts" as separate from the "knowns." The paradigm of the value-free proposition providing informed, research-affirmed guidelines for action is generally viewed as the scientific base on which the profession's claim to competence rests. The value component is not subject to the same methodological tests for truth; it is appreciated for its significance in the process of negotiating the ends to be sought, not the means of achieving them. Omitted from these propositions and preferences is the ethical imperative that would help the practitioner decide whether what can be done should be done. To correct for this omission, we shall consider how one recognizes an ethical issue and how one goes about making an ethical assessment.

AMBIGUITIES

Workers frequently must choose among alternative intervention strategies that, at best, are chancy. For example, when a worker applies eligibility criteria in a public assistance program, or chooses among various placement options for children who must be moved from their own home, or considers commitment of a client to a mental hospital, or wonders whether the time has arrived to terminate treatment in a therapeutic relationship, he or she is usually confronted with ambiguities that are perplexing.

These uncertainties, which may lose their equivocal attributes as facts are clarified and as supplemental information is provided, seldom involve ethical predicaments. When the addition of knowledge removes the doubt, an informed judgment is facilitated. For example, consider the not uncommon practice situation with the frail elderly. As a risk of injury from unsupervised living arrangements increases, the decision must be made to provide protective services in the home or placement in an institution. The more knowledge one has of the particular person involved and all the relevant contextual factors, the better one can evaluate these alternatives with some assurance of likely outcomes. Such added information can alter what might have been a cloudy choice to one in which informed judgments can be made. However, where ethical issues are involved, the additional clarification that facts provide may increase one's doubts. Thus, in the example cited, added knowledge also may make it evident that basing the choice on likely outcomes, which the worker judges are in the client's interest, can involve a paternalism of the type, "doing good for the client's sake." Where either choice is morally right for the aged recipient of the service—recognizing that each involves some relinquishing of the client's autonomy and independence—is moot. In this situation, the ethical issue remains even when the consequences of actions are least obscure. The measure of positive and negative benefits can be stacked against the right of freedom of choice, which ought not be abrogated without full representation of the client's consent. The client may express a preference for a future free of supervised restraint even if this increases risks of physical injury. Unlike those ambiguities that ignorance inspires in practice, ethical ambiguities may become even more sharply delineated as ignorance is dispelled. Thus, knowing more can clarify choices and consequence, while concurrently highlighting an ethical dilemma that stems from the conflict of a good versus a right.

Similarly, examples can be cited where two goods are in conflict. For example, a client's interest and that of the client's family may be at odds in weighing protective services in the home or institutionalization. Or two rights may be in conflict, as when efforts to provide for the civil rights of a client require the sacrifice of another client's right to confidentiality.

From the preceding, it should be clear why the worker must seek to clarify all that can be known about the situation involved. While this is a common sense conclusion for any aspect of professional practice, it is often not appreciated in seeking to assemble those elements without which an ethical appraisal is likely to be faulty.

WHEN ETHICAL ISSUES MAY SURFACE

When the worker seeks to act in an ethically ambiguous situation, she or he is bound to consider the practice principle that directs and commands the actions. Practice principles consist of two elements that have frequently been thought of separately in the literature. First are the propositional statements, "if this . . . , then that" or "from this in time to that." Whether derived from theoretical science generalizations or from experience, such propositions inform the practice principle, giving it the strength it has to direct the worker's action.

The second element in a practice principle is some commendation derived from an ethical imperative. The "ought," "should," "will," and "must" that are always incorporated in practice principles provide the strength such principles need to command the action that the proposition directs the worker to follow. Thus, when the worker appeals to a practice principle for clarification of an ambiguous situation, he or she is seeking theoretical and ethical guidance, assembled in a single prescription. Fortunately, workers do not often have to seek such guidance, because much of practice is rule-governed. (Rules are directives for action that spell out the process the worker is expected to follow in practice. They are intended to provide uniformity and control over practice. Principles, which frequently provide the justification for rules, are guidelines formulated to allow maximum freedom of choice and innovation in their application.)

When operating by rule, the directive and command elements that constitute the rule are sufficiently clear and compelling to permit routine, almost habituated responses in situations for which rules are appropriate. When a person questions a rule and appeals to a practice principle that seems to recommend a different action than the rule, an ethical issue may be identified.

Similarly, when assessing the situation and circumstances that will require intervention, if the worker concludes that she or he should not do so and so and therefore will not, and justifies the "should" on grounds of what is "good" or "right" for the client, an ethical issue may be present.

Consider, for example, the position endorsed by some people that manipulation—including lying or presenting half-truths—is justified in professional practice when such falsehoods are believed to advance the interest of the client. The need for truth telling in interpersonal relationships has received considerable attention in the literature of science. When a person is engaged in scientific work, failure to be truthful is equivalent to a betrayal of a rule for assuring a fundamental trust. Reordering the presentation of information in science is accepted as a necessary condition for establishing truths but it is prohibited activity when its intention is the opposite. Can social work, which lays claim to a scientific grounding for its actions, ignore this ethical imperative of science? One is tempted to dismiss the position of those who try to justify falsehoods, for this and all the reasons one can list for rejecting practices that destroy trust in any human relationship. Nevertheless, a more detailed analysis of the reasons offered to justify lying can provide some guidance in our concern to develop a sound ethical assessment procedure.

CONFLICT AND CONTRADICTION

Practice in social work is intended to assist the recipients and concurrently to advance a useful social purpose. Thus, a worker advances the well-being of an aggregate—the community—by an intervention that improves the well-being of its individual members. This part—whole conceptualization makes social purpose and professional function congenial, so long as one assumes an overarching commonality of interests shared by all its members. Communities differ in their compositions—by race, sex, social status, religion, class, and ethnicity, for example. An overarching community of interests must take account of these differences. It is easily documented that communities vary in their interests and that such interests may be in conflict. A seemingly congenial union of purpose in function may, in real communities, resemble a Roman Peace: the "purpose" of controlling interests swallowing the practice "function;" the lion at peace with the lamb, the lamb inside the lion.

Practitioners are rarely unaware of the contradictions such differing interests generate. They are constantly made aware of their implications by agency programs and procedures that communicate in fairly certain terms, whose interests are to be advanced in the aggregate. The practice task would seem to require that only those interests of the recipient of service that in the aggregate advance the community's interest are to be pursued. What is the worker to do if it appears that the client's interest would, if realized, advance a purpose that is not acceptable to all groups, but only to the group that determines the policies and procedure of the service program? Should the imperative that client interests come first be violated?

Methods for bridging the gap between community, group, and client interest have been proposed, but all appear to require acceptance of some time delay before they can be achieved. In the interim, for a particular client, the practitioner must ask what remedy is to be offered. Enter here, the tactic of falsification, manipulating the system by half-truths. Little white lies, misinformation, omission—in short, using a trust-destroying procedure on the client's behalf, advancing the client's interest while outwardly professing adherence to a strategy that would promote the common good as defined by those governing the service program.

The ethical issues posed are complicated. For example, agencies frequently prepare budgets and justify funding on the basis of exaggerated or misleading claims as to the manner in which the funds will actually be spent. Among those who engage in such practice there often appears to be an understanding that such distortions are necessary and expected, since they pacify the unrealistic expectations of those who support services. Rather than attempting to use the budgeting process as a tool to educate funding sources, the funding presentation provides justifications that are acceptable to the funding body and that, in the long run, assure services that the agency leadership believes essential. This obfuscating practice raises doubt about the ethics of those who engage in it.

But some people advance another perspective on these deceptive budgetary practices. They argue that administrators of programs need to exercise professional judgment in the expenditure of program funds. They note that agencies exercise some control over the choices open to the practitioner while recognizing that oversight in professional practice must not deter the worker in using professional judgment in the helping transaction. Similarly, the budget process allows for supervisory control to be exercised by those to whom the executive and board may be accountable, but ought to allow the executive and board choices without which program implementation would not be possible. These people reason that the benefits achieved by the deceptive practice, in situations where the funding body would otherwise unduly restrain the judgment needed to advance the program, exceed the cost—the obligation to provide the funding body with a more accurate picture of how funds will be used. Obviously, these alternative interpretations of an ethically ambiguous situation do not provide an assessment. While they help clarify the substantive issues involved, they hardly resolve them.

In the author's view, an assessment ought not be so constructed as to deny a function to guiding imperatives, reducing choices to situational preferences of individual actors. In the example cited, the ethical imperative is to tell the truth. Where a worker finds herself or himself pressed to manipulate information and, by so doing, manipulates persons on the basis of falsehoods, the imperative of truth-telling affirms such practices as unethical. The problem posed is how to alleviate the pressure for such falsifications in order that the client's interests be served and the community of interests be furthered. Rather than promote a tolerance for ethical deviations, the assessment should fuel opposition to the circumstances that, to the worker, appear to make such unethical practices necessary. Often, the efforts to alter these circumstances produce situations giving rise to additional dilemmas.

Another aspect of the assessment is also highlighted by these examples. The conflicts that are pervasive in a society are not likely to be absent in a professional practice generated by that society. If, for example, a community discriminates on the basis of sex in the opportunities it offers persons, practice will evidence such discrimination in the difficulties presented by persons seeking help and in the way in which the help is offered. The imperative that seeks to advance equity through the promotion of equal access for all will be perceived in its absence as a cause to be advanced in an ethical practice and a function to be carried out in the methods employed in that practice.

In addition to considering the imperative, the worker must recognize that psychological as well as logical influences enter into the formulation of an ethical assessment. There is evidence that consistency in rational behavior and satisfaction with anticipated outcomes—both essential in practice decisions—are best achieved if the choices made are not intended to answer the question, "What do I want now?" but rather, "What will I feel then, after the choice is made?" Moreover, the way an action is understood may affect the actual experience of its outcomes. The adoption of a decision frame is an ethically significant act in itself. For these reasons, the choice of any assessment approach is not value-free. It will reflect the ethical preferences of those designing it, including in this instance, the author of this essay. (This author's preferences are for social justice, self-realization, fraternity, and freedom of choice in the realization of those "goods" noted in the second paragraph of this essay). An unethical act in an ambiguous situation may be judged the best alternative, although recognized by the worker as deficient in standards and appreciated as a signal to work toward changes necessary to make an ethical choice possible. What is unacceptable is to assert that an immoral act is ethical.

CONTENT OF AN ETHICAL ASSESSMENT

Mila A. Aroskar suggests the inclusion of answers to the following as core data on which to base an ethical assessment:

Action

1. Who are the actors involved? What are their histories and involvement in the situation?
2. What is the proposed action or actions?

3. What is the setting or context of the proposed action or actions?
4. What is the intention or purpose of the proposed action?
5. What are the probable implications or consequences of the proposed actions?

Decision

1. Who should decide?
2. For whom is the decision being made? Self, proxy, other?
3. What criteria should be used? Social, legal, psychological, economic, psychological, other?
4. What degree of consent by the client or subject is needed? Freely given, coerced, none?
5. What, if any, moral principles are enhanced or negated by a proposed course of action? Self-determination, truthfulness, beneficence, justice, or fairness?

Others have proposed a problem-solving approach to the consideration of ethical issues.

Unhappily, a person can answer all the substantive questions and yet not reach a viable ethical decision. Such information serves an orienting function, alerting the assessor where to look and what to look for. It does not provide guidance as to the essential processes that the decision maker must carry out in his or her own head. The remainder of this essay addresses these processes.

CHOOSING AMONG ALTERNATIVES

A practitioner responsible for making an ethical assessment will approach this intellectual task in a manner not unlike that which she or he has come to favor in carrying through the usual diagnostic effort. The worker will want to organize all information available within the time constraints dictated by the practice situation, in a manner that suggests answers to his or her inner-directed questions: "What am I to do?" and "How ought I proceed?" The assessment is more likely to yield a useful decision if its logical form is congenial with the reasoning favored by the worker in her or his diagnostic efforts.

Propositions that inform choices and shape decisions are acted on by the worker as if they were matters of fact. For example, the worker will take as a given the proposition: "If clients participate in the decision that affects them, they are more likely to act on that decision than if they are not party to its formulation." The truth of this proposition is confirmed by the worker's observations of consequences that follow when it is acted on and when it is ignored. The worker may also seek to anticipate consequences entailed in the resolution of an ethical issue. Past experience, the reported experiences of others, and anticipated outcomes provide the worker with some measure of likely losses and benefits that alternative actions will produce. The worker's measure of the rightness of the act may be based on the judgment that any other course would not have as high a utility for this client and all those affected. This form of hypothetical reasoning, when used to assess ethical acts, resembles the logic the worker uses in confirming for him- or herself the truth claims of a propositional statement. Necessarily, it suffers the same limitations: for example, a chronic lack of adequate information and unavoidable distortions because of subjective and contextual factors influencing the worker's judgment. For these reasons, an approach that depends on an evaluation of consequences is likely to yield a tentative choice of action, subject to revision or modification during the entire service transaction, constantly responding to new data generated by the service process itself. The approach is appealing, in that it favors the bias of the practitioner who prefers to be seen as an "objective" actor in the service drama.

The worker who employs a formalist approach reasons from general ethical imperatives or duties intended to provide overall guidance in all instances in which such imperatives or duties have relevance. For example, the worker may believe with Alan Gewirth that freedom and well-being are the critical maxims, thus he or she decides to sequence choices based on the order dictated by these maxims in particular cases. For a worker electing a formalist approach, the weighting of consequences are of lesser or no concern in deciding on an ethical course. Consistency with the guiding imperative is the proof sought in judging the rightness of action.

Thus, if such duties as fidelity, reparation, gratitude, justice, beneficence, and self-improvement are accepted as intrinsically right, an act may be judged morally required if such a duty can be identified. Or if a worker accepts as binding the duty to distribute unequal benefits so as to advance the expectations of the least advantaged, she or he may believe that the resulting allocations will reflect a form of justice that is fair. Having accepted a maxim, the duty it entails, and the knowledge that no more stringent duty can override it, the worker would not be prompted to measure consequences in order to decide on a course of action. He or she would seek to determine if the chosen action is consistent with the guiding imperative.

The commendation that commands, not unlike the proposition that directs, may be justified on the basis of different rationales. Each such rationale for a particular choice may be grounded in an ethical theory that dictates how choices are to be made. Conflicting scientific theories may coexist in the repertoire of the worker and serve useful purposes, so long as each is used to justify a different proposition, or all concur in the justification of the same proposition. This is not necessarily the case with ethical imperatives. The need for ethical consistency presses the worker toward adopting a single belief system to guide action when confronted with ethical choices in professional practice. This assumes that ethical imperatives are not newly formulated to deal with each instance where an issue surfaces, despite the obvious unique features of each situation and the possibility that some ethical theories may be more helpful than others in certain situations. In this view, an individual response, free of any prior practice principles or rules for deciding problematic choices, may easily come to represent opportunistic, unprincipled behavior.

AN EXAMPLE OF A STRATEGY

If, as is suggested, there are rules that can guide the ethical decision-making process, what are they and how ought they be applied? The following discussion seeks to answer this question, using a purposefully simplified case to illustrate a recommended logical strategy for arriving at appropriate decisions.

Returning to the case of the frail elderly, we have the situation in which Mr. K, eighty-four years of age, living alone, and quite independent of outside assistance in managing his affairs, repeatedly falls and injures himself. After his last injury, he is confined to a wheelchair and bed. He has home-aide services that he repels by burdening the aide with aggravating actions and verbal abuse. A neighbor, who in the past had helped with Mr. K's shopping, is now unable to assist in this area. Mr. K, a lifelong bachelor, has no children or relatives to call on for assistance and no friends still living or well enough to help out. The agency providing the home-aide service for Mr. K decides that he is at excessive risk if he continues to live alone at home. It recommends that he seek placement in an institution. Mr. K, mentally alert and in control of his own preferences, does not wish to enter an institution and insists he can manage on his own. The medical opinion on Mr. K's condition is quite discouraging. The doctor does not anticipate an early or complete healing of his last injury and is certain that, without constant supervision, he will experience additional injuries with less and less probability of recovery. His physician agrees with the agency that anything less than full-time supervision will be inadequate. Such supervision cannot be provided in the home even with a full-time live-in aide.

Referring back to the core data that Aroskar suggests should be used as the basis for an ethical assessment, we have here the actors—Mr. K, the home aide, the agency worker, the doctor, and the friendly neighbor. There are sufficient data on the situation to anticipate past and current involvements that are relevant. We have not explored financial information that, while relevant, would not significantly alter the ethical issue we shall address. The action proposed is to place Mr. K in a nursing home. We've described the context of the proposed action and its purpose, and have considered, in part, possible consequences if the action is not taken. We are now positioned to consider the decision theory dimensions. These entail the questions: Who should decide—Mr. K or the agency and worker? What criteria should be used? What degree of consent by Mr. K is needed?

Obviously, in keeping with the practice principle of maximizing a person's participation in decisions that affect him or her, Mr. K is able to and should decide, without coercion, on the course of action to be followed. But there is an undesirable consequence to his choice not to enter a nursing home—that is, a further threat to his well-being. Let us consider a sequence of logical steps that could be followed in assessing the ethics of the situation and see what conclusion would be reached for further action. We shall assume that all parties to the situation are involved for the best of motives—they have Mr. K's interest at heart.

1. *In relation to the propositional element (that is, if . . . then) in the situation, a consequential analysis should be carried out.*

In this instance, if Mr. K stays in his inadequately supervised residence, he will probably suffer further injury, experience more limited recovery with each injury, and make heavier demands on medical and home-aide services, with little or no chance of altering a steady or accelerated degenerative process. If he is moved to the nursing home, protective supervision will minimize risk of injury and make for more efficient care under constant medical supervision. The anticipated consequences obviously favor placement. But Mr. K is proud of his independence, detests the idea of entering a nursing home, and finds dependence on others an unacceptable intrusion on his autonomy and privacy. There is no doubt that his autonomy and privacy will be affected if he must leave his residence and enter the home. It is also probable that, with the deterioration of his condition, much of the freedom of action and decision-making autonomy he enjoys in his residence would be lost as increasing care taking by others would be required. Again, in the balance, it would appear that placement would have a positive consequence in the long run, even if measures of autonomy are used as criteria.

2. *The ethical imperative justifying the action that the proposition commends should be identified and a formalist analysis carried out.*

In this instance, following a Gewirth formulation, Mr. K's voluntary choice and well-being ought to take precedence over any consequences that follow from the exercises of these rights. Since he is competent to appreciate his situation, and mentally alert and clear as to what he can expect, he ought not be coerced into a decision against his wishes. However, it is apparent that Mr. K's well-being and voluntary action are in conflict, and that well-being may be thought to take precedence. Were this found to be the case, then placement in the home would appear to be justified on formalist grounds, if the threat to well-being far outweighs the possible loss of freedom Mr. K will sustain.

3. *Where both analyses—the consequentialist and the formalist—suggest the identical choice to be preferred, act on the suggestion.*

In this case, place Mr. K, even if coercion is necessary "for his own good."

4. *Where the analyses yield different results, evidencing similar strengths, follow the consequentialist-derived guidance, provided the action does not directly contradict the guidance offered by the formalist analysis.*

Thus, in Mr. K's situation, the consequential analysis remains as previously described. There is question whether the threat to well-being is sufficient to warrant sacrificing the client's freedom of choice. Thus, the formalist analysis is inconclusive. In these circumstances one would be well-advised to press for placement, preferably with Mr. K's reluctant approval but by coercion if necessary.

5. *If the consequential analysis directly contradicts the formalist analysis, the formalist analysis should prevail and provisions be made to work at eliminating the influences producing the contradictions.*

In Mr. K's situation, if may be that his well-being is not as clearly in danger as the earlier analysis suggests. Hence, coercion is not justified, even though the consequentialist analysis remains unchanged—that is, it finds placement to have more positive consequences than remaining at home. Here the client's rights would be given precedence over what is thought to be for his own good. Nevertheless, the worker and the physician may seek to persuade Mr. K to accept their recommendation.

6. *Where the consequentialist analysis is weak, lacking in adequate detail or measurable results, act on the formalist analysis, but restrict such action to as limited a scope as possible, while seeking to strengthen the conditions necessary to make a sound consequential analysis.*

In Mr. K's situation, if the consequences of either choice, placement or remaining at home, are equally negative or uncertain, then the client's rights should be protected but the consequences of the exercise of rights should be carefully monitored to assure review of the decision if the consequential analysis changes based on new information and modified circumstances.

7. *Where both analyses cannot be carried out because of lack of needed information, understanding of influence, and prior experience with consequences: (a) follow the guidance suggested by the incomplete formalist analysis; (b) periodically review the possibilities for taking step 4 or 5, moving to one of these as it becomes feasible.*

8. *In cases where the formalist analysis is adopted and there is conflict among duties and imperatives, act on the priority order that the particular formalist approach commends, keeping in mind that the choice must respond to the client's interests that: Jointly encompass the futures the worker and those whose professional judgment she or he respects deem likely to satisfy the client's needs and desires and, if realized, would be acceptable to both the worker and client.*

Thus, if in Mr. K's situation, it is decided to honor his request not to be placed, this decision does not relieve the worker of responsibility for pursuing the soundness of the assessment and reevaluating the decision as circumstances change. Knowing that Mr. K's wishes would be best realized if both his autonomy and well-being could be assured, it should be the aim of the worker, doctor, and home aide to do as much as possible to help him realize these goals.

9. *Having arrived at a choice of duties and imperatives to be followed, giving precedence to the guidance suggested by the formalist analysis, the requirements of step 5 should be kept constantly in mind.*

The sequenced rules apply both consequential and formalist approaches to ethical evaluations. The branching alternatives are explored when conflicting outcomes are generated by the two approaches. It should be fairly obvious to social work practitioners that the decision tree proposed does not differ substantially from clinical assessment processes employed in direct practice diagnoses. An ethical assessment always must be seen as tentative and ongoing, as is true of diagnoses in practice. Circumstances and conditions, attitudes and behavior, are always in flux, providing new evidence that injects new influences to which interventions must be responsive.

POINTS TO BE EMPHASIZED

This discussion has considered the need for ethical assessments, the ways in which ethical issues can be identified, approaches to ethical evaluations, the preconditions for decision making, and how one systematically decides what to do on the basis of the assessment. The points to be emphasized are the need for greater sensitivity to ethical issues on the part of practitioners and their awareness that the intellectual processes involved in ethical decision making are congenial with prevalent assessment processes in clinical work.

Chapter 12

The Whistleblower and the Whistleblowing Profession

Lewis uses a case in which he was actively involved to examine the issue of whistleblowing and, through this issue, broader questions regarding the ethical obligations of social workers to employers and to society, particularly in those instances where such obligations conflict with the client's interest.

A social worker, a supervisor in the Brooklyn Office of Special Services for Children of New York City, turned over confidential records to the newspapers, exposing questionable practices in his agency's dealing with clients. Poor practice, incompetence, and inadequate services had, in his view, resulted in death for nine children and suffering for many more. An internal study by the Inspector General of the agency found the agency negligent in seventeen out of twenty-two cases cited by the worker. For violating confidentiality and breaking the law, the worker was demoted, fined, and transferred to another department. The conditions that led to the problems he identified are only now being addressed.

Without detailing all that occurred, certain facts should be noted: The worker had complained to his immediate and proximate superiors about the alarming practices. When no action was taken, he contacted members of the City Council of New York, one of whom was a social worker. When nothing came of these efforts, he sent copies of case files to the Governor, who did not reply, and to the Children's Aid Society, which returned them. He contacted religious, ethnic, and service organizations, but most refused to support him. He contacted me and, in response to a request from his attorney, I agreed to testify on his behalf if his case went to court. The City Board of the NASW, while recognizing the seriousness of his charges, voted not to support his request for financial support from the NASW Legal Defense Fund. He appealed to the national NASW office, which extended a grant of $600. Through the efforts of the New York Deans' Association and the Community Welfare Council, a Committee of Concerned Persons was organized; it pressed the City for an investigation into the allegations. The Inspector General's report was, in part, a response to this pressure. Finally, after the case again made

Presented at Simmons College, October 4, 1984, and originally published in the *Journal of Clinical Social Work with Children*, Winter 1985.

the press, the Mayor first endorsed the disciplinary action taken against the worker, then reconsidered and removed all the disciplinary measures, reinstating the worker. Concurrently, the Mayor established a regular procedure through which complaints such as those presented by this worker would be heard and acted on without threat to the whistleblower.

In a letter to me written in August 1983, the worker noted:

> During the past four years I have been maligned, harassed and attacked by fellow workers and my union, resented (and severely fined thousands of dollars) and indicted by others without a trial, just because I tried to save children's lives. I could not have done less.

In a letter to me some months later, he wrote:

> I'm sorry to bother you with my personal problems, but it now seems certain the City will fire me. A job in social work isn't possible—if you know any people who might be willing to train me—or if you have any other ideas, please let me know.

This worker, as far as I could determine followed all the prescribed rules for airing a serious concern through agency channels. Even after exhausting the agency route, he sought help from key, responsible persons. Finally, he went to the press. He broke one rule, and that rule was imbedded into law. Thus, he earned the punishment for breaking a rule, and was not punished—other than in his conscience—for following the rules. Note, I could find no personal benefit to be gained by this worker for breaking the rules, except the ease with which he could live with himself and his conscience. What can be learned from his case, and what implications for ethical practice in social work are suggested by its outcome?[1]

ETHICAL PRACTICE

Lydia Rappaport (1968) once described social work as the conscience of society. She believed it was our professional destiny to speak out in opposition to the social injustices we encounter in the course of providing services to our clients. For more than a century, as our profession has matured, its leadership has urged its practitioners to bring to public attention the evils wrought by unfair social policies and practices, and to document their cost in anguish, pain, sorrow, and poor health. Those who have accepted and acted on this challenge have also experienced the inevitable attack on their person. It is common practice to condemn the messenger who brings the bad news. Those who have spoken out have been labeled as hairbrained idealists, unrealistic do-gooders, bleeding hearts, arrogant busybodies, all attributes normally assigned to those organizational whistleblowers who protest injustices in the system of which they are a part. One does not make friends by calling to the attention of outsiders the evils perpetuated by existing programs and practices. One generates enemies among those whose failings are exposed and whose prestige, power, and income are threatened.

During the past four years, the incident involving a social worker who "blew the whistle" in a public child welfare agency, gained national attention. The media—including the *New York Times,* the *Village Voice,* the *Daily News,* the *New York Post,* the *New Yorker,* the *Hastings Journal,* the *National Newsletter* of the NASW, and others all carried stories about this happening, and all appeared to be sympathetic to the whistleblower, who admittedly had broken a law. In reviewing this case, with which I was involved, I find it useful to first consider the whistleblowing that is our professional destiny, to establish some perspective for viewing the whistleblowing in the case to be discussed.

Lydia Rappaport's description contained an important truth that can be generalized for all professions. In their domain of expertise, professions should be the conscience of society. They should deliberately blow the whistle on social conditions and practices that contribute to the problems evidenced by people seeking their services. Doctors, nurses, lawyers, teachers, journalists, and clergy, no less than social workers, should be judged less than deserving of the social sanction with which their practice is endowed if they allow the evils their practice uncovers to remain "professional secrets," and by failure to speak out do nothing to end them.

In the ethical sense, the responsibility for speaking out is a duty owed the society that assures the profession certain privileges, protections, and status. In the social work profession, this duty is also an obligation, incurred in the very process by which entrance into the profession is earned. A socialized profession, one in which the overwhelming number of its practitioners are employed by social agencies, it educates its initiates in part by placing them in these very same agencies. In the vast majority of cases, students earning social work degrees are in some way supported by public funds given directly as scholarships, indirectly as support to the schools offering their training, and to agencies that provide the field work opportunities in which students test their learning in practice. The concern for students often expressed that their untrained practice in field work may represent an unethical intrusion into the lives of persons in need is a healthy concern. The rationale for maintaining such field practice opportunities leans heavily on the anticipation of an obligation being incurred, which justifies this practice. Given the safeguards of close supervision, carefully selected cases, student selection, and the overall support of the agency function built into all aspects of its work with clients; and recognizing that in most social work practice the clients seek the service of the agency, not the service of a particular worker, it nevertheless remains true that the ethical obligation incurred is critical to a justification of such field practice learning. This obligation is part of the unwritten contract the student makes with the client, the agency, and school, to use the competence the education will provide to serve clients, agencies, and in the widest sense, society. The worker thus takes on a function that he or she is duty-bound to fulfill.

If, in the course of their training, students encounter evidence of social conditions that help generate the problems clients bring to their service encounters, they are expected to consider ways in which such conditions can be altered. Rarely can a student engaged in field work practice avoid confronting evidences of the kind noted, and thus early in their induction into the profession students are cautioned and/or encouraged to speak up about such evidence, even to speak out about it. More difficult, yet a necessary part of the learning, is for students to find the most effective channels for voicing their concerns. Here we come to the nub of the whistleblowing function. Where the profession challenges the evils it recognizes as contributing to the problems confronted in daily practice, it brings to the consciousness of society concerns that many would rather remain unexpressed. For those who feel that the socially troubling secret should remain unspoken, when the social work profession speaks out, the profession, may be heard as "having a problem that is giving it trouble." When the profession persists in seeking to remedy the evil-producing situation, it is perceived as "making trouble about its trouble." Just as the student will most often be guided to follow the normal hierarchy of authority in the agency and school, to register his or her concern, so the profession will be encouraged "not to make waves," but to work "within the system" for change, or risk being expelled from the system entirely. Of course, students find ways of protesting while concurrently living within the range of agency- or school-defined limits. They may be tolerated as heretics when they speak up so long as they do not engage in heresy by speaking out.

So also will the profession relate to those who challenge the system of which the profession is a part. The ostracizing of such a person as Bertha Reynolds because of her belief in the need for a change in the political economy of our society, manifests the treatment accorded heresy. Prior to her advocacy of so radical a position, she was recognized and respected as a heretic for the many iconoclastic ideas she espoused. When the profession blows the whistle on a national administration whose policies further disadvantage the most disadvantaged, it, too is viewed by some as outside the pale. It, too, is subject to severe political and economic pressures, similar to the treatment accorded Bertha Reynolds by her own professional colleagues.

But most often the profession recognizes its duty to blow the whistle. Much of the recent discussion of private versus agency practice touches on this incurred obligation and the potential for fulfilling it. The agencies in which students learn their practice skills serve relatively disadvantaged persons. It is especially, although not exclusively, to these populations that the primary obligation is incurred. They have the greatest need and fewer options and consequently more opportunity to be abused. Some fear that such populations are not likely to be served by private practitioners. But, possibly more important, they worry that private practice may be less socialized practice, and the obligation to engage in whistleblowing is not likely to be perceived as germane to such practice. Thus, the obligation incurred in the educational contract may be less likely to be fulfilled, and an ethical duty will go unattended. However, ethical obligations and duties are basic components of all types of professional practice.

THE PROBLEMS OF WHISTLEBLOWING

Within the social agency there are hierarchies of professional responsibility, with some social workers supervising others who, in turn, are under the supervision of still others. Most agencies have line workers, supervisory workers, and administrators, all of whom may hold professional social work degrees. Do these imply different degrees of obligation to expose and seek to correct poor or inadequate work? When the line worker blows the whistle, is the failure of the supervisor to join the whistle chorus a sign of unethical behavior (granted the validity of the case), or is it the result of other obligations toward the organization that are heavier, and more likely to counterbalance those due the client and potential client? What if the whistleblower implicates other social workers, including those above him or her in the administrative hierarchy? Is that a violation of collegial respect, or simply an inevitable byproduct of the bureaucratic structure of social agencies? What if the whistleblower in one agency blows the whistle on another where both agencies employ professional social work staff? Is the usual expectation of collegial exchange being violated? Given different levels of skill in practice—at what point does poor practice become malpractice, and whose judgments should prevail if the practice is exposed by a whistleblower?

Obviously, blowing the whistle on "society" may be dangerous to one's future health and well-being, but may win support from colleagues and friends. Blowing the whistle on colleagues and fellow workers, on the other hand, may ostracize, malign, and blackball, even if the wider community honors, respects, and approves. For very good reason, one thinks carefully and a long time before inflating the lungs, puckering up the lips, and blowing.

CONFIDENTIALITY

This introduces us to the case of the social worker who blew the whistle on the practice of the agency in which he was a supervisor. Everything that one might anticipate could happen to this worker did, although in the end he was vindicated. First, consider the specific issue of confidentiality. The ethics of confidentiality are intended to protect the client, not the agency, and in this instance the client was dead. As a matter of fact, it is not possible to guarantee confidentiality for any client. Long ago, Helen Harris Perlman (1951) addressed this issue in *Social Casework* and more recently, Sissela Bok (1982), and Tom Beauchamp and James F. Childress (1983) commented on this impossibility in health care and professional work in general.

The issue then gets translated into one of trust. The client is expected to trust the agency or worker who promises that information about the client will be used only where it advances the client's interests, and will be denied to all others. This introduces the more vexatious issue of motivation. When the client trusts the worker's competence, he or she yields control to the sanctioned authority of the service provider. But when the worker or agency asks the client to trust its intentions—i.e., how it will use the information obtained—it is not competence, but integrity that one must address. To force a client who has no other choice but to use the service offered, to believe in the integrity of the service provider, is to exercise an authoritarian option, not one justified by sanctioned skill. In the case cited, many workers in the agency had information about the practices cited by the worker—either from experience in their own or other workers' caseloads, or in the twenty-two cases cited, through having the situations brought to their attention by the worker. Within the agency, trust, not confidentiality, was already the guiding imperative. That the worker did not receive support from other colleagues is puzzling, but I have not seen or heard this aspect discussed in detail by any of the persons involved.

Now the "trust" of motivation is significantly dependent on crucial ethical guidelines that are encapsulated in our professional *Code of Ethics*. The Code states that the social worker "should share with others confidentialities revealed by clients only for compelling professional reasons." The Code also states that "the social worker's primary responsibility is to clients;" that the social worker "should adhere to commitments made to the employing organizations;" and that "the social worker should promote the general welfare of society." Finally, the Code states that "the social worker should take action through appropriate channels against unethical conduct by any other member of the profession." If we are to follow these guidelines in this illustrative case, one would have to establish "compelling professional reasons," be clear on the nature and scope of "commitments made to the employing organizations," show how actions taken promote the general welfare of society, and demonstrate that appropriate channels were followed. But more crucial than any of these requirements is the one that puts the client's interest first, as the worker's primary responsibility. Nowhere in the Code is a definition of the client's interest provided, and having spent some time trying to operationalize this concept, I can assure you, reaching agreement on the meaning of this requirement, in particular, is difficult.

Given the preceding, why should the client trust the worker and the agency, when the guidelines that will be followed to warrant the trust remain in possible conflict, one with the other, and ambiguous when applied to specific cases? Another, deontological, approach to this issue of trust, as it relates to confidentiality is, I believe, more helpful.

Consider, for example, the interests of future clients of the agency, if it becomes known that confidences will not be respected. On what grounds could one expect their trust, and would not the loss of this trust discourage persons needing the service from utilizing it? In short, the agency can argue that its interest in the client's interest is as compelling as that of the worker, if one includes potential users of the services as well as the current client's interests. To avoid inconclusive arguments that such a debate will inevitably generate, why not start with a lexical order of imperatives, along the lines developed by Gewirth (1978) and Rawls (1971). Assume that well-being, freedom, equal opportunity, and self-realization are imperatives that taken together provide for the dignity of persons whose interest we intend to serve. Where well-being is threatened, the service providers respond to this threat, which takes precedence over the other three imperatives. Similarly, the other imperatives shall be acted on in the order noted.

Applied to the case at hand, the worker acted properly in seeking to protect the lives of the children involved, and of future children who would be equally exposed to danger because of the practices he identified. The neglect/abuse families involved did not seek the agency's service; they were compelled by law to accept it. Freedom not to participate in the service was not an option. Being compelled to participate or face a possible removal of their child, by definition the service itself placed priority for well-being over freedom. The worker, through his review of the case records, identified twenty-two cases that were not properly served. In a practical sense, they did not have an equal opportunity to access the protection the agency was expected to provide. Thus, the worker's action can be viewed as intended to promote equity, by calling this inequality to public attention. Finally, the issue of self-realization is moot, where severe neglect and possibly death threaten existence itself. Unless the prior imperatives are acted on, this last is not likely to be realized.

It is interesting to note that almost all the public and professional discussions of the case focused almost entirely on consequences with a utilitarian emphasis, when analyzing the merits of the worker's actions and those of the agency and profession. My preference for a formal, deontological analysis does not exclude the use of a consequentialist assessment as well. But given the vague and ambiguous guidelines of the Code, and the difficulties in evaluating consequences, I opt for the deontological. It was based on this approach that I agreed to testify on the worker's behalf. Moreover, it was based on my view of social work as a whistleblowing profession and what many of us have experienced personally when fulfilling our obligations in this regard, that I urged my colleagues to stay with the issue and not focus on the person, so that the usual treatment of the messenger be avoided.

What can the profession take away from this experience? First, that issues of ethical behavior in work that directly affects the lives and well-being, the freedom, equity, and self-realization of participants in such work are likely to have serious consequences. They may not offer clear choices, and will require decisions in uncertain situations. The *Code of Ethics* offers some guidance in thinking about ethical issues, but is not likely to provide sufficient grounds for resolving dilemmas as they occur. Part of what constitutes competence in practice must, for these reasons, include the ability to make an ethical assessment (Lewis, 1984) that is as demanding in what it requires as any other assessment the practitioner is called upon to make in practice.

But because the ethical issues are of significance to agencies and the community, as well as the particular individual cases in which ethical issues are addressed, it is increasingly important that agencies establish ethics review committees, analogous to the tissue review committees in hospitals. Such committees would be expected to conduct periodic reviews of agency practices to determine their adherence to ethical imperatives that operationalize the values that form the agency's goals and objectives. This committee would also be responsible for reviewing cases of malpractice judged to involve lapses in ethical standards, and to recommend policy to correct for such lapses. Finally, the committee would accumulate a case record of its own actions that could be used to orient new staff to this important dimension of agency work.

Schools, of course, should seek to implement the new accreditation standards that require ethical assessment skills in the curriculum. I'm convinced, having taught courses in ethics for some years, that unless field work agencies develop ethics review committees, and students in placement are helped to address issues in which such committees are involved, there will be considerable resistance to introducing such content into all areas of the curriculum. Whatever one's view of the centrality of field work in social work education, students consistently value the practice experience more than any other in their education, and schools sensitive to this attitude tend to be practice-driven in the design and implementation of their curricula. Educational offerings for persons serving on such agency-based committees would generate the more advanced training in axiological reasoning and analysis that electives can offer.

One final word about the "case" discussed. Standing up for one's principles can be an isolating, depressing, and career destroying experience. Usually, deciding to challenge a practice on ethical grounds can result in considerable cost to the challenger. Yet, we need persons courageous enough and committed enough to blow the whistle when such action is indicated. Unhappily, many of my colleagues evaluated the person rather than the issue he posed. When he needed support most, it was not always given, and when given, was given reluctantly. True, there are instances of bizarre and unjustified whistleblowing, of victimization of innocent persons and programs. But before interpreting a happening in this light, it is a humane as well as sound practice to listen, to check out, assess, and convince oneself that the charges are unfounded. If we can act in this way toward all who challenge our profession as well as the whistleblowers within the profession, we will more likely come to recognize our friends, more clearly identify our detractors, and inflict less uncalled-for psychological damage on the heretics whose actions help keep us honest, even when it hurts to see ourselves through their eyes.

Chapter Note

1. This incident was the subject of a lead editorial in the *New York Times*.

BIBLIOGRAPHY

Bok, S. (1982). The limits of confidentiality. In *Secrets*. New York: Pantheon Books.

Beauchamp, T., & Childress, J. F. (1983). The rule of confidentiality. In N. Abrams and M. Buchner (Eds.), *Medical ethics* (pp. 23–27). Cambridge, MA: MIT Press.

Gerwirth, A. (1978). *Reason and morality.* Chicago: University of Chicago Press.
Lewis, H. (1984). Ethical assessment. *Social Casework, 65*(4), 203–213.
Perlman, H. H. *(1951).* The caseworker's use of collateral information. *Social Casework,* 23, 325–333.
Rappaport, L. (1968). Creativity in social work. *Smith College Studies in Social Work, 38,* 145–146.
Rawls, J. (1971). *A theory of justice.* Cambridge: Harvard University Press.

Chapter 13

Teaching Ethics through Ethical Teaching

Using the NASW Code of Ethics *as a framework, Lewis applies the Code's principles to social work education with some interesting results. In the context of an increasingly unethical society, he addresses such concerns as the responsibility of teachers to be honest about the limits of their knowledge and to translate their ethical principles into action outside of the academic setting.*

There has been a resurgence of interest in applied ethics among the human service professions (AAAS, 1980; EVIST, 1978). Reflecting this interest, the National Association of Social Workers (NASW) recently revised its *Code of Ethics* (NASW, 1980) and schools of social work, to be accredited, must now incorporate content on ethics and values into their curricula (CSWE, 1984). Courses have integrated ethics content and new courses have been initiated, on the assumption that in this way students will learn what they need to know about values and ethics in order to practice their profession (EVIST, 1978). The extent to which this objective can be achieved outside the formal curriculum, communicated to students by the behavior of their teachers and a school's administration, has been ignored. Since I believe that "do as I do" may be as helpful as "do as I say" in communicating ethics content to students, what such doing may entail for teachers will be explored in the remainder of this essay.

Teachers educate in part by modeling the behavior they expect of their students. Where teachers adhere to ethical standards in their behavior, what is "caught" by students may be more significant than what is "taught." One would be hard put to decide in the case of that great teacher, Socrates, which was more significant to his students' understanding: his dialogues about ethics, or his choice of hemlock over betraying principles in which he believed.

Teachers confront ethical dilemmas in seeking to discharge their professional obligations. Faced with complex, ambiguous, and uncertain situations teachers are often at a loss to know which, among many alternatives, constitute those actions that are ethically justified. Their task is often made more difficult by the context within which they teach.

Originally published in the *Journal of Teaching in Social Work 14*(1), Spring–Summer 1987.

Ethical teaching is difficult to achieve in an administrative environment that condones unethical behavior (Gummer, 1984; Levy, 1982; Thompson, 1985). It is even more difficult to engage in ethical teaching when students behave unethically. It is hard to judge the extent to which a community and national atmosphere that breeds distrust and fosters contempt for the civil rights and well-being of its citizens affects the expectations of all actors in the social work education drama. Nevertheless, such an atmosphere undoubtedly influences the extent to which ethical teaching can be sustained. The discussion of a teacher's behavior that follows must be appreciated in light of the context in which teaching occurs. While the context is not fully discussed, it is a "given" that places the entire discussion in perspective.

As best I can determine there is no formal Code of Ethics for higher education teachers. Most of the unexpected behaviors have been incorporated into policy statements by the AAUP (1980). Human service professionals who teach in colleges and universities are also guided in their ethical standards by the codes of their professions. It seems appropriate, then, to utilize the recently revised NASW *Code of Ethics* as an analog to help us consider some of the difficulties a teacher may encounter in seeking to model what the profession considers ethical behavior. A few of the major principles enumerated in the Code will serve illustrative purposes. Wherever the Code refers to a social worker, I will substitute the word "teacher." Whenever the Code refers to "client or recipient of service," I will substitute the word "student."

COMPETENCE AND PROFESSIONAL DEVELOPMENT

The teacher should strive to become and remain proficient in professional practice and the performance of professional functions.

How do teachers recognize that they are deficient in the knowledge and/or performance requirements of their function? How do teachers know that they do not know? Knowing what one does not know is the hardest knowing of all. Moreover, in a professional education program, there is usually a clinical component to be taught. How does the teacher know that he or she has mastered the skills required for competence in clinical work? If it is difficult to judge what one does not know, it is possibly more difficult to evaluate what one does not do.

Is peer evaluation the answer? Will student evaluations detect lacks and caution about shortcomings? Can a self-monitoring procedure flash warning signals? Each of these possibilities has been considered, and in many programs has been incorporated into contracts and personnel procedures. But there is doubt as to their reliability and validity as tools for judging adherence to this ethical imperative. Each has recognized limitations. Nor are these limitations overcome when evaluations are concurrently applied to arrive at a definitive judgment. For example, these measures do not tell us much about a teacher's integrity, courage, commitment, and fairness attributes that play a significant role in shaping a teacher's behavior.

Thus, in relation to the requirement of currency and competence that is so crucial in judging the ethical behavior of a teacher, we are deficient in means for knowing how to measure performance and have yet to determine who might best do the measuring.

RESPONSIBILITY TO STUDENTS

The teacher's primary responsibility is to the student.

The teacher's function is to communicate to students what they need to know, do and be, in order to qualify as a member of the social work profession. Each teacher seeks to meet this responsibility in an assigned area of the curriculum. Hopefully, the school's program as a whole integrates these various efforts in a way that enhances students' opportunities to realize this objective. The major stumbling block in meeting this ethical imperative is usually not a lack of agreement about responsibilities, but a difference of opinion on how one defines the student's interest. Only when there is agreement on what constitutes this interest, and how it is affected by other interests—including the teacher's, the school's administration and, ultimately, the likely consumers of social services—can one judge whether the teacher is responsibly attending the students' needs, acting in a manner that conveys evidence that the teacher's primary responsibility is to the students.

This principle raises questions about the responsibilities of professional education in the university. Should the primary responsibility of the professional school be to prepare a pool of competent practitioners who will serve consumers of social services? If one answers in the affirmative, how then justify the charge that the teacher's primary responsibility is to the student? While these responsibilities may not be mutually exclusive, neither are they always congenial. One need only consider how professional schools have wrestled with the implications of such responsibilities when they conflict—in deciding on admissions to a program; in selecting field work settings; designing elective offerings; determining content to be emphasized in class and field, etc. What may be in a community's interest may not be in the career interests of a particular student. When conflicts between a perceived social good and an individual good surface in the day-to-day operations of a school, they invariably impact on the various activities going on in the school, as well as on the teachers and their teaching.

If one views concurrent responsibilities as requiring choices from among competing interests, one is likely to generate consequentialist resolutions to ethical dilemmas (Held, 1984). This problem-solving approach to ethical issues entails enumeration of positive and negative utilities that can be shown to result from alternative choices, assigning weights to each, and hopefully arriving at a measure of consequences. This utilitarian calculus hopefully suggests the alternative to be preferred because it yields the maximum overall good. If the conflict is viewed as requiring choices from among competing rights, those of students and those of the community of consumers, for example, a deductive mode of reasoning may be employed. Starting with the ethical imperatives that define these rights and concluding with a lexical ordering of imperatives that determine the priorities among rights, it will suggest the choices to be preferred. In this deontological mode of reasoning, consequences are of little or no significance. Judging from the professional social work literature, partisan positions on interests and rights have been debated, but practically nothing has been done to establish guidelines for reasoning about such conflicts (Levy, 1976; Lewis, 1984; Loewenberg & Dolgoff, 1982; Reamer, 1982). It is of little solace to note that the NASW *Code of Ethics* is unenlightening on ways to establish what constitutes a client's interest, and on how one ought to reason about conflicting interests in social service practice.

A third principle in the NASW Code addresses ethical responsibility to colleagues.

ETHICAL RESPONSIBILITY TO COLLEAGUES

The teacher should treat colleagues with respect, courtesy, fairness, and good faith. The teacher has the responsibility to relate to the students of colleagues with full professional consideration.

It is relatively easy to recommend to members of a faculty the kind of civilized behavior with regard to colleagues that they would expect for themselves. Respect, courtesy, fairness, honesty, integrity, and good faith are what all persons would want shown them by others. Unhappily, in the academic colleagueship, complicating difficulties arise that are not without their ethical conundrums.

Consider the simple case where colleagues disagree on what is to be taught and who is best able to teach it. Where the disagreement is substantive in nature, the temptation is great to dismiss the opposing view as a reflection of the colleague's intellectual or experiential limitations. Not infrequently, it is the person, not the problem, that gets analyzed. Where the disagreement is ideologically based, labeling the opposition in a derogatory way often colors the discussion with insulting and threatening innuendoes, which may then be embellished with power plays based on rank and tenure differentials. As some studies have suggested, academics seem to associate intellectual depth with negative criticism and intellectual superficiality with positive evaluation. Where this operates, respect and fairness are sacrificed to oneupmanship. This may be particularly stressful where colleagues are in competition for a limited resource, promotion, tenure, or a very desirable assignment.

The second requirement of this principle—suggesting how one ought to relate to students of colleagues—makes heavy demands on the first. Students can be neglected and abused. Failure to attend to their needs, often by acts of omission, not commission, jeopardizes students in course and field work. Students can also be unknowingly drawn into conflicts among faculty members, and abused in situations not of their own making. Failure to implement a field-advising function not infrequently contributes to neglect. Discouraging students from registering for a colleague's course for reasons that are unrelated to the student's educational needs can contribute to abuse.

The two parts of this principle often are involved in a single activity having serious ethical implications. For example, when a faculty member lends an encouraging ear to student complaints about a colleague or more directly supports the complaint, promoting its elaboration, without cautioning the students to discuss the complaint with the teacher being judged and sharing with the colleague the fact that a complaint has been registered, serious ethical issues are raised. Or, as not infrequently occurs, a faculty member may initiate a complaint about a colleague to the Dean ("his students haven't learned a thing") without first discussing the complaint with the colleague involved. While it is unreal to expect a total absence of rumor, gossip, and innuendo that normally accompany the informal operation of a school, one does expect that such distracting and sometimes destructive behavior be discouraged.

One noteworthy failure to adhere to principles is exemplified in situations where a teacher uses the classroom to advocate a personally favored ideological or theoretical position without providing the students the opportunity to consider other conflicting views that are known to exist. Using the classroom to advocate a particular dogma is especially reprehensible when a colleague's differing position is used to force students to take sides, not on the merits of the positions espoused, but on the basis of allegiance to the instructors involved. Such occurrences are almost always destructive of sound learning, particularly where the substantive content of a course involves efforts to establish "truths," or "truths" that are not long-lasting.

The obverse side of the classroom as platform issue, is the threat to academic freedom that is involved when teachers are threatened because they present unpopular or deviant points of view for consideration by their students. The McCarthy period is still in our memories to warn against such threats, with the harmful effects on scholarship and free discussion. Recently, papers have carried the news of a renewed attempt to stifle free expression on campuses, sponsored by a right-wing conservative group (AAUP, 1985; *Newsday*, 1985; *Science*, 1985). They are instructing students to report teachers, particularly in the social sciences, who are "liberals" and who fail to present adequately the conservative point of view. Having unknown informers in one's classroom, and an organized self-appointed censure group ready to act on such informer reports, is threatening to academic freedom, and the underlying assumptions that inform this ethical imperative. The recent acknowledgment that the President of the United States at one time acted as an FBI informer on his colleagues undoubtedly sets up a model of duplicity that this principle is intended to discourage. Clearly, schools wishing to encourage adherence to the principle of collegial relationships, would be well advised to provide, within their structure, for procedures that will protect academic freedom for their teachers, even as teachers are encouraged to demonstrate the behavior this principle is intended to promote.

Another ethical imperative in the NASW Code addresses the teacher's responsibility to the school administration and the college. It states:

The teacher should adhere to commitments made to the employing organization.

Let us take a given, the expectation that administrators of schools and colleges will adhere to their commitments made to the teacher. This assumption may be the root of many evils, because it is often not the case that commitments made by administrators are adhered to. But assuming such adherence as a "given" simplifies a discussion of the reciprocal responsibility of the teacher.

One expects the teacher to live up to obligations and duties agreed to in the employment contract. But ethical issues concerning these commitments surface prior to the contract being agreed to by all parties concerned. There are job applicants who verbally commit themselves to accepting a position while negotiating for a position elsewhere, ending up as "no-shows." Schools have lost lines for a year or more because of no-shows. There are applicants who provide incomplete or inaccurate information, deliberately misleading the employer. There are applicants who plan other time-demanding involvements yet sign contracts knowing that such outside commitments would disqualify them as applicants for the position. The examples of departures from this ethical principle that occur before contracts have been signed are limited only by the creative imagination of unethical applicants. When students learn of such behavior on the part of their mentors, and they do, an unfortunate example is set.

But once having accepted a position, failure to fulfill the obligations and assumed duties that come with the job constitutes a major breach of ethical behavior. Arriving late for class; engaging in outside work that interferes with the performance of duties; failing to meet deadlines when returning papers and grades; comments that leave students confused as to what was missing or unacceptable in reports or term papers; starting class sessions late and ending early; failing to provide appropriate course outlines, bibliographies, criteria for evaluating performance and grading; being unavailable for individual appointments with students; ignoring requests to serve on key committees and assist in administrative tasks required to assure the success of the overall program; and so on, all may, in certain circumstances, constitute unethical behavior, violating agreed-upon commitments to the school, college, and students as well. Judgment in these situations would have to identify behavior that suggests a pattern of consistent failure to perform duties assumed in agreeing to serve in the teaching position. Guidelines for making judgments in such cases are sorely lacking and inferences of unethical conduct must be drawn with caution. Nevertheless, failure to press for rectification of such behavior can result in some students being denied the quality education provided others.

An unusual aspect of this principle flows from the nature of academic personnel procedures, where colleagues conduct peer reviews when considering candidates for retention, promotion, and tenure. The procedures followed in such reviews require integrity, honesty, and all the other attributes noted earlier but, in addition, ask of the reviewers that the needs of the school and university, as well as the needs of the colleague, be considered. Not infrequently, the two may not coincide. An otherwise meritorious performance may be increasingly irrelevant to the changing mission of the school. In accepting to serve on such a peer review body, a commitment to the school is essential, and this may override a commitment to particular colleagues. Failure to accept the responsibility that this position demands can have short-term effects on faculty morale, and long-term effects on the quality of education the school can provide for its students. Both in the process whereby members of such peer review bodies are selected or elected, and in the willingness of respected colleagues to serve, once chosen, there are opportunities to department from this principle in spirit, if not in relation to a formal contract.

Another principle in the NASW Code addresses the responsibility of the teacher to the profession.

RESPONSIBILITY TO THE PROFESSION

The teacher should uphold and advance the values, ethics, knowledge, and mission of the profession.

A confusion that can result from the implementation of this principle stems from the dual identity of the social work teacher. Which of the two professional functions—educator or social worker—is the social work teacher expected to uphold and advance? Some would say both, while others would straddle the ambiguity by cautioning "it depends." What can be agreed upon is the need to be governed by ethical guidelines in either function. It is useful, nevertheless, to note some critical differences that are associated with these two functions.

The teacher is engaged in assisting students to master skills preparatory to becoming a knowledgeable practitioner. This is the primary good to be realized. Ethical commendations that guide the teacher are intended to operationalize the value that promotes this "good." Social work practitioners are primarily engaged in promoting the well-being of consumers of their service. The "good" here is achieved by helping recipients realize personal health, security, justice, education, self-realization, and aesthetic satisfaction, and helping society provide supportive resources in each of these areas. Thus, granted overlap in values to be realized, the differences in the purposes of each function can't help but influence the roles each—the teacher and the social worker—will be expected to enact. For this reason, while the teacher may serve as a "model" of ethical behavior for the student, others, particularly the field work supervisor and practitioners in the field work agency, can have equal or greater influence as "models" from whom ethical behavior for the practitioner can be "caught." Thus, if this principle is to be realized in practice, it requires that not only the teacher, and the school, but the field work instructor and the field work agency hold to standards that maintain the integrity of the profession and that promote the mission of the school and the profession.

To uphold and advance the values and ethics of the profession, it is necessary to advocate for the goals and objectives of the profession. This requires partisan activity, favoring programs and policies without which these goals and objectives will not be realized. Thus, to implement this principle the social work teacher is expected to engage in social action, with all its consequences. The teacher as educator *is* expected to be open to conflicting views, serving as a detached conveyor of truths, not a rigid adherent to a particular cause. As professional and educator, he or she can feel pressured to both advocate and remain detached, yet conflicted in trying to do both. There are many opportunities for the teacher to participate in social action, and also to present a rounded view of program and policies. He or she need not take advantage of all these opportunities, and is free to select issues he wishes to address. What the teacher is ethically prescribed not to do, is to ignore all opportunities to act on this principle. Teachers who identify themselves with particular causes that are consistent with the profession's values and goals, are important role models for initiates into the profession. In carrying this obligation with courage and conviction, they need not depart from the other ethical imperatives already discussed. Teachers who manage to act on this principle with integrity and creativity are among the most admirable practitioners of their craft.

The NASW Code also addresses the teacher's ethical responsibility to society.

ETHICAL RESPONSIBILITY TO SOCIETY

The teacher should promote the general welfare of society.

It is hard to imagine a social work teacher who would deliberately set out to undermine the general welfare of society, assuming the definition of welfare is congenial with the point of view of the teacher. It is how one defines the general welfare and what one believes are appropriate actions to promote it that create ethical dilemmas for the teacher.

A teacher may believe in incremental changes as the primary or only way in which the general welfare can be advanced. Where this results in a perspective that requires a more tolerant view of inequities that are long-standing, even if recognized to be unfair, the teacher holding this belief may be perceived by some students as willing to accept injustices as a necessary condition that cannot be corrected in a timely fashion. Another teacher may believe that radical reform of social institutions is the only way in which the general welfare can be advanced. This latter perspective may be critical of existing practices that perpetuate the injustices that reform is intended to rectify. The teacher holding this belief may be perceived by some students as insensitive to the day-to-day needs of individuals. While neither of these extremes need typify any one teacher's stance, communicating a belief in the unity of "cause and function," of social purpose and personal service in each instance of practice, is difficult. We have yet to establish criteria that are universally accepted as measures of the extent to which a teacher's behavior provides evidence that he or she is promoting the general welfare of society. When a teacher is especially caring and attends to individual student's peculiar circumstances and needs, does such activity on behalf of the student's private troubles promote the general welfare? One would have to weigh the cost of such attention to one student's needs against depleted teacher time and resource that other students may have to pay. It may be argued that the teaching function is primarily educational and diverting energies from this function to a caring one is not in the interest of the general welfare, even if caring can be shown to promote the central educational purpose of teaching. The stricture that student counseling not be confused with psychotherapy, that it remain focused on its educational intent, touches on this issue.

Conversely, when a teacher is especially concerned with advocacy on behalf of professional values and goals, taking time away from students, who thereby miss opportunities to receive individual counseling, can such behavior be considered consistent with this ethical imperative? Ideally, if every teacher activity concurrently advocated for a social purpose as it promoted an individual service, the tensions generated by adhering to this required behavior would be minimized. Unfortunately, as is true of so many issues involving the relationship of ends and means, life does not provide easy choices, and seeking to do good while fulfilling a requirement to do what is right is ever a rich source for ethical dilemmas.

These six illustrative ethical principles, adapted from the NASW Code, serve to identify the difficulties teachers face in seeking to engage in ethical teaching, i.e., in behaving in an ethical fashion, setting an example for students to follow. Based on the discussion of these principles, I will conclude by suggesting practice principles that, if followed, could promote teacher behavior that models the ethical imperatives advanced in the Code.

1. Teachers should assume that in all areas of activity associated with their teaching function—in class, field, counseling, administration, or when pursuing a scholarly purpose—their roles will necessarily confront them with choices that involve ethical issues.
2. Teachers should consciously and appropriately share with colleagues and students their own difficulties in trying to resolve ethical dilemmas that surface in their work. Teachers ought to solicit from colleagues and students evaluations of their—the teacher's—personal judgments about problematic ethical situations. Such observations should be used to monitor their own understanding and behavior.
3. Teachers should sensitize themselves to how one reasons about ethical issues; how to recognize when, in fact, an ethical rather than a practice issue is involved.
4. Teachers should realize they are always on stage for their students. In the drama of social work education all the actors influence the behavior of others, all contribute to their understanding of what is ethical and what is not. No situation is ethically neutral.

BIBLIOGRAPHY

American Association of University Professors (1980, December). Statement on professional ethics, in R. Chalk, M. S. Frankel, and S. B. Chafer, eds., *Ethics project*. Washington, DC: AAAS Committee on Academic Freedom.

American Association of University Professors (1985). *On accuracy and academic freedom*. Washington, DC: Author.

Commission on Accreditation (1984). *Handbook of accreditation standards and procedures*. New York: Council on Social Work Education.

EVIST (1978). *Resource directory: Ethics and values in science and teaching*. Washington, DC: Office of Science Education, American Association for the Advancement of Science.

Gummer, B. (1984, Winter). Ethics in managerial behavior (Come on! Who are you trying to kid?). *Administration in Social Work, 8*(4), 97–109.

Held, V. (1984). *Rights and goods: Justifying social action*. New York: Free Press.

Levy, C. S. (1976). *Social work ethics*. New York: Human Sciences Press.

Lewis, H. (1984, April). Ethical assessment. *Social Casework, 65*(4), 203–211.

Loewenberg, F., and Dolgoff, R. (1982). *Ethical decisions for social work practice*. Itasca, IL: F.E. Peacock.

National Association of Social Workers (1980). *Code of ethics*, revised. New York: Author.

Newsday (1985, October 13). Accuracy in academia.

Reamer, F. G. (1982). *Ethical dilemmas in social services*. New York: Columbia University Press.

Science (1985, August 29). New group targets political bias on campus, 841–842.

Thompson, D. F. (1985, September/October). The possibility of administrative ethics. *Public Administration Review, 45*(5), 555–561.

Chapter 14

Ethics and the Private Non-profit Human Service Organization

Lewis expands upon his discussion of the distinctions between non-profit and for-profit organizations in "Management in the Non-profit Social Service Organization" to incorporate the ethical dimensions of these differences. In particular, he analyzes the effects of the blurring of sectoral lines on the ethical conduct and obligations of non-profit agencies.

There are a variety of meanings associated with the term non-profit. For our purposes, a recent definition used in New York's not-for-profit corporation law, will serve to convey what is meant by the term:

> A not-for-profit organization is . . . one exclusively for a purpose or purposes, not for pecuniary profit or financial gain, and no part of the assets, income, or profits of which is distributable to or ensures to the benefit of its members, directors, or officers. . . . Their financial structures differ [from for-profit]: a business corporation borrows its capital funds or generates them internally, and pays taxes on its profits. A non-profit corporation accepts donations, usually tax deductible, from the public, and is permitted to reinvest its profits without being taxed. (Collin, 1987)

We assume that the public sector must carry major responsibility for coverage and sustaining health and welfare services for all citizens. Individual, foundation, and corporate philanthropy, taken together, constitute a small fraction of government expenditures for these services. We also assume that the private non-profit sector is relatively free to contribute to innovation, advocacy, criticism, and reform. The relationship among public sector, private non-profit, and private for-profit modes of human service delivery is increasingly complex and changing. As a result of policies adopted in the public sector, both non-profits and for-profits in the private sector have become heavily dependent for their revenues on tax-levy

---

This essay is based upon a paper presented at a conference, "The Future of Non-Profit Management and the Human Services," San Francisco State University, November 1987. Originally published in *Administration in Social Work 13*(2), 1–14.

monies and third-party payments. Having to depend on the same sources of revenue, private non-profits and for-profits have become more and more alike in the services they render, and the personnel they employ.

Moreover, faced with shrinking revenues, private non-profits have moved to increase their sponsorship of for-profit subsidiaries, which evaluate their success using criteria common to for-profit corporations. No wonder, then, that some are led to consider a convergence thesis, anticipating in time a blending of private non-profit and for-profit modes of service delivery. Despite these developments, this essay does not adopt the convergence perspective, choosing instead to focus on fundamental differences that distinguish the private non-profit from the for-profit organization in the human service arena. These differences are discernable in the metaphor "gift giving."

GIFT-GIVING RELATIONSHIPS

The community may choose to ignore the service needs of recipients as frequently as it seeks to provide for such needs. Those who shape community policy set ceilings on expenditures, exercising control over the quality and scope of human services. Typically, policy makers prefer to calculate consequences in market terms, that is, in terms of what they believe the community will accept and can afford. For those whose altruistic motives cause them to extend the criteria beyond those that policy makers are willing to support, operating "in the red" may represent a preferred alternative to ignoring identified needs. Their willingness to supplement allocations, using their own personal and financial resources, may be viewed as a form of gift giving.

Such gift giving can be considered from three perspectives: the giver, the recipients, and others not immediately involved in the exchange. Each perspective can be described in terms of the motivations, opportunities, and capacities of the participants. The ethical imperatives entailed in a gift-giving relationship provide guidance for acceptable moral behavior and attitudes. In addition to the perspectives of the actors and their ethics, there are the imperatives that guide the practice, the organization, and the societal context. While a full appreciation of the gift-giving relationship requires a detailed analysis of all these elements in their interaction over time, the scope of this essay will permit only an initial discussion of the key perspectives.[1]

MOTIVATION: THE PROVIDER

The primacy of an altruistic impulse that is inherent in a giving relationship, more than any other factor, distinguishes the private non-profit from the for-profit human service transaction. Giving because of guilt or pressure, or giving because one wants to, and the range between extremes, all entail an altruistic element so long as the expectation of the giver is a beneficial outcome for the recipients, not personal profit for themselves. This, of course, does not exclude a concern for consumer benefits in a for-profit transaction where motivation for consumer benefit is extremely strong. It does, however, signify an intention to help for reasons exclusive of the profitability of the service. From the altruistic impulse of sponsors of non-profit services, one can derive a conceptualization of altruism as a commodity and note how often it is in short supply.

The products produced by non-profit human service organizations are peculiar commodities (Lewis, 1983). They have many of the attributes of gifts (Murray, 1987). Typically, the motivations of those who provide the support for the production of these services are presumed to be altruistic in nature. Satisfactions are not assured by dividend payments for stock ownership, or by impressive cost:benefit ratios. Ideally, while concerned to obtain the most good at the least cost, concern for quality and effectiveness is subordinate to a wider interest, that of rendering services that reflect the type of society they prefer and hope to achieve. For those persons associated with the outcomes of private non-profit human service organizations, the goals sought in their objectives include "fostering a sense of connectedness among people, acknowledging the universality of basic human needs and desires, and protecting the dignity of persons (including their bodies)" (Murray, 1987, pp. 36–37). Support for such private non-profit organizations reflects the belief that it may be better at times to produce and distribute human services utilizing non-market systems. It is thought that systems generated by the generosity of the human spirit are more likely to assume obligations that assure a minimal standard of caring for those unable to satisfy their common human needs. Thus, the altruism that motivates those who support private non-profits is itself a commodity that endures that may, in fact, expand rather than be expended with use (Murray, 1987).

However, when viewed as a scarce resource, it is possible to distrust the power of altruism to generate needed human services. Combining such distrust with a strong belief in the "market" yields a decided preference for policies that favor strengthening the for-profit sector. Trust in the power and efficacy of altruistic motives, when combined with a strong belief in the duty of the community to engage in gift giving, may promote policies that favor strengthening the private non-profit sector.

MOTIVATION: THE RECIPIENT

The recipient of human services may reveal motivations more attuned to those of the market economy. In a society dominated by a market economy, it would not be unusual for those whose needs cause them to seek resources on their own behalf to be self- rather than altruistically motivated. Such potential consumers would seek to position themselves to favorably compete for these relatively scarce resources. The recipient who is neither in control of money nor provided with alternatives, and is not free to choose the conditions under which service can be obtained, can only exercise control over his or her use of self in exploiting access opportunities. For such recipients, altruistic motivations are usually subordinate to a self-serving interest, which the conditions of eligibility tend to require. Acceptable behavior and attitudes, for recipients having no choice, are dictated by the provider who sets the standards of morality that must accompany the recipient role.

For the recipient with options from which preferred choices are possible, the motivation that sponsors the service may be significant. It is possible that the recipient who is free to choose believes that the service offered is provided as a gift and may be favorably disposed toward receiving it. Knowing that profit is not the motivating factor may lead to more trust in the service provider's intentions. More likely, however, is a consumer preference to avoid a dependent role.

Thus, for the recipient, as well as the provider, motivation is a factor that influences the scope of activities that are likely to generate ethical commitments. It is important to realize that among private non-profits that originated out of an altruistic motive, some may not sustain this motive. Such organizations take on the attributes of the for-profits, including dependence on market conditions rather than need assessment when making operational decisions. On the other hand, there is also the possibility that a for-profit operation may provide a service for a special target population at a loss, providing evidence of its motivation to contribute to the community's well-being.

OPPORTUNITIES

Private non-profit organizations often restrict access to their services to specific target populations. Religious, ethnic, gender, age, geographic, and financial criteria frequently determine who will be eligible for access to the service. The for-profit service is more likely to limit access on the basis of market factors and cost:benefit calculations, for understandable reasons. Competitive considerations often determine market shares and turf battles for control of the market can be costly. For-profits are likely to limit access on the basis of attributes of the potential consumer where purchase-of-service contracts specify such restrictions. The private non-profits, on the other hand, will tend to respond to the commitment of contributors whose motivations for establishing the service include identification with a target population with which some communal associations are involved. Typically, in the provision of human services, where public monies underwrite the cost of such services, both private non-profits and for-profits may modify their access conditions to reflect the interests of the funding source. Thus, in human service programs, where so large a share of financial cost is paid by tax revenue monies, the differences between private non-profits and for-profits may be less discernable, but nevertheless remain and can surface very rapidly when tax levy funds are curtailed.

Access to service is critical if opportunities are to be realized. However, equity in access requires that unequals be treated unequally. It is not enough to provide all with the same opportunities. But, assuring fair access to service can be costly. Ability to pay for service, the extent of outreach needed to achieve equitable participation for the most disadvantaged, and the added demands on resources that accompany the most difficult cases, all caution against an unrealistic expectation that equity of access will be assured if the usual market mechanisms are allowed to determine outcomes. Experience strongly suggests the contrary. In the ordinary operation of the market, the "poor pay more" (Caplowitz, 1967); and, they are the last to gain access to needed resources. Even among the poor, it is the most deprived who are further deprived of opportunities to use services unless deliberate special interventions are made on their behalf. And such interventions are costly.

CAPACITY

It has always been difficult to evaluate the helper's capacity to offer assistance and the recipient's capacity to utilize the offer. In the private non-profits, the helper's capacity is likely to be judged by broader outcome measures. Given the altruistic intent and the basic goals associated with efforts to contribute to the community's welfare, sustaining a condition that might otherwise get worse, or improving a situation that cannot be avoided may be viewed as evidence of effectiveness, as much as prevention or cure. All contribute to the overriding intent to serve the community, reinforcing the altruistic motivation of the sponsors of the service. Caring for one's own, be it kin, neighbor, ethnic member, etc., offers its own justifications—a measure of success rarely used in a for-profit service evaluation. In relation to the recipient as participant in the service drama, claims on service attributable to membership in a targeted group may enhance the recipient's capacity to command resources in a way not likely to be manifest in the for-profit service.

The for-profits, using market criteria, also find it difficult to evaluate the helping capacities of the service provider. Unlike the private non-profits, the ability to operate at a profit will most likely serve as a measure of greater significance than the contribution made to the communal welfare. In such organizations, consumer satisfaction may be represented by demand for services. Other consequences of intervention may serve as indirect measures of purposes achieved. Here again, recipient capacity is measured by the extent of funds available and willingly paid to access the service.

What is important to recognize, from an ethical perspective, is that the consequences sought will vary for the for-profit in contrast to the non-profit. In relation to both organizations, the difference in consequences intended affect the perception of both the helper and recipient. In turn, the duties and obligations assumed by the service providers and recipients in the service transactions will vary.

This brief discussion of the motivations, opportunities, and capacities of the actors in the service drama need to be viewed in the context or scene in which practice occurs.

THE CONTEXT

It is useful to view the not-for-profit human service organization as a social environment having significant impact on the actors in the service drama, including their actions, functions, role, and purposes. It is equally helpful to perceive the organization as being nested in an encompassing environment, including a market-responsive economy and political commitment to maximize the benefits that such an economy generates. The achievements of this surrounding political economy and cultural environment, and its shortcomings, necessarily have a significant impact on the work of the private non-profit human service organization. Ethical issues generated by the work of the organization are embedded in the political economy of the milieu, the particular organization, and the internal environment, and are shaped by the behavior, effect, and cognition of those who do the work of the organization. The quality of the ethical components can be judged against standards used to judge behavior, effects, and cognitions, as well as the standards derived from professional and organizational codes.

THE COMMON GOOD

The non-profit is, in the view of the sanctioning community, intended to serve the health, welfare, and educational needs of its citizens, particularly the most vulnerable. Its tax-exempt status is bestowed in recognition of this fact. Should anything occur that suggests that the organization seeks to act like a for-profit corporation, the tax-exempt status is challenged on at least two grounds. First, that the organization's commitment to the primacy of the common good may be weakened by a commitment to personal gain. Further, that once it has entered the competitive for-profit market, tax-exemption serves as a subsidy giving it an unfair competitive advantage.

The importance of the primacy of commitment to the community's well-being is evident in the expectations that flow from it. Administration, staff, and board are expected to operate in a manner that reflects this commitment; resources are allocated on the basis of a lexical ordering determined by this commitment. While recipients of services and applicants as well may believe that their interests take precedence in allocating the organization's resources, this is only the case where their interests coincide with the organization's commitment to the common good. Where the consumers' interests, or those of the organization's participants, do not coincide with the common good the organization is committed to serve, it is expected by the sanctioning bodies that precedence will be given to the common good. For-profit organizations are expected to give precedence to the financial gain of their sponsors, although this need not be detrimental to the common good. Similarly, consumer interests, evidenced by a willingness to pay for the service, may also take precedence over the common good in for-profit organizations because for-profits will depend on such a willingness to pay. In part, the payment of taxes on profits earned may be viewed as contributing to a pool of public monies that may then be allowed to promote a common good, but not necessarily one of benefit to those whose needs the organization is seeking to meet. Thus, in a fundamental way, the altruism that sponsors a non-profit organization, as well as the philanthropic and tax supports that fund it, also serve to promote an expectation of socially responsible behavior on the part of the organization and those who participate in its operations.

From this overriding ethical commitment, there flow certain obligations and duties that the actors in the non-profit drama are expected to assume:

1. Distributive decisions should be based on ethical imperatives that give precedence to the common good—for example, unequal benefits would be justified if they raise the expectations of the least advantaged in the pool of potential consumers—following the Rawlsian difference principle.
2. Quality of life decisions should enter into the calculations of consequences and should carry at least as much weight as coverage in community benefits. This principle, when linked to the previous one, protects the utility of an intervention without sacrificing a just allocation of the resource.

When profits are the bottom-line measures of organizational success, most often cost:benefit calculations will focus on efficiency of operations intended to maximize the financial gains of the corporation while minimizing the sacrifice of quality and coverage that may be necessary. The underlying ethic seeks from consumers the price they are able to pay, and provides to each consumer the service they, the consumers, can afford. The contrast of this ethic with that underlying the two principles noted for the private non-profit is clear. If adhered to, those two principles accept from consumers the price they are able to pay and provide to each consumer the service he or she needs. This latter ethic, if followed, would result in many private non-profit organizations operating at a deficit, requiring philanthropic and government subsidy if their services are to be sustained.

Clearly, these different ethics reflect the influence of different purposes on the lexical ordering of virtues that may be required. The actors in the service drama are all capable of virtuous behavior. All may be honest, fair, self-sacrificing, sensitive, empathic, responsible, etc. The functioning of either type of organization need not press them to behave otherwise. When the aim is to provide the service one needs, the expected behavior will differ from that where the aim is to provide service for persons able to pay. The actors in the service drama will be harder pressed to justify restrictions in access and quality when they view their function as intended to promote a just and fair distribution than if they view their function as intended to provide an affordable service that is profitable as well. The emotional and physical examination that accomplishes the ethical battering experienced by the former is in sharp contrast with the monetary satisfaction that entrepreneurial acumen provides. In addition to the wish to make better use of hard-earned skills, and the freedom to organize one's practice with greater independence, human service workers who shift to private practice may also find more satisfaction in the financial rewards of entrepreneurial practice and concurrently suffer less stress than accompanies work in the non-profit sector. Altruism is not necessarily the primary motivating factor in their choice.

RIGHTS AND OBLIGATIONS

Private non-profit and for-profit human service organizations agree on certain obligations incurred in accepting to produce and market their commodities. Both seek to assure access to their services, to be sensitive and responsive to individual differences, to sustain the necessary supports that recipients need in order to manage an appropriate use of their program's resources, and to protect the privacy of recipients of their services. The degree to which these obligations are fulfilled, however, may vary when different criteria are used to determine organizational success. These criteria include the following:

Sensitivity

Respect for the dignity of persons seeking help requires sensitivity to their special needs and responsiveness to individual differences.

Sensitivity to special needs and responsiveness to individual differences can be expensive to sustain in a human service organization. Both require great skill in the assessment of need and of persons. Such "quality" components in programs absorb costly resources without increasing income. Evidence suggests that for-profit as well as some non-profit organizations are more likely to screen out persons who cannot afford the quality services they wish to provide or whose problematic situations are likely to make extraordinary demands on program resources.[2]

Sustained Support

To be truly available an offer of service must include sustained support in managing an appropriate use of service.

Lacking such support, those in greatest need are less likely to benefit from the offer and may be further disadvantaged.

Sustained support in managing an appropriate use of the service provided assumes the organization accepts an obligation to the recipient that goes beyond making the service available. Such an obligation is often costly, particularly in the multi-problem recipient and typically among the more disadvantaged. To avoid the deficits promoted by efforts to fulfill this obligation the for-profit, more so than the non-profit, is likely to limit this obligation.[3]

Privacy

Respect for a recipient's autonomy is enhanced when confidences that build trust in a helping relationship are protected, are shared with others only with recipient approval, and are utilized only when such use can be shown to benefit the recipient.

The recipient's right to privacy obligates the organization to give precedence to client confidences unless pressed to do otherwise for a more compelling good. Unhappily, the choice to maintain confidences, a professional obligation, may be in conflict with maintaining a profitable operation (Rosner, 1980). For-profit operations frequently seek recipient permission to share confidential information in order to assure payment (third-party or public) for services. The non-profit organization may also be pressed to do likewise, if only to meet accountability required by funding sources. Thus, both for-profits and non-profits may bend the confidentiality rules. There is some evidence that suggests for-profits are less likely to resist such pressures than are non-profits (Jacobs, 1982/83).

In light of the problems inherent in the implementation of these rights in for-profit and non-profit organizations, we should anticipate differences in the manner in which ethical imperatives will serve to provide guidance in their organizational practice.

CONCLUSION

It is in the interest of the most disadvantaged, and those who wish to help them, to preserve and strengthen the non-profit sector of human service organizations. Altruistic motives and a desire to contribute to a common good jointly justify the ethical imperatives that guide their programs. Weakening these programs results in cutbacks in the supply of just and caring human services provided to the most vulnerable and needy.

Initially, we noted recent trends, accelerated by policies at the national level and in the public sector, that threaten the continued existence of private non-profit human service organizations. Non-profits have experienced cutbacks in tax-levy funding, increased competition for tax-levying supported contracts from the for-profit sector, and increases in the number of multiproblem families unable to gain access to the public and for-profit sectors. Some have compromised their moral justifications by accepting market criteria in evaluating their services. They have taken on for-profit service programs and have shifted the most costly cases to the unreceptive public sector.

In the past, altruism and serving the common good have helped sustain the humane concerns in our human service programs. These concerns should be sustained, lest we suffer the loss of a major claim we make to being a morally responsible society.

Chapter Notes

1. This essay avoids discussion of the usual assertions that non-profits assure access to public goods at the lowest possible price, are subject to the same controls as public organizations, do not cost society as much as for-profits, are better suited to provide service their customers cannot evaluate, and provide employees the best kind of environment. The empirical data needed to establish the correctness of these assertions are in short supply and conclusive evidence that they are facts, not myths, is lacking.

2. The experience of New York City may not be exceptional. *The New York Times* (September 11, 1987) reported that Dr. Lois Marcos, head of psychiatric services for the municipal hospitals of New York City, said the private, non-profit hospitals of New York City are reneging on a commitment to treat more of the indigent mentally ill: "Some private hospitals tended to restrict psychiatric admissions to less seriously disturbed patients with health insurance, leaving municipal hospitals with the burden of treating the most disturbed and indigent patients." Such practices were described by Marcos as "taking the cream from the top."

3. Testifying before the Sub-Committee on Domestic Marking, Consumer Affairs, and Nutrition, House Committee on Agriculture (May 5, 1987) Robert Greenstein, Director of the Center on Budget and Policy Priorities, cited the following as an example of a violation of the principle of welfare reform, that those who work or who participate in employment and training programs should not be disadvantaged by this participation.

> Several states have found an anomaly in the new employment and training program regarding child care. If a recipient must incur child care costs to participate in a program, reimbursement for these costs is limited to $25 a month. This, of course, is far below typical child care costs virtually anywhere in the country.

BIBLIOGRAPHY

Caplowitz, D. (1967). *The poor pay more: Consumer practices of low income families.* New York: Free Press, 1967.

Collin, R. W. (1987, Spring). Toward a new theory of non-profit liability. *Administration in Social Work, 11*(1), 15–24.

Jacobs, S. (1982/83, Winter). Advocates for children v. Blum. *The Advocate* (Publication of Advocates for Children of New York).

Lewis, H. (1983, November). The social work service commodity in the inflationary 80's. *Journal of Sociology and Social Welfare, 10*(4), 550–563.

Murray, T. H. (1987, April). Gifts of the body and the needs of strangers. *Hastings Center Report, 17*, 30–38.

Rosner, B. L. (1980, December). Psychiatrists, confidentiality and insurance. *Hastings Center Report, 10*, 5–7.

Chapter 15

Values and Ethics in Agency Practice for a Caring and Just Service

Again using the metaphor of the drama, in this essay Lewis links the roles and behaviors of actors in a nonprofit agency to the definition of our civilization. He articulates an ethical framework that integrates a charitable view (that emphasizes skill enhancement) with a justice view (that promotes social reform) and, thereby, provides the ethical basis for a resolution of these competing perspectives.

Values serve many purposes. They constitute one's belief in what is good and right. They spell out the elements in human relationships that are to be preferred. In combination, they provide the building blocks for differing ideologies. They act as persistent reinforcers, supporting sought-after changes in attitudes and behavior. In helping relationships through which services are provided, where changes in attitudes are intended to produce changes in behavior, and vice versa, the changes achieved are less likely to be sustained if not accompanied by changes in values.

For our purposes I'll assume we all believe that persons ought to be viewed as having the inherent right to be treated with dignity and respect. Their right to autonomy and privacy should be protected. All should have equal opportunity to realize their own potential, even if this requires that unequals be treated unequally. All should be secure in their persons, free from physical and mental threats and so on. I'll also assume that these values are to be realized in the behavior and attitudes of board members, volunteers, staff, and administration. Now, what if these assumptions are unfounded? What if there is not agreement on the values that are to be valued by the agency's programs and policies. Would it make a difference in agency practice?

Only if each acted on the basis of his or her different beliefs. As usually prescribed, values are generalized abstractions. They are most frequently cited to justify goals and purposes, equally general and abstract. If they are to make a difference they must be acted on, and this requires guiding principles, adherence to which assures their implementation. Such guidelines are provided by ethical principles or imperatives. Where such imperatives are lacking, it is doubtful that

Paper presented at Westchester Family and Children's Services, May 1988.

relevant values will find expression in practice. Values would then hardly matter, and different ideologies would persist without their assumptions being challenged.

Thus, to pursue an interest in ethics is a dangerous business. It can bring disharmony and conflict to an otherwise smooth functioning operation. On the other hand, not to pursue ethical issues may prove uneconomical and dysfunctional. It can lead to a practice that is effective and efficient in doing the wrong thing, even if occasionally one does the right thing for the wrong reasons. The collective interest of board members, volunteers, staff, and administration in value and ethical issues is prompted by the joint obligation they have assumed to deliver a social service under the auspice of a family agency. The different functions of the participants in this service drama result in differing perceptions of which values are to be emphasized.

The ethical imperatives that guide those seeking to act on these values likewise will vary for participants. But unless there is overall agreement on core groups of values and ethical imperatives to justify the goals and objectives of the agency, the danger is ever present that an unprincipled practice may result. I will not use our time together to pursue in detail the core values I expect all concerned would accept as justifying the agency's purpose. Instead, I will focus on ethical imperatives and some of the dilemmas they pose for the actors in the service drama. For convenience sake, these imperatives will be considered under three headings: virtues, obligations, and duties. Together they constitute the common good. The service drama will be viewed from the perspectives of the actors, action, agency, scene, and mission. If my approach succeeds in its intent, I should be able to summarize my major points in a statement of practice principles that are appropriate to a service that is both goal-oriented and ethical.

First, let us consider the scene: The ethical context in which current agency practice is framed. A new journal entitled, *Ethics: Easier Said Than Done* summarizes, in its lead editorial, the scene in which value and ethical issues are currently being addressed.

> In 1987, revelations of the Iran-Contra deceits, Ivan Boesky's greed, Jim Bakker's hypocrisy, Gary Hart's arrogant insensitivity, and dozens of lesser stories of selfishness, dishonesty, and moral weakness presented a major challenge to the self-image and self-esteem of Americans.

This occurred after Watergate, which demonstrated that a president lied, and that a public trust could not be taken for granted. The names of Michael Deaver, Lynn Nofziger, Edwin Meese, and at the local level, Mannes, Meyerson:[1] all persons of note tainted with the smudge of unethical conduct. When industrial and financial leaders, government officials, major sports figures, and religious spokespersons are publicly censured for unethical behavior, we must wonder what values underpin their dishonest, unfair self-serving activities. Their example promotes a deeply felt distrust of government, business, and political organizations. This distrust can't help but affect how social service organizations are viewed by their clientele as well. Coming at a time when our national priorities have decimated human service programs and have contributed to an increase in the number of persons living below the poverty line, is it any wonder that clients who see their common human needs denied also question the motivations and intentions of organizations and personnel supposedly there to help them? During the past decade it has become increasingly more difficult to help people, and the troubles of people have become more pervasive and unyielding to professional intervention.

Earlier, I noted that for an agency to succeed in its purpose, the participants in the service drama must agree and act on a common core of shared values. I am nevertheless sensitive to the misleading nature of a moral consensus. Recently, one of my doctoral students sought to test the ethical judgments of field education supervisors. Using a set of vignettes, each depicting an ethical dilemma that could well occur in their practice, the supervisors were asked to select among alternative decisions they might make in seeking to resolve these dilemmas. There was a high level of agreement among supervisors, and based on the scale of moral maturity used in the study, with few exceptions all evidenced a high level of maturity. Unhappily, when asked to explain the basis for their choices, there was little agreement, with some offering no explanation, other than a "gut feeling." In short, as the philosopher Stephen Toulmin (1986) observed in a comparable situation, "they could agree what they were agreeing about; but, apparently, they could not agree why they agreed about it." Or, as another scholar observed, "Scratch a moral consensus and you will find a chaos of principles." I expect this state of affairs is prevalent where ethical dilemmas are being confronted in all aspects of our daily living, but especially in an agency offering a caring service.

We know that ideas and experiences are not independent because everything we feel is modulated by what we know, and everything we know is influenced by how we feel about it. We know, for example, that all civilized societies would, ideally, seek to promote the health of their members, assuring them the benefits of a just and secure environment; promote knowledge and aesthetic satisfaction; and provide opportunities for them to realize their full potential. Any one of you would want these needs met for yourself and others, particularly those near and dear to you. We also know that achieving these ideals is not easy for the individual or family unit. Thus, all civilized societies have a health care system, economic structure, legal structure, and an educational system; they promote the arts, and hopefully, provide support for individuals and families seeking to realize these goods.

The major mission of social service agencies in our society is to enhance opportunities for individuals, families, and communities to realize these goods even for their most disadvantaged members. In this respect, the staffs, boards, volunteers, and clients of social agencies help, by their actions, to define our civilization and to serve as civilizing agents. Belief in the moral right of persons to realize these common human needs can serve to justify the core values for the actors in the service drama. But while we know these things, we are not as clear as we might be as to how we feel about them.

For example, a startling aspect of the most recent focus on the poor, in statements of various religious bodies and presidential candidates, is the lack of a crusading intention to do away with poverty altogether—not by feeding the poor to the lions, but by inviting them to share in the abundance long evident on the tables of the affluent. In contrast to the spirit that characterized the 1960s, there is now a significant body of opinion that believes the poor will always be with us; that these "less fortunate," unsuccessful ones are born to their lot; are paying for their follies; are inferior in their abilities and morals; in short, deserve to be poor. The very idea that there need not be poor people in our society, that policies and choices made by our leadership can be designed to eliminate poverty from our midst—(a view more prevalent in the early 1960s when the War on Poverty was launched by the Johnson Administration)—appears to be a marginal view today. In the past decade, the increase in the number of people living in poverty has furthered the more pessimistic view. The reason for this pessimistic view may be gleaned from our experience with the War on Poverty in the 1960s.

To win that war, we would have had to confront the possibility of total destruction of life on this planet, and opt for the alternative of a peaceful and competitive coexistence among nations. If the choice had been for peace, the energies devoted to the production of bombs and bullets would have instead been devoted to shaping the plowshares for harvesting a previously unimaginable plenty. Instead, the arms race continued, resulting in the dilemma of a steadily increasing military power and steadily decreasing national security. The wealth of nations spent on military account has been more than the entire national income of all poor nations combined. The hungry one-fifth of humanity, and the malnourished one-third would clearly have benefited from the diversion of resources to agricultural research and education. Unhappily, for all Americans, not only the poor, the perspective embodied in the Economic Opportunity Act of the mid-1960s was not pursued.

Thus we are confronted with the results of our immoral behavior, our own unfortunate choices—evidenced in homeless people crowding our shelters and sleeping in our streets; school systems failing in their mission for lack of resources; a large segment of our population not covered by medical insurance and lacking in adequate health care; chronic underemployment and increasing job-loss in basic industries; decaying bridges and roadways; depleting housing stocks, etc.

But possibly of greater interest is the state of our economy, sharply delineated by Black Monday, when the market crashed on October 19, 1987. For the first time, the possibility of a breakdown in the international as well as national economy was openly discussed by key financial bodies in our country and abroad. The devastation such a meltdown of the financial community would cause for the most vulnerable in our population is too awful to contemplate.

For social agencies that serve families in need, not only are shrunken budgets and inadequate resources byproducts of our present economic policies, but the problems their clientele experience are more severe than would otherwise be the case.

Since the end of World War II, movements seeking justice and fairness in the treatment of the sexes, racial minorities, and handicapped and otherwise disadvantaged populations have challenged all Americans to re-examine our consciences. In short, the discouraging lack of morality in our national leadership, and the conscionable disregard of the needs of the most disadvantaged, have contributed to the scene in which our social service agencies find themselves, as they move to a critical examination of their own ethical behavior.

THE ACTORS

The actors in the service drama are the worker, the client, and in a more indirect fashion, the administrator and board members. For our purposes, I will limit my focus to the lead actors, the worker and client, leaving to later consideration the other actors as they participate in the agency's work. The critical ethical concern of the lead actors in the drama is encompassed in a wish to protect the quality of the helping relationship, most often designated as a concern to protect standards. To the actors, tampering with the helping relationship, by reducing resources, restricting available service time in order to increase coverage of cases, altering the manner in which services are rendered in order to conserve resources, etc., represents departures from high standards. In a worse case scenario, the client becomes a means rather than an end. The worker's and client's integrity and autonomy are sacrificed to another end—efficient use of insufficient agency resources.

While the agency is seeking to do good as best it can, it is viewed by the actors as failing to refrain from doing harm and engaging in a process that promotes distributive injustice. The results achieved by departures from standards are manifest in worker burnout and client distrust. Standards degenerate from the ideal for practice. The challenge to the worker/volunteer and the client is to advocate more forcefully on the client's behalf, to achieve a more just allocation of resource for the particular client without doing so at some cost to other clients. The inevitable dilemmas that stem from seeking to do good and to protect rights in conditions of insufficient resource are too well known to require elaboration.

THE ACTION

There are a variety of approaches to practice on which the actors can draw for guidance in the conduct of a helping relationship. None of these approaches—psychosocial, behavioral, problem-solving, systems, ecological, existential, etc.—are value-free; each encounters ethical issues that generate dilemmas. These issue include paternalism, definition of the client's interest, confidentiality, determination of whose goals are to be worked on, who controls the helping process, how problems are defined, etc. All of these issues surface in the helping transaction and involve ethical judgments. Where limitations are placed on the scope of permissible actions by factors other than the needs of the client and the efficiency of the intervention approach, the action itself may prove to be generative of an unprincipled practice. An often-cited example is that of doctors, faced with a range of possible tests that can be justified in seeking to assess a client's condition, who may first be compelled to do a "pocketbook" diagnosis, since the patient can not afford the battery of tests that could be justified. There is always the possibility that the client's problems will be redefined to fit within the scope of what the agency can afford, rather than what the clients need.

THE AGENCY

Pragmatism is the philosophical preference of agency-sponsored social service programs. Viewed as social instruments, agencies usually opt for a consequential analysis in arriving at resolutions of ethical dilemmas. As the philosopher Rawls observed,[3] justice is to institutions what truth is to science. Social work services, historically, have been rendered by organizations, and social workers for agencies have always had a deep commitment to justice in the treatment of client claims. But social workers have consistently served primarily the poor and most disadvantaged. From extensive experience, social work has evolved a deep concern for the fair allocation of resources.

From close association with institutions and the poor, social work has developed its commitment to strive for distributive justice. No other human service profession has as its primary value the commitment to distributive justice that dominates social work's world view. Thus, for agencies providing social services, the obligation to client and community entailed in implementing societally designated mandates generates critical choices entailing very complex ethical analyses. But such analyses are made more complex than they might be where distrust permeates a relationship. If truth telling is doubted, scientific claims are distrusted. Where justice is lacking, the first element in the relationship to go is trust. When agencies do not fulfill their duties and obligations, they generate distrust and burden the helping relationship with clients. When the societal context is conducive to distrust, as noted earlier, the tasks of the agency and staff are made more difficult to perform, or in some instances, impossible.

Thus far, I have commented briefly on four of the five elements in the service drama—the scene, actors, action, and agency. What remains to be considered—the mission—is of particular interest to the board and the wider community.

Where an agency takes a "charitable" view of its social purpose, it usually sees adjustment and acceptance as the other side of a self-improvement and self-elevation expectation of clients. Where the focus is on justice, the agency adds an expectation of the community, that it will provide resources that the agency needs to achieve the self-realization of its clients. The charitable view emphasizes the skill component in agency work, and the justice perspective emphasizes the social reform component. When both are integrated in agency practice, one achieves a competent practice.

For policy to reflect this competence, attention must be given to ethical issues dealing with the common good. Particularly in times of expanding need and contracting resources (incidentally, a chronic condition in social service programs) triage-type choices are often approximated in intake policies, defining target populations, retaining staff and support services, and deciding who/what program/services shall survive when not all can survive. Such choices are a pressing concern of boards and financing bodies. The need to set priorities involves the decision makers in both fact-finding and purpose-clarification actions.

Inevitably, facts are significant but inadequate for ordering value priorities. Criteria for determining priorities necessarily require the guidance that ethical imperatives provide, if goals justified by values are to be manifest in objectives, justified by ethical imperatives. Typically, priority choices, to be congruent with the need to act in a just manner, require that equals be treated equally, and unequals, unequally. The order of priorities ought not further disadvantage the most disadvantaged, and in fact, ought to raise the expectations of the least advantaged. Provision needs to be made to assure participation by those affected by resource allocation decisions. These and other ethical imperatives are commended as likely to promote the common good of the community, not only the good and rights of the immediate recipients and providers of service.

As should be obvious by now, the impromptu drama I describe is not like any ordinary play. There is no director, there is no script, and it is constantly responding to the task of a changing audience. It is an historical process that reflects the conditions prevalent in our society at any one time. Its creative merit is achieved by the original contribution of the actors, and its effectiveness is achieved by the way in which the agency organizes the action. In the remainder of this presentation, I'll note some crucial ethical imperatives that I believe should govern the provision of services that would be both charitable and just, and will enhance the relationships that need trust in order to be effective.

Among those who have struggled with ethical issues that confront professional service providers, there is agreement on at least four ethical imperatives that ought to guide all practice. These imperatives cover the concerns of recipient and worker alike:

1. Promoting the autonomy of the actors in the drama.
2. Beneficence or doing good.
3. Malfeasance or avoiding doing harm.
4. Justice—assuring a fair and equitable service.

Autonomy, and the need to protect the privacy and confidentiality of the parties to the service transaction, have received considerable attention in recent years, particularly as our nation has confronted the AIDS epidemic. A guiding imperative in this area is the caution that we should refrain from seeking information that is not relevant to the service transaction. It is also commended that recipients of services participate in decisions that affect them, and where incapable of such participation, have their interests represented by an appropriate surrogate, preferably not the agency providing the service. Assuring the recipient of opportunities to make choices is fundamental to the commitment to promote autonomy.

Doing good, and the need to protect the rights of those intended beneficiaries of such "best intentions" efforts, usually confront issues related to paternalism. In providing services to the elderly and to children, and to other often dependent populations, the provision of services may call for sacrificing the recipient's rights for the recipient's own good. The recent cases of homeless street people who were forcefully "housed" against their will, highlights a far more prevalent practice in providing what we have come to consider "protective services." The overriding principle in these situations recommends priority be given to rights, where rights and "good" are in conflict. When rights are to be sacrificed, provision must be made to see that the sacrifice will benefit the recipient who makes the sacrifice.

Refraining from doing harm is particularly difficult in times of scarcity, when limited resources are insufficient to satisfy identified need. One ought not further burden those already overwhelmed by deprivations, in order to promote a desirable purpose such as may be reflected in a cost-benefit ratio. Policies that discriminate on the basis of characteristics—such as gender, age, race, ethnic origin, etc.—which are not directly relevant to the satisfactory provision of a service ought to be avoided. Granted that community neglect, for reasons of cost or prejudice, may make the task of the agency and staff a trying one, it is imperative that the agency and staff not contribute to such neglect by its own practices, and by failure to press for more adequate provision by the community. The most general statement of this imperative is to avoid treating the recipients as a means to an end, rather than as ends in themselves.

The justice provision, as a minimum, asks the service provider to respect the three imperatives noted, but further to make special provision for those disadvantaged by circumstance of birth and social conditions. This requires, as I earlier noted, that equals be treated equally, and unequals unequally. In this category Affirmative Action efforts are commended, and a useful principle formulated by the philosopher John Rawls is applicable: that unequal benefits can be justified if they raise the expectations of the least advantaged.

I'll end now, with the understanding that further discussion is needed to make more explicit the implications for practice and policy that adherence to these imperatives will generate.

Chapter Note

1. The President of the New York City Borough of Queens (Donald Mannes) was implicated in a corruption scandal.

BIBLIOGRAPHY

Rawls, John. (1971). *A Theory of Justice*. Cambridge, MA: Harvard University Press.

Toulmin, Stephen E. (1986, March). The ambiguities of self-understanding. *Journal for the Theory of Social Behavior, 16*(1), 41–55.

Chapter 16

Morality and the Politics of Practice

This essay was the first in U.S. social work literature to apply the ideas of John Rawls to the development of practice principles. In addition, well ahead of his time, Lewis integrates an application of such issues as privilege, power, self-esteem, and trust into his discussion. "Morality," he argues, is critical because "[it] produces a set of values and seeks to generate trust and justice in reciprocal human relationships."

Science first developed as a method, then as a body of knowledge, and, more recently, as a social institution. Scientists now overwhelmingly assume roles as professionals employed by large organizations, universities, and governmental agencies. Human service professionals similarly have found themselves emphasizing their methods, their knowledge base, or their institutional self-interests at different points in their history. The concern for consequences that justify practice and the values that direct such concerns are frequently overlooked in the history of science but can hardly be ignored in the development of a profession. When such values are evident in the product of professional effort, they constitute its morality.

Our nation and the helping professions are currently experiencing a moral crisis. This crisis is manifest in every issue confronting the social work profession, challenging its very existence. Questions of manpower, professional and paraprofessional; of auspices, public and voluntary, profit and nonprofit, religious and nonsectarian; of advocacy and treatment; of generalist and specialist; and of policy and practice cannot be understood without confronting the moral crisis and cannot be resolved without some commitment to deal with the issues posed.

Although the sciences have helped orient us to issues affecting our means, and the applied humanities have oriented us in our choice of ends, our profession utilizes a blend of both, formulated as principles and guidelines for practice. These practice principles define the performance expected of the principled practitioner

---

Originally published in *Social Casework 53*(7), July 1972.

and his commitment to a moral practice. Morality produces a set of values and seeks to generate trust and justice in reciprocal human relationships.

The reluctance of professional social work to engage in authoritative services—to doubt the possibility of a professional service in circumstances where the recipient is an unwilling participant—stems in part from assumptions concerning the minimal moral maturity essential for a truly helpful relationship. The worker who assumes willing engagement and freedom of choice is reluctant to initiate a relationship of fearful dependency with an obedience and punishment orientation. He or she is equally reluctant to enter into a self-serving reciprocity where contact and exchange are characteristically egoistic and opportunistic. As a minimum, almost all of the psychological approaches that provide the conceptual underpinnings of practice imply at least some conforming to a stereotypical image of natural role behavior. The conforming may be only a concession to please with a "good-boy" intention. Where this minimal implication is absent, the recipient is likely to resist involvement in a service relationship that expects some degree of commitment on his or her part.

The recipient who is motivated to use the help to be given and who evidences a willingness to conform to rules is more commonly found. He or she behaves in an appropriate manner, as defined by the service source, even when rules and behavior may be viewed by him or her as burdensome additions to the conforming role—necessary and entered into only because failure to fulfill them can deny him or her access to the resources that he or she badly needs. Studies of helping relationships usually find such recipients among the more successful cases of short-term service—able to sustain their participation in the helping process long enough to transact the transfer of resource that prompted their seeking help and maintain their conforming role behavior.

This degree of commitment, nevertheless, is rarely seen as sufficient for achieving a more ambitious psychological influence in a counseling transaction. For long-term helping, conforming behavior would seem to require adherence to shared standards, rights, and obligations involving a contractual, legalistic orientation, based on mutual willingness and expectation of positive consequences. This level of moral maturity usually cements the relationship with mutually satisfactory intentions, releasing energies for growth-yielding experiences generally seen as major goals of long-term service. It is only one step further in moral maturity for the recipient to pattern his or her behavior on the basis of conscious and universal logical principles founded on mutual respect and trust. The recipient who has achieved this level of moral maturity is more likely to be psychologically free of handicapping attitudes and behavior. He or she can initiate and terminate engagement in the helping relationship with minimal need for structure—rules and procedures.

These levels of moral maturity depict different degrees of morality, evaluated from the perspective of the profession's view of a recipient's mature behavior in a helping relationship. Although these levels suggest a progression with reference to dependence-independence, they evidence no such progression with respect to commitment to behavioral norms appropriate to each level. For example, at the lowest level of morality, dependence on outside rules is greatest; at the highest level such dependence is practically nil. The degree of the recipient's involvement with the helper, however, will fluctuate at any level of the dependence-independence continuum. Professional authority is appropriately exercised in relation to the recipient since this authority is earned through furthering the moral maturity of the recipient in his or her service role. In sharp contrast, the exercise of professional authority to compel commitment and the involvement in service it would entail is more appropriately viewed as authoritarian and unprofessional. This difference is fundamental and poses the central issue that confronts the human service professions in our country today.

There is work to be done in achieving a level of self-trust that supports one's risking independent behavior when the professional worker helps contribute to the clarification of tasks, monitors behavior, identifies weaknesses, and expands on alternatives. The consequences of such effort is evident to the recipient in his or her own experience. The recipient, in effect, is able to know and claim his or her own growth. He or she can willingly yield some control to the helper, whose authority is knowingly based on the recipient's belief in the helper's capacity to provide the service needed. It is an authority based on means, not on ends.

Commitment, on the other hand, is a matter of trusting the other's intentions, not his competence. It depends on factors affecting, but extending far beyond, the relationship. Thus, in a society where social practice and policies evidence a lack of regard for distributive justice and privacy, trust is the earliest victim. Such practices and policies are increasingly evident at all levels of our own national life. A pervasive immorality is contributing to deterioration of the humane context of professional practice. If this destruction of trust is allowed to continue, it will, in time, no longer be possible to engage in an ethical social work practice. Instead, a dehumanized welfare service, void of a caring human interface, will take its place. Such dehumanized service will provide a computerized, plastic, and efficient tool for national pacification, programming people who will be known by the company that keeps them and by their code numbers in an omniscient surveillance memory bank.

IMPORTANCE OF TRUST

Consider what characterizes a relationship without trust. A relationship without trust is burdened with fears. It entraps the parties involved in a labyrinth of unfathomables: guessing intentions, deciphering motives, or searching for meaning that arouses or placates doubts. Without trust, a relationship may breed contempt when it intends respect or create anxiety when it wishes to comfort. Lacking this element of reciprocity, it will also be deficient in friendship and love.

Social workers experience circumstances in their practice that foster distrust in their clients and themselves. Common to such circumstances are requirements that foreclose on choices by limiting alternatives. In social work practice, choices are most often denied where resources are lacking. The poor and powerless, those with the least and needing the most, are frequently the victims of such denials, promoting their distrust. Thus, in service encounters that ask for mutual engagement for good and humane reasons, the expectation of mutual trust may, for many, be most unreasonable. Certainly, in times such as we are now experiencing, where social workers and services are being separated from the poor by deliberate national and state policies, there is good and sufficient reason for distrust.

In a helping relationship, trust functions to support dependence without fear of self-effacement; to inculcate an expectation of joint, mutually beneficial effort—despite differences in kind, frequency, and intensity of involvement; to reinforce the belief that assigned obligations will be fulfilled and cooperative effort sustained, reassuring participants who might otherwise fear betrayal. Trust serves as an organizing device that facilitates the communication of a moral tone to a helping relationship. These functions, composed of elements that signal the basis for trust, may be evidenced in the circumstance, in the process, and in the participant's attitude and behavior in the relationship. It will be undermined where racial, class, cultural, and ethnic differences deny equal and fair access to available resources. A society—its institutions and welfare programs—that fails to see all persons as ends in themselves (whether they be Vietnamese or Americans), fails to give equal weight to the interests of each person affected by an action, or which departs from this equality in a way that grants unequal benefits without regard for the expectation of the least advantaged, is necessarily unjust in its distribution of resources and is not to be trusted. It is crucial for the social work profession to develop and support practice principles that will instill trust in the helping relationships associated with its services. Such principles should generate rules that would commend agencies and workers in the offer of service and the helping situation to act in a trustworthy manner.

PRACTICE PRINCIPLES

The first set of practice principles deals with fair and equal access to service. These principles assume that an absence of justice in the offer and initiation of service will seriously undermine that confidence on which trust relies.

1. *The conditions that determine the availability of service should be unformly applicable to all partaking of it. Deviations from these conditions are justified only when they can be shown to be to everyone's advantage.*

This principle recognizes that trust develops with the expectation that each request for help will receive the same consideration, will be evaluated on the basis of appropriate and similar criteria, and will be judged by its intrinsic merit as a claim on service resources. No person will be privileged without good and apparent reason or without some provision for those thereby disadvantaged. An example of privileged consideration in keeping with this principle is the selection of a request for special care and treatment where potential for enhancing new knowledge exists. An example of privileged consideration that contradicts this principle is the bypassing of a waiting list in order to facilitate access to service resource for a recipient who makes claims based on friendship, kinship, or some other irrelevant criteria. This principle also recognizes the chronic limitation of available resources; it cautions against exhausting their supply without provision being made for those who will be unserved for reasons over which they have no control and that otherwise are not grounds for exclusion.

2. *No more should be asked of the recipient in a service relationship than is necessary and sufficient to transact the intended service. Involuntary involvement of a recipient in service for his or her own protection or that of others should provide for the defense of the recipient's rights by persons and procedures not under the control of the service source or an agent pressing for such involvement.*

This principle proposes an allocation of resources and provision of procedures to protect a recipient against unwarranted intrusion upon his or her privacy. Where privacy is denied an individual against his or her wishes, he or she is thereby deprived of an essential element of trust: the choice to share a part of him- or herself that he or she can otherwise choose to keep from public view. In such intimate relationships as love and friendship, the granting of access to one's otherwise private self is frequently the most convincing expression of trust. Requesting information in a service relationship must clearly demonstrate its relevance to the use the recipient will make of the service and to his or her appropriate participation in it. Only under these circumstances can the recipient exercise choice in self-revelation and trust the intentions of the offer of service.

Compelling a person to enter into a relationship that inevitably must subject parts of his or her thoughts, attitudes, feelings, and behavior to the scrutiny of another is tantamount to victimizing him or her by robbing him or her of an area of personal authority and thereby arousing his or her distrust. External authority, when imposed and not contracted for, communicates to the person imposed upon intentions that are suspect, for they threaten his or her freedom of choice and self-determination. Without a reasonable and adequate appeal against imposed authority, it will convey an authoritarian tone to the relationship this imposition establishes. The intervention without request—whether motivated by an intention to protect others or to protect a person from his or her own self-destructive behavior—is most often justified on grounds that the person involved cannot be trusted to behave in a socially acceptable manner. This distrust breeds further distrust, which, although it can never be totally removed, can be mitigated by providing access to a higher authority empowered to subject the intrusion to a test of validity, under circumstances not entirely in control of the instigating authority.

An example of the application of this principle would be in a process whereby eligibility for public assistance is determined on the basis of the specific, immediate, and shared evidences of financial need. Another example of the application of this principle would be in a child neglect case in which a presentation to a court makes provision for an attorney to represent the client, overseeing the interests of the family charged with neglect. An example of the failure to comply with this principle is determining eligibility for a service through requirements concerning political, religious, ethnic, or other personal preferences having no direct bearing on the determination of need for the resource requested.

3. *The restraints implicit in the conditions for offering or making claims for service should not be posed as a threat. The risks and obligations entailed in a service relationship should not unfairly burden any one participant.*

Given the excess of demand over supply associated with the provision of services, preferences must be exercised. In arriving at such priority decisions, some recipients will be disadvantaged. Such disadvantage will frequently ask of the group affected that they risk the uncertainties of delay and incomplete provision and undertake greater obligation of justification of need than is otherwise required. Recognizing this fact, this principle requires that such differential treatment be based on legitimate and relevant criteria, be openly arrived at and uniformly applied, and be subject to ongoing review lest a just procedure in time perpetuate an unjust burden. Where the recipient perceives unequal treatment as unjustified, fairness is doubted and distrust promoted.

This principle cautions against surrounding otherwise fair and equal access to service with conditions that promote privileged treatment based on unequal talents and status. It is unreasonable to expect persons seeking help to have confidence in processes and procedures that evidently channel their requests into categories of service provision differing in quality and quantity when such assignment is based on social status and conditions over which they have no control or natural differences not subject to alteration by their own conscious and reasoned effort. The application of criteria that are unrelated to the elements relevant to the request and that are not subject to the influence of a helping resource as a condition of access must inevitably deplete the recipient's image of him- or herself as a source of power and influence over his or her own condition. This depletion threatens one's sense of self-determination. Similarly, priority considerations determined by such criteria do not order preferences on the basis of need, motivation, or capacity, but on competitive evaluations. These evaluations are likely to penalize, for reasons over which they lack control, those persons who are most disadvantaged. Fair and equal access must anticipate natural and social restraints and not be conditioned by them.

An example of this principle is the fair manner in which provision is made for a waiting list and fee assignment in a child guidance clinic. An example of the failure to apply this principle is the practice of "first come, first served" allocation of resources, without consideration of unequal opportunity or capacity for initiating request. This lack of consideration is often evident in the allocation of concrete resources such as day care, homemaker, camping, or financial emergency relief funds.

4. *The offer of essential concrete services should include alternatives for the intended beneficiary. Lacking alternatives, the offer should be made as a matter of right, as free of conditioning tests as possible.*

This principle primarily concerns the provision of such basic human needs as food, clothing, shelter, and medical care. Where survival depends on access to these resources, it is unrealistic to expect persons needing such assistance to trust a relationship that intervenes between their request and access to the resource. To the applicant who understandably assumes his or her own continued survival to be a fundamental right, a requirement that limits this right represents a threat to his or her existence. He or she can hardly avoid the implication that the claim is in some way doubted and that he or she is not entirely to be trusted. Under these circumstances, reciprocal involvements intended to enhance social and psychological functioning may be viewed as barriers, not aids, to access. They would appear to hold little promise of effective consequences.

An example of the application of this principle is the provision of unemployment compensation as a right. Another example is the provision of emergency medical care after natural catastrophes. An example of the contradiction of this principle is in the uniform requirement that indigent recipients participate in a counseling service as a condition for emergency relief or medical care.

5. *The recipient of service should have the opportunity to experience his or her role in its provision as a test of its fairness and not be expected to assume such fairness as a precondition for service.*

This principle accepts as an unavoidable accompaniment of a trusting relationship the risk entailed in revealing oneself to another, relinquishing thereby some element of personal autonomy and self-determination. Deciding on what and how much to risk involves the recipient and helper in ambiguous situations whose scope and consequences cannot be entirely anticipated. Thus, each new encounter with a helping process requires of its participants a willingness to consider the intent of the other partly on the basis of past experience, but always on the basis of performance in the here and now. Foreclosing an existential criterion by which participants can evaluate fairness limits the choice to risk based on what is new and different in this encounter. This limit denies to each participant the opportunity to be judged anew. Emerging changes and growth may in these circumstances be discounted for the sake of relative certainties projected from earlier evidences. In some ways, such projections may become self-fulfilling and in other ways may undervalue existing potential. In either case, a fair hearing of a current request may be denied.

An example of the application of this principle is the provision for an initial phase in service for mutual exploration of the resources requested, the resources available, and the conditions for their utilization. An example of the contradiction of this principle is the requirement of detailed, personal history data on application forms, without any explanation of their intended use nor any clear statement of their relevance to the decision affecting the applicant's access to service.

The second set of practice principles pertains to the need to provide opportunities in each service encounter to share risks, engage in frank and responsible expression of feeling and thought, and evidence dependable and consistent behavior in order to promote trust among participants in a helping relationship.

6. *The worker should seek to enlarge on choices available to the recipient, including those proposed by the recipient and those newly developed in the course of rendering the service.*

This principle regards choice as significant in moral behavior. Choice is as essential for trust as opportunity is for self-realization. Choice increases opportunities for error. Where there is no possibility of error, there is also no basis for trust. Willingness to act in uncertain situations is a necessary condition for determining one's commitment to the goals of a relationship that entails some risk to one's self.

Without choice, decisions are foreclosed. The recipient, denied the option of selecting among alternatives, is limited in the risks taken. Where the offer of service is tightly bound by requirements and where resources are limited, the recipient may be faced with a take-it-or-leave-it decision. In these circumstances, neither the worker nor the recipient has reason to experience together the exploration of alternatives so essential to a trusting relationship. Enlarging choices thus constitutes a significant source of evidence on which convictions about intentions and expectations can be developed. Where new choices evolve from the worker–recipient interaction itself, a natural bond can evolve that cements the relationship with the commitment of both parties. The binding nature of joint discovery reinforces in the explorers a sense of their mutual competence and importance. Finally, the attitude that conveys an intention to seek after options is likely to be one that is hopeful. An atmosphere of hope, associated with choice, communicates belief in potential and thereby encourages trust.

An example of the application of this principle is a community's providing a range of supervised housing services for the aged, with varying degrees of supervised care provided. Such provision makes possible relevant choices based on recipient need rather than making do with limited alternatives that may further undermine the full potential for self-care of the aged person involved. An example of the failure to adhere to this principle is a community child welfare program in which a lack of provision for halfway houses, specialized institutions for the emotionally disturbed, sufficient foster-home care, and care away for home perpetuates conditions of child neglect and dependency through the very structure of service intended to alleviate such conditions.

7. *Potential recipients should be informed about programs for which they are eligible. Participating recipients should know when resources sought and promised are no longer on hand. Failure to utilize a service or sustained participation in a program of service ought not be based on ignorance of the facts concerning the availability of resource.*

It is not uncommon for channels of communication to handicap further those already handicapped. The lack of awareness of available services on the part of economically and socially deprived persons has been documented many times over. Failure to reach eligible populations in need with information of their rights and opportunities reinforces in them a deep disbelief in the intention of those offering a service and a distrust of procedures used to determine eligibility for the service. Similarly, doubt as to program intentions is inevitable when recipients are initially involved in a relationship on the basis of a promised provision of resource and subsequently are sustained in this relationship despite knowledge on the part of the service source that the original resource requested has been exhausted or is no longer available.

An example of the application of this principle is the program of the Veterans Administration, which utilizes a variety of channels to inform veterans of their rights and of available resources. A further example is the provision of ombudsmen services to protect the clients' rights to services that are promised by programs in which they are involved.

An example of the failure to apply the first element in this principle is the denial of public assistance in many instances to poverty-ridden persons primarily because they remain ignorant or misinformed of their rights. Failure to apply the second element in this principle is illustrated by the commitment of persons to institutional care for purposes of treatment when, in fact, treatment resources are so scarce as to be practically unavailable to the recipients who are thus retained in a custodial setting with little expectation of a change in their condition.

IMPORTANCE OF DISTRIBUTIVE JUSTICE

Clients of social service programs are among the most disadvantaged persons in our society. Social workers employed in these programs normally serve such disadvantaged clients directly or work with persons interested in promoting services for them. A principal moral justification for professional social work practice, therefore, is to be found in the dedication of the practitioner to the improvement of the circumstances and expectations of these clients. A helping profession not based in a morality inspiring a just order risks encouraging a practice that promotes an unjust one.

Distributive justice, while by no means the whole of a just order, is a particular concern of a helping profession serving the disadvantaged. If it penalizes the least advantaged, it defeats efforts intended to aid the disadvantaged.

An ethical imperative intended to guide the behavior of persons seeking distributive justice has been proposed by John Rawls (1971). Professor Rawls utilizes social contract theory and a set of value expectations that rational persons may be presumed to want (that is, liberty and opportunity, income and wealth, health and educated intelligence, and self-respect) and proposes the following necessary conditions for distributive justice:

1. Each person is to have an equal right to the most extensive basic liberty compatible with a similar liberty for others.
2. Social and economic inequalities are to be arranged so that they are both:
   a. reasonably expected to be everyone's advantage, and
   b. attached to positions and offices equally open to all.

Rawls assumes a framework of social institutions in which fair equality of opportunity obtains. His second condition suggests an ethical imperative: ". . . the higher expectations of those better situated in the basic structure are just if and only if they work as part of a scheme which improves the expectations of the least advantaged members of society." He also assumes that the first condition must be satisfied before the second can be met. Thus, the principle of equal rights to liberty becomes a preliminary condition to the establishment of justifiable inequalities. These conditions and the derived ethical imperative seem compatible with the goals of service voiced in the professional literature of social work and in statements expressing program intentions of social service.

Social institutions incorporate into their practices those established patterns of behavior that they are charged to maintain in the society that supports them. While they may differ in their functions in relation to the *status quo*—some primarily concerned with control or maintenance, others with the restoration or restructuring of social relationships among competing groups—all are directly involved in activities or events that inevitably favor some and may discriminate against others.

With knowledge of the role of social institutions in any society and of the ethical imperative earlier annunciated for achieving distributive justice, it is possible to formulate principles intended to promote distributive justice that should enhance the work of social workers, whatever their practice concentration.

Practice Principles

1. *The profession and its associated institutions must, in the work and attitudes of their constituents, combat unfair discriminatory practices or be judged as perpetrating the disadvantages they entail.*

This principle includes in its formulation a denial of the possibility of a neutral stance toward racism. This principle assumes that one cannot enter the stream of community life and remain dry; nor can one avoid some deflection of its flow. Either the worker imparts a principle in his or her practice or departs from it; his or her actions provide the evidence by which his or her adherence to principle can be judged.

2. *In choosing program goals and purposes, it should be assumed that ability and motivation among the disadvantaged are more widespread than is opportunity.*

This principle carries with it the implicit expectation that the worker will be knowledgeable in actions intended to change institutional structures as well as actions intended to structure personal and interpersonal change. It does not assume that these need be separate or qualitatively distinctive actions. The principle further recognizes that institutional arrangements in troubled communities must not model professional and organizational goals but serve them. If the profession is to act in accordance with its commitment to distributive justice, it must be prepared to transform itself and other community institutional structures and agencies employing social workers.

3. *Institutionalized restrictions that limit opportunities, as well as the personal shortcomings of the client that may curtail his or her options, are legitimate targets for change.*

This third principle visualizes a societal and personal component in every service encounter. In seeking to maximize the client's utilization of resources, the worker's causal interests direct him or her to focus on personal and social restraints, which determine the current opportunities available to the client. He or she would be so directed whatever the nature of the client's problems, whatever the etiologies. Utilization of service appears in practice as action and, in the context of the helping process, is an important form of social action. It is not likely to be enhanced without client involvement on his or her own behalf. Nor can it be enhanced where opportunities available for improved utilization are so limited as to deny choice.

4. *Opportunities to participate in the development of programs, in the formulation of policies and procedures, as well as in the practice decisions directly affecting their lives, must be afforded the disadvantaged as a minimal expectation of organizations and practices intended to help them.*

It makes little sense to see individuals and institutions as beneficiaries of service, while denying them a central role in its development. The fourth principle, therefore, requires organizations and professionals intent upon helping people to include those for whom their services are intended in all phases of the social processes whereby needs are identified and resources are organized and distributed to meet these needs. The knowledge basis for the propositional element in this principle has received extensive documentation in the literature of social work, particularly as a result of the experiences of recently developed antipoverty, community mental health, and client self-help programs. This principle does not require that those who are intended to benefit directly from the program have control of it, but it does not exclude this possibility. There is increasing evidence that many client groups favor such control, and experience may prove that it is an essential ingredient for sound practice. Conceivably, client control may provide one of the more important opportunities that traditionally have been denied to the disadvantaged in our country.

CHARACTERISTICS OF THE PRACTICE PRINCIPLES

All the principles cited may be generalized to cover a variety of immoral practices known to be prevalent in our society, including denial of fair opportunity to racial and religious minorities, women, handicapped persons, the aged, and the poor. The propositional elements are derived from known facts about social institutions and their functions in any society, about discrimination and its impact on all groups thereby disadvantaged, and about changes that are required if evident inequities in opportunity are to be eliminated. The ethical commendations are derived from the ethical imperative accepted as essential for the achievement of distributive justice and trust. Together, these propositional and value statements justify the principles proposed. The experiences of social workers also serve to justify them in a way that encourages their acceptance in practice.

The social worker, in his or her professional and nonprofessional experience, has the opportunity to observe and evaluate the unjust and untrustworthy practices of the community in which he or she lives and works. He or she stores in memory these perceptions of prevalent social inequalities and refers to them when he or she seeks to understand events and circumstances new to his or her experience. Certainly, life experiences differ among social workers and such differences extend to the social context and circumstances of their encounters with various forms of discrimination. There are workers who have been the victims of unfair behavior and others who have practiced such behavior without a conscious awareness of its implications. There are, undoubtedly, some who have rationalized the injustices they have observed, attributing evident inequities to the influences of fate, faith, or fundamental biological differences. Whereas some workers would find support for the suggested practice principles in their total life experience, others would view these principles as contradictory to what nonprofessional and even certain professional experience would suggest.

Workers who would accept these principles for professional practice but deny their applicability to their own behavior when not involved in professional work would have to manage serious inner-directed conflict. One may suppose that the mental compartmentalization of behavior norms that must accompany such contradictory directives is likely to be successfully maintained when reinforced by external influences. Social structures, community norms, and institutions appear to facilitate and reinforce mental compartmentalization of behavioral roles by supporting differential role expectations in different settings. Increased dependence on such external structures to sustain mental compartmentalizations would ultimately deprive the worker of considerable freedom to respond imaginatively to client need situations, reinforcing a more rigid, habituated role-dominated practice. This is a heavy price to pay, but probably unavoidable if inner-directed conflict is to be controlled.

Experience teaches us to accept as a matter of fact the ability of most persons to engage in inconsistent behavior; we accept it as normal provided that contradictory behaviors are not simultaneously evident in the same social context. A helping profession (and its associated institutions) that promotes such inconsistencies, however, cannot expect to compartmentalize them so readily. Policies and procedures are never entirely private in an institution; the tensions generated by contradictory policies are communicated to the practitioner and his or her clients and are not likely to be fully absorbed in intraorganizational stresses and strains. The profession can hardly afford to be inconsistent in its principled behavior lest it be judged dishonest to the degree that its rules subvert professed intentions. If, for the individual, inconsistent behavior in professional and personal activities can be depleting of energy and resource, for the profession it can be calamitous.

There is a process, not clearly understood, whereby the principled behavior is achieved. For the individual worker there is the need to determine for him- or herself that the propositions and ethical commendations of the principles to be followed are true and right, and this determination normally requires the worker to experience in practice the positive consequences that follow upon their application. He or she may, in relation to the principles proposed, find personal and social reasons for supporting their directives, recognizing that they are intended to increase the choice open to recipients. As he or she works with recipients and discovers how personal and social factors contribute to the conditions he or she seeks to change, he or she will compose for storage in memory the self-confirming proofs that develop and sustain convictions and will be more willing to act on them.

One cannot legislate an inner-directed adherence to an ethic or truth, but one can promote a context that encourages such adherence. A practice environment that is increasingly intolerant of workers who profess ideals but fail to evidence conviction about them in their work is likely to inspire principled behavior. This fact is sensed by workers seeking employment in such agencies who assume that they will be encouraged to do likewise.

The social work profession attaches considerable importance to its code of ethics and similarly seeks a community environment that is sympathetic and encourages the profession to act on the basis of its convictions. While the profession is aware of its limited capacities and deficiencies in skill, there is much evidence of community restraints and deprivations that harm programs employing social workers, severely limiting their opportunities to achieve at the level of their known capacities.

A measure of a practitioner's skill is the ability to comprehend both the recipient-situation and worker-situation and develop a balanced perspective that frees him or her to act on the basis of practice principles. The processes that the practitioner experiences in developing and sustaining a conviction to act on the principles must include work and the opportunity to observe the consequence of his or her work. The assumption long held by social work educators that methods are mastered in their application rests in part on the necessity to do in order to know what acting on a principle really means.

Patterns of worker activity provide the vehicles through which guiding principles are actualized. "By their deeds ye shall know them" accurately describes the role of action in the appraisal of professional intentions.

THE POLITICS OF PRACTICE

Practice principles impart a moral component to professional service when they influence the worker's use of self in action, guiding his or her political choices. Politics concern the processes whereby priority decisions affect the allocation of resources (including the worker's own professional competence) and in this sense no professional practice can be apolitical. Given the ethical imperative that we have chosen to inform the principles cited, it is possible to define a morally destructive practice as one in which rational, programmatic, or personal priorities evidence preferences that further benefit the advantaged without increasing the expectations of the least advantaged. Such priorities can only be enforced by coercion, compelling those they further disadvantage to accept them. It is such coercion we call authoritarianism and that we identify in professional practice as unprincipled.

The priority question, "What should be the order in which I (we) do what I (we) can for this recipient (program)," is necessarily complex. It seeks a list of possibilities among which a choice must be made, some measure of their interdependence, and the sequence in which those possibilities chosen will be acted on. Thus, three different questions are incorporated in the one: What can I (we) do? How does the choice of one influence the others? What order of actions is required? These three questions differ in the type of answers they seek. The first requests information; the second asks for a propositional statement establishing the relationship recovered in answer to the first; the third resembles what John M. O. Wheatley calls a deliberative question, wanting a decision. In answer to the first question, a "true or false" test may be applied. In response to the second, one can propose a procedure for proving whether, in fact, the relationships specified are what the proposition asserts. For the third, what is called for is a decision rather than an assertion: an answer that is neither true nor false. The first and second questions seek knowledge—"know-that" statements, for example; the third draws on imperatives. Since decisions are dispositions to behave in certain manner if certain conditions are realized, the value component entailed in an answer to the third question is clear. What the enquirer wants in answer to the decision question is not a prediction, but suggestion or advice.

The social worker employed by a social agency is not free to exercise his or her preferences in determining the clientele, workload, or problem to be dealt with in practice. Priority decisions that have culminated in the program of services offered by the agency limit his or her opportunities. It is not difficult to identify the many prior decisions that have shaped an agency's program and the political and economic interests they reflect. These decisions are manifest in program budgets of financing bodies and in the attributes of persons serving on those bodies that pass on plans and policy. The agency's goals, purposes, policies, and procedures are themselves conditioned by prior decisions and, in turn, set limits within which the worker's choices are exercised.

The worker must deal with two situations that necessitate personal priority decisions, given the constraints flowing from agency program preferences. He or she must, at any one time, decide how to allocate his or her personal resources among all clients requiring his or her services. He or she must also decide on the allocation of those resources designated for a particular client. These two decisions undoubtedly have their distinctive, as well as common, attributes. These personal priority decisions can be contrasted with the priority decision process occurring in social policy and planning activities.

It is customary in social work to think of priorities as an aspect of the planning and policy decision processes of groups, organizations, and communities, but rarely, if ever, as an integral part of the worker's practice wherein he or she decides how to budget and allocate his or her own personal resources. Actually, the worker's efforts to cope with value-preference issues in practice evidence all the issues identified in planning and policy choices situations if we accept the following list of such issues as indicative:

- There are conflicting values at stake.
- Value questions must often be posed in an "as if" form.
- It is difficult to clarify just what the prevalent values or preferences are.
- "If" values are not always transitive.
- There is often dispute as to whose choices are relevant or most relevant to the decisions to be made.
- It is difficult to translate technical issues into their value consequences in a completely objective fashion.

The social worker may accept as a given the agency's allocation of its resources, recognizing the priority choices such allocations evidence in its programs goals. He or she may also accept as a given the preferences expressed by clients regarding problems to be worked on, the nature of help desired, and acceptable outcomes. The worker, nevertheless, must then ask, whatever are the restraints of these givens circumscribing the choices: How shall I allocate my own resources? What investment of self ought I make in a particular service transaction? In what order should my abilities be committed in meeting the demands evidenced in this one practice encounter?

The approaches to decision making suggested for those concerned with problems of valuations in social policy and planning hardly suffice for this inner-directed choice process. The concern in the former is with processes and procedures for enabling others to achieve consensus on goals and purposes, often in conflict-laden interpersonal situations. Self-directed valuations, having as their intent the recovery of guides for actions that realize the worker's allocation of his or her own resources, involve other matters.

For example, while compromise is often an acceptable ploy in social planning, one does not compromise with one's self—one compromises one's self. Consensus is important to social planners, but one does not look for consensus or majority opinions in inner-choice decisions, nor does one avoid the need to choose by delegating the choice to others. Such delegation is itself the choice. Dividing the circumstances conditioning the need for the self-directed professional priority question may be helpful; involving others in identifying the alternatives and their consequences may clarify and focus the worker's perspective; but in the end he or she, and he or she alone, will have to decide how to allocate his or her resources in each practice encounter within the givens that limit his or her options.

In seeking to recover guidelines for action, the worker's theory and value preferences no doubt point in certain directions and limit the range of possibilities to be considered in arriving at "inner" priority decisions. The external parameters that circumscribe the available possibilities, such as the agency and client conditions, certainly restrict the range of choices and serve a justifying function as well as an orienting one. The "realities" to be reckoned with are likely to be accounted for in the theory and goal preferences of the worker. These realities would tend to assure, whatever the worker's choices, that "what is" in practice will largely determine "what should be." Another element that will influence the worker's choice of theory and values will be his or her own response repertoire, which sets limits on what he or she can personally consider as possible choices.

The worker must also establish a tentative agenda that maps this inner-directed inquiry. This agenda sets forth a set of problems to be dealt with in order that the priority decision appropriately relates to the practical intent of his or her efforts. Thus, the worker must determine: (a) whether the recipient has a legitimate claim on his or her resources; (b) what the recipient would have to do to in order to avail him- or herself of these resources; (c) what the worker would have to render the agency's services in this instance; (d) what other claims on the worker's resources are conditioned on this particular allocation and the relative merit of each; and (e) what resources are to be allocated in light of the answers obtained to questions (a) through (d).

The substantive materials that constitute the content that characterizes these agenda items are generated in the interaction of worker and recipient. Whereas the worker may be aware of this inner agenda relevant to each service request, he or she is only able to establish the order and scope of the consideration of these agenda items through the exchanges with the recipient that occur in the "intake" process itself. Thus, the prevalent view that service begins with the process of determining eligibility and does not wait on priority decisions seems realistic. It is inevitable that a certain amount of worker resource be expended in determining his or her time and energy allocations, and this expenditure necessarily influences the future direction of relationships that will obtain with the recipient. This item apparently ranks first in whatever priority scheme he or she later evolves.

The worker's inner-directed agenda must not be confused with the program of work that the worker and recipient jointly agree upon to govern their contacts. Although the "inner" agenda is, as noted, dependent on the "outer" agenda in certain respects, it is neither temporally nor spatially bound by the latter. The worker's professional questions which he or she puts to him- or herself, while similar to those entering into any priority decision process, nevertheless have their own characteristics.

The worker's complex self-directed question assumes that there are possibilities—that a choice exists—and he or she would want all likely ones to be listed. It does not, as far as he or she is concerned, assume that there is an indeterminate number of such possibilities. The worker seeks answers that commit his or her existing capacities. Moreover, he or she has been oriented by agency and recipient conditions and by his or her own professional theories and values to remove from consideration all possibilities that do not meet certain special qualifications.

The "special qualifications" that serve to limit alternatives for the worker differ from those that may limit the range of possibilities considered in the social policy and planning situation. In the first (approximation of possibilities), the worker will be guided by "thou shalt nots" that prescribe prohibited cases and focus his or her attention on recoveries that can count. This internal censorship clearly cannot prevail in social processes wherein the various interests influencing the priority choices must first reach agreement on those "shall nots" in order to proceed with the listing of possibilities.

Establishing the interdependence of possibilities, in order to arrive at the number of truly independent choices available, and determining which choices necessitate others as prerequisite or consequences can only follow, not precede, the listing of possibilities.

This sequence, of course, is not unlike that which is evident in the interplay of preferences in interpersonal and intergroup priority processes. In the self-directed query, however, both the possibilities and their associations are presumed to be likely and in the interest of the recipient. In the social policy and planning choice situation, this is hardly the case where heterogeneous interests are represented.

In any case, the initial priority decision cannot precede some approximation of responses to questions noted at the outset of this discussion of priorities. This order of precedence does not mean that the worker is committed to an unbreakable chain of consequences in arriving at his or her initial decision. All possibilities and their interdependence probably will not be recovered or discovered in time for the initiation of action. The process is a continuous one, with feedback serving to open new options not previously stored in memory. Stored options are sometimes recognized as appropriate only after the worker–recipient interaction develops.

In the social planning situation, collective decisions are reached usually after considerable investment of effort on the part of those whose interests are represented in the process. These decisions are not easily altered and are not as susceptible to change through the corrective influence of feedback transmitted in the course of their implementation. Resources committed to one purpose often deny sustenance to others—terminating certain interests' representation in the bodies responsible for policy, planning, and decision making and denying them further claim to a voice in setting or altering priorities.

The decision taken in response to the self-directed questions may be more readily altered as a result of experience in its implementation. It is private in the commitment it entails and more open to self-correction, not having to contend with the fault-finding that publicly admitted error in political judgments normally provokes. It is true that the worker's resources are limited and allocations to one purpose will deplete resources to be used in another. To the degree that the decision is the product of a single judge, however, judgments will be contingent on self-selected criteria reflecting the worker's natural preference for flexibility in the investment of his or her self in a given practice engagement.

A unique aspect of the self-directed question is its monostylous nature. What the worker finds attractive will more than likely influence his or her preferences. Because the alternatives to be ordered are inseparable from the style in which they are formed, the elements of style-conflict or style-complementarity that are present in interpersonal decision processes are absent in the worker's inner choices. Stylistic bent affects inner-directed query in another fashion that is somewhat unique. The worker anticipates that what he or she decides will be what he or she has to carry out in practice. Knowing this, he or she is likely to prefer those alternatives that he or she judges will prove, in application, most congenial to his or her own style. Thus, style influences the possible alternatives selected for consideration and affects their ranking. It is not surprising, therefore, to observe how often diverse situations requiring dissimilar activities on the part of the worker manifest his or her individual style in their realization.

The social and the personal priority determination processes have deliberately been contrasted in order to use their differences to clarify elements peculiar to the inner-directed query. The comparison was also intended to highlight similarities, which suggest the "political" attributes of professional thought processes. Although deserving more discussion than it has been given, this subject seemed important to identify. The worker's priority decisions inevitably influence his or her practice, yet rarely are recognized for what they are: *An approximation of his or her view of just and trustworthy behavior.*

The reluctance to engage in authoritative services previously noted stems in part from assumptions concerning the minimal moral maturity essential for a truly helping relationship. Levels of moral maturity were used earlier to identify the recipient's behavior. The same analysis applies to the moral behavior of the worker, particularly as such morality is manifest in his or her inner-priority decisions—his or her practice politics. Finally, the context of practice—our society's morality or immorality as evidenced in its priorities can support the reciprocal relationships of the human service professions but currently is undermining them by destroying trust, invading privacy without which trust is impossible, and perpetrating distributive injustice on a massive scale.

BIBLIOGRAPHY

Eckland, B., and Kent, D. P. (1968). Socialization and social structure. In *Perspectives on human deprivation: Biological, psychological, and sociological*. Bethesda, MD: U.S. Department of Health, Education, and Welfare, Public Health Service, National Institutes of Health, National Institute of Child Health and Human Development.

Hamblin, C. L. (1967). Questions. In *The Encyclopedia of philosophy* (vol. 7). P. Edwards, ed. New York: Macmillan.

Kahn, A. J. (1969). *Theory and practice of social planning*. New York: Russell Sage.

Kohlberg, L. (1968). *Acquisition and development of values: Perspectives on research*, Bethesda, MD: U.S. Department of Health, Education, and Welfare, Public Health Service, National Institutes of Health, National Institute of Child Health and Human Development.

Rawls. J. (1971). *A theory of justice*. Cambridge, MA: Harvard University Press.

Sebeok, T. A. (1960). *Style in language*. Cambridge, MA: MIT Press.

Warren, R. L. (1970, April). Toward a non-utopian normative model of the commuity. *American Sociological Review 35*, 219–228.

Wheatley, J. M. O. (1955, January). Deliberative questions. *Analysis 15*, 49–60.

Part III

Essays on Social Work Education

Editor's Introduction

By the time he retired as Dean from Hunter College School of Social Work in 1991, Harold Lewis was one of the senior deans in the United States and an acknowledged national leader of social work education. Despite his prominence in the field, he never hesitated to express views that were contrary to the conventional wisdom, both explicitly and implicitly. Lewis was often outspoken in his criticisms of the content and structure of social work education, as several of the following essays make clear. He attacked what he regarded as the imposition of self-serving interests on the field under the guise of a variety of rationales. He also believed that contemporary models of social work education perpetuated dysfunctional dichotomies between theory and practice, means and ends, and class and field education.

While a strong proponent of the intellectual aspect of practice (his 1982 book was entitled *The Intellectual Base of Social Work Practice*), Lewis expressed a broad view of what constitutes intellectual work and scholarship. In an era in which most social work scholarship became increasingly narrow and methodologically driven, he stressed the role of imagination and cultural sensitivity, the importance of critical thinking, and the use of analogic reasoning in educating students for practice. Drawing upon the influence of the Functional School at the University of Pennsylvania and his longstanding appreciation of art, Lewis also identified the role of time and space as critical components of the educational process.

Throughout the essays in this section, Lewis draws frequently on artistic metaphors and the relationship between national and international events and social work education. From his final, retrospective paper it is clear that the Cold

War and its consequences shaped not only the environment of social work education but Lewis's views on the relationship of education and practice. In this essay, it is also clear how wider developments in the field, particularly the increased attention paid to issues of racial, ethnic, and cultural diversity, influenced Lewis's views. He accurately predicted that the post-Cold War world would be dominated by the issue of "respect for the dignity of persons and for the differences among peoples." In his essays, he tried to incorporate an awareness of these cultural differences into a justice perspective and concluded that "issues of distributive justice can only be resolved within the wider framework of social justice." He understood that his vision of the common good would, by necessity, be seen in the twenty-first century through a multicultural lens.

Chapter 17

The Intellectual in the Practical

In this essay, Lewis provides an overview of the intellectual basis of social work practice. He argues that "A practice without theory is said to be blind, just as a theory without practice is thought to be sterile." Stressing the role of imagination and of analogical thinking, he sets forth principles that would enable the intellectual aspect to fulfill its primary function: to enable the profession to incorporate both knowledge and values into its work.

Intellectual work comes in many attractive packages, evidencing as much variety as manual work. Wizards, shamans, professors, and professionals are as clearly identified with work of the mind, as carpenters, sailors, fishermen and plumbers are identified with work of the hand. Human services, those depending primarily on the relationships between two or more people in which a helping or educational purpose is implemented, involve primarily mental effort, and fall under the rubric intellectual work. This essay explores some of the implications that follow where persons engage in such intellectual work.

Where a condition exists that one wishes to alter in a preferred direction through the expenditure of effort, the possibility that work will be done is also present. In this sense, both physical and mental work are distinguishable. The difference between the two becomes more evident when one explores the tools used in the effort to bring about the desired changes in the existing condition. Tools for thought do not resemble the tools used in manual labor. A concept, theory, ethical imperative, or principle are frequently employed in mental effort. They are, of course, in the mind of manual workers as well, but hardly share the material attributes of the hammer, wrench, wire splicer, or fishing net, each crucial tools for the tradesmen who use them. Of course, the distinction between the mental and the manual becomes somewhat blurred as one focuses on the technical in disciplines, where the microscope, retort, computer, and electronic network are so closely attuned to the mental manipulations of their users. Nor is the distinction as clear in the hands-on performance of the professional, such as the surgeon, dentist, and nurse. But we need not confront this difficulty here, since in the human services the technical and manual are minor in contrast to the conceptual.

Written in April 1987 for unpublished manuscript entitled *Ethical Practice in Troubled Times: Papers, 1955–1985.*

Mental work is usually subsumed under the concept "thought." When philosophers such as Descartes locate the distinctive feature of "being" in the act of "thinking," it is not merely a prejudice in favor of their trade, but a belief that thought is so unique and tangible a product of human effort it can readily serve as the minimal assumption necessary to prove one's own existence. Of course, all thought is not intended to be intellectual work as previously defined. [One may play with a hammer, as my grandchild loves to do, without doing work as we define it.] One can contemplate many things without engaging in intellectual work. But when thought is involved in work, it benefits from the assistance provided by mental tools in accomplishing its purpose, and such tools carry with them attributes that are of major interest to human service professionals.

One important attribute of an intellectual tool is its capacity for ordering otherwise chaotic situations. For example, if given the sequence 14, 23, 28, 34, 42, 51, 66, 72 and asked to make sense of these numbers, for most people it would appear to be a random series. For the informed New Yorker, the algorithm is obviously local stops on the Seventh Avenue IRT subway in Manhattan. Substitute a series of behavior symptoms and attitudinal dispositions for the numbers, and to the average citizen what is judged to be a withdrawn character, is catatonic to the educated professional. A good intellectual tool manages to achieve this type of economy in thought and precision in description.

A second attribute of an intellectual tool is its capacity to provide a rationale where there appears to be chaos, and for the order achieved by the algorithm. The overzealous hug of the two-year-old, when allowed to embrace his two-week-old brother, is more than affectionate enthusiasm, when seen in light of a theory of sibling relationships. The theory, in fact, would have correctly anticipated the hug moving to become a stranglehold in this expression of familial affection. The power of theory to explain in turn explains why theories are so frequently sought after by intellectual workers. A practice without theory is said to be blind, just as a theory without practice is thought to be sterile. Both infirmities merely point to the importance of intellectual tools that can prevent, not merely treat, these deficiencies.

A third attribute of intellectual tools is the ability to communicate guidelines for action. For professions, they communicate guidelines for action in uncertain situations. Consider, for example, the guidance offered administrators: "When you don't know what to do, appoint a committee or delegate to another responsibility for action, or postpone actions, etc. If none of these can be done, then do the least you can as slowly as possible—hopefully doing nothing at all—letting nature and time take its course." The guidance offered derives its utility from its applicability to diverse administrative decision dilemmas, flexibility in allowing for more time and place considerations, and its relatively modest claim of certainty in uncertain situations. It is, of course, most helpful to have laws that are true for all situations to which they apply, as for example, the laws of motion in physics, or the laws governing the transmission of genetic characteristics in biology. But in professions it is even more important to have principles that may be oriented to the parameters dictated by such laws, yet formulated to provide for the application of such orienting knowledge in practice.

A fourth attribute is the capacity of intellectual tools to incorporate values into the tools themselves, in contrast to manual tools whose users retain the ability to designate the purposes to be achieved. Intellectual tools for thought are internal to the minds of their users. There are no barriers that physically limit the influence that values may exercise on the choice of goals and objectives. Thus, the guiding practice principles that one employs in the performance of professional tasks is informed by theory and knowledge, and is also justified as an "ought" by ethical imperatives and values. In professional work, where intentions are crucial in making choices among alternative forms of intervention, this power of the intellectual tool to incorporate both knowledge and value in its directive and commands, shaping its rules for action, is significant.

On the other hand, this attribute introduces another that distinguishes the intellectual from the manual tool. A hammer is a hammer, whether employed to drive in a nail in India, Brazil, or Chicago. It tends to be culture-neutral, although it has incorporated in its structure a good deal of past culture (e.g., the steel-making process, the design of head and claw, the length and shape of the handle, etc.). Intellectual tools, on the other hand, because they incorporate values in their form, are much more culturally sensitive and more readily reflect the peculiar societal and historical conditions in which they evolve and are employed.

A sixth attribute of intellectual tools that gives them unique strengths is the manner in which tools relate to each other in a hierarchical order. Knowledge, theory, propositions, and directives form a pyramidal hierarchy, each capable of independent application, but each able to draw on lower or higher order tools to enrich their capacity for doing intellectual work. Thus, knowing that siblings, particularly those whose ages are proximate, often evidence competitive as well as loving behavior, may suggest a theory of sibling rivalry that, while not a truth in the sense that knowledge is truth, nevertheless provides an explanation of the knowledge that otherwise would remain simple information. Theory, in turn, may suggest testable propositions for use in forming practice principles, or may provide insights that extend the meaning of knowledge, and deepen our understanding of it. Propositions, in turn, justify directives for action, and when experientially derived, may initiate formulations that lead to corrections or innovations in theory. Thus, this knowledge hierarchy permits a number of theories to flourish concurrently, each explaining a different piece of the known; a number of propositions to be tested, not necessarily subsumed under any theory; and directives that simply are followed because they work even when no propositional statement has been formulated to provide a rationale for their use.

The value hierarchy differs from the knowledge hierarchy in crucial ways. Values justify ethical imperatives that, in turn, justify commendations that are incorporated in practice principles, and all justify the commands that, when wedded to directives, provides the rules that shape a practice. [For our purposes, merely to note this pattern suffices to sensitize our discussion to these unique attributes.] What implications for practice flow from these attributes of intellectual tools? How do we prepare persons for practice in a profession that depends primarily on mental rather than manual work to achieve its purposes?

IMPLICATIONS

Clearly tools for thought because they are themselves mental formulations are not readily demonstrated in the same way one demonstrates the use of a plane in woodwork. They must first be conceived by the learner, and then held in mind as their utility is demonstrated. To hold them in mind, given the competing thoughts that constantly seek entry into consciousness, requires an emotional as well as a mental exertion, and not all learners are capable of both exertions in equal amount. This condition for communicating to learners the nature, structure, and application of intellectual tools must help sustain both exertions in proper amounts. Balance here, of course, is critical, lest the emotional overwhelm the mental, and dogmatic learning subvert the intellectual. The emotional investment may, in turn, be insufficient. [We are familiar with the expression "in one ear and out the other," which translated in this context suggests failure in interest sufficient to sustain an information input for the required time in short-term memory, time enough to transfer the input into long-term memory.] Obviously, education here is a difficult business for both the teacher and the student, and a good demonstration is a golden nugget, hard to mine, even harder to rid of its impurities, and while malleable, is very dependent on the knowledge, value, and style of the toolmaker for its attractions and power to inform.

Skill in the use of intellectual tools is similar to skill in any performance; it depends on what one knows, what one can do, what one values, and one's style. The use of intellectual tools necessarily requires ability to reason well, ability to formulate inner-directed questions that enlighten even as they seek to discover, and ability to entertain doubt in circumstances in which we are prone to feel certain.

Imaginative ability often goes unattended in the literature of educators and practicing professions in the human services. One reason for this inattention is that imagination involves a form of thought, analogic, which is the most frequently used in applying intellectual tools to mental tasks, yet which remains incompletely understood.

ANALOGIC

Reasoning by proportion, "this is to this as that is to that," is essential for survival. The infant who avoids fire after the first contact with a flame or a slapped hand followed by the cautioning "No!" quickly learns such reasoning, long before formal logic and dialectic become part of his or her intellectual equipment. Analogical reasoning, in formal education, is most often identified by its shortcomings; the risks entailed in false or misleading analogs; the vagueness of its anticipations; the unequal distribution of a talent for creating heuristic associations; all dictate caution in its use. The more robust predictive power of dialectics relegates analogy to a minor role in proof and in the demonstration of certainties. But, and this is an important codicil, analogs are crucial to discovery, which depends so much on imagination. The so-called art of a professional practice often represents a misnomer, because style that gives a practice its attractions is not what is meant. Rather, the reference is to the unique use of analogy, enabling the creator to explore uncertainties, allowing for the inclusion of unproven assumptions in making assessments, and encouraging risk in situations where the unknown must enter into decision to act, lest timely opportunities be lost.

Consider, for a moment, the peculiar calculus of analogic. One does not add in this logic, one assembles. Think of the artist painting from internal imagery, without a model, adding on a wrinkle here and bulge there, to create a whole person aging, as it were, before your eyes. In this logic, one does not subtract, one discards. Think of the sculptor slicing off a chunk of clay here, a glob there, shaping a figure by chipping away at the marble. In this logic, one does not divide, one partitions. Think of the map maker locating territorial units within a political entity, or the playwright or composer deciding where to end a scene or terminate a movement, in order to move the creation forward, while keeping mentally intact the fullness of the total work. In this logic, one does not multiply, one overlays. Think of a matrix, where each additional dimension creates new subunits, somewhat like the development of additional cells by cross-classification or of subordinate colors by the overlay of primary colors. Thus, in the calculus of analogic, assembling, discarding, partitioning, and overlay are mental procedures for managing imagery.

It is necessary, also, to appreciate another unique characteristic of this logic. As illustrative cases of analogs are stored in memory, for recovery when needed in practice, the binding glue that keeps the mental image intact is an emotion, an attachment that connects inner feelings aroused at the moment of storage to the image being stored. Recall of such imagery includes the recovery of a feeling associated with it, and this personal, inner-experienced marker, provides a powerful indication as to whether a particular resemblance qualifies as a compatible analog for the new situation being momentarily experienced. In short, it may "seem like" this new situation resembles a previous one, but it may not "feel like" it does. Unlike formal and dialectical logic, analogic includes feelings, and hence draws on the whole gestalt of the person's disposition in creating and recovering its composition.

If you think further about this logic, it will become obvious to you that the mental work involved is best described as designing. All practice involves the practitioner in design, and hence the importance of analogic in professional practice. These few observations that analogic should suffice to introduce a final and practical conclusion to this essay: What implications follow for educational programs preparing persons for the intellectual work described?

The first is the most obvious: Such persons should be systematically trained to think analogically. This, of course, has been appreciated by all professions, and the use of the case method basically responds to this need. The "case" is a most productive source of analogy, anchoring the imagery as well. It also permits the learner to associate practice principles and rules with instances in which they are applicable. This facilitates quick recovery of action guidelines in practice. Learning by doing—field work—also provides a rich source of analogy and not surprisingly, it is also encouraged by most human service professional educational programs.

The second is the need to teach "design." Designing programs, designing methods of intervention, designing approaches to evaluation—all offer opportunities to learn how to apply analogic to concrete situations.

It is useful to distinguish between scholarship that seeks to add to knowledge and scholarship that seeks to demonstrate new applications of knowledge. The former aims to produce laws, the certainties that define the claims of the disciplines. The latter seeks to evolve and test principles of practice. The difference is one that Simon recognizes when he refers to a theoretical science in contrast to a practice science. To engage in a useful practice, one must design a program of service, implement the design through the delivery of the service, and evaluate it. It requires making clear and specific the principles the design seeks to demonstrate, the rules that make the principles operational in a given context, while being fully aware of the relevant orienting knowledge and values that command and justify the principles being demonstrated. Such a practice requires that its designer have, as part of his or her mental preparation, substantive knowledge of the practice to be demonstrated, as well as skill in its design. Necessarily, it would best be undertaken by a practitioner who has mastered the intellectual "tools" of the profession, and who is, therefore, prepared to innovate through designing new applications of the known.

Chapter 18

Educational Preparation for Practice

This is one of a series of papers in which Lewis offered a stinging critique of contemporary social work education. He was particularly critical of the accepted "split" between education and practice, which he regarded as "a misleading formulation of their relationship." He identified the different forms of reasoning used in social work education and analyzed the potential role of each in preparing students for professional practice.

Education and practice differ in significant ways. In educating for practice, failure to appreciate these differences while concentrating on similarities can lead to unrealistic expectations, mechanistic approaches to curriculum design and teaching methods, and confusion in sequencing educational programs. That we should overlook such differences and choose instead to focus on similarities is understandable. Our intent is to establish linkages between learning and doing, and focusing on differences can be counterproductive to this intention. It is analogous in many respects to our recognition that all beings have much in common, pressing us to seek ways of meeting their common human needs. But we can be guilty of serious oversights when we consider sexual needs, for example, and fail to appreciate the not inconsiderable differences between men and women.

Nevertheless, the separation of education and practice is a misleading formulation of their relationship. All worthwhile education is a form of practice, and practice that does not educate is likely to be less than adequate. Thus, education and practice differ at the same time that they share much in common, and in reality interpenetrate one another. The very idea that there can be education without practice or practice without education is questionable. It is as if one can have a magnet without both north and south poles. By definition each is an element that makes the other possible. Cut off one, and so long as the other exists it will naturally generate its interpenetrating opposite.

Practice means to "work at." Professional education for practice is the supervision of instruction for work. When education becomes otherwise focused, it changes its nature. Thus, in Schools of Social Work when the focus shifts entirely to the self-development of the student, the program can readily be described as

---

Presented in Bloomington, Indiana, March 1978.

therapy. While one can argue that there is learning in therapy, the learning we intend focuses on the doing, the practical application in work. This is the crucial criterion for distinguishing professional education for social work practice from other forms of education.

What practice and education share in common unites them. Their differences, and efforts to deal with these differences provide the fuel that generates changes in both, and in their relationships. It is, therefore, entirely plausible to imagine a circumstance where contextual forces exacerbate these internal differences to a point where a rupture occurs between education and practice, resulting in the birth of a new practice, and an altered educational program. [Since the last revision of the Council on Social Work Education Curriculum Policy Statement in 1969, there have been indications that certain fields of practice, such as psychotherapy and policy development, were finding existing educational programs so lacking in response to their respective perceptions of new demands for their services as to threaten just such ruptures. In my discussion I will first consider some of the differences that distinguish education and practice.]

1. *Historically, practice preceded formal educational efforts to prepare for it.*

This is not surprising because in the entire spectrum of knowledge, with few exceptions, practice precedes the theory that informs it, and without theory, training, not education. The uneven stages of their development inevitably produce tensions that promote strains and stresses, but fuel change as well. Recall the long period of indecision, when the field was reluctant to associate its training schools with formal academic institutions, and the earliest period of such tensions can be noted. Currently, the reluctance of the academy to take on the trappings of trade schools has inhibited its response to demands for in-service, on-the-job training, particularly stressed by public welfare departments concerned to exercise control over course content taken by their personnel at their agency's expense. To discuss these differences as minor irritants is to ignore basic issues that must be confronted and dealt with. These issues that threaten the relationship of school and agency are potentially the most fruitful for growth-producing resolutions.

2. *The packaging of what is to be learned may differ in form and substance from the packaging required for the delivery of service.*

Thus, the educational program may stress concentrations in health; family, child, and adult development; justice; education; and the world of work, while the field may stress specialties in hospital social work, child welfare, corrections, school social work, or income maintenance. While obviously related, the curricula concentrations intended for enrichment respond to a different set of criteria than specialties intended to focus and deepen narrower areas of competence. These differences can produce friction between education and practice, but these sources of stress can also promote efforts to conceptualize specializations that are responsive to these differences.

3. *The sequence in which learning occurs differences from that in which work is carried out in practice.*

Learning may require the attainment of one set of skills before moving to another. For example, one needs first to understand elements of probability theory and inferential statistics when one wants to develop skill in decision theory. This does not imply more or less intellectual demand in mastering any phase of the sequence. In practice, however, the skills encompassed in each of these intellectual tasks may be concurrently tapped in a moment of action. Thus, the tasks in the order of their appearance in practice are not necessarily the tasks in the order in which they should be learned. Curricula that fail to recognize these differences often omit consideration of prerequisites for sound learning; depend heavily on hands-on learning, with mistaken notions of what intellectual skills are being achieved; and are prone to produce task-oriented, in contrast to practice-oriented practitioners. The difference between these two orientations is the difference one recognizes between a technician and a professional. Yet recognition of the difference in sequencing that characterizes the learning and doing in education and practice can result in clearer and more useful guidelines for determining priorities in their distinctive functions.

4. *In learning, progression from the simple to the complex is usual. In practice, combinations of two or more simple requirements often yield extremely complex demands.*

In fact, what may be a complex educational achievement, such as learning to discipline one's style, once attained, may become a habituated, relatively routine element in practice. This difference between education and practice is at the heart of efforts by the profession to develop compatible schemata for an educational continuum and a practice job-classification. The efforts to define "core" and "superstructure" in education and practice likewise will defy clarification so long as this difference is not dealt with in depth.

5. *The time it takes to know differs from the time it takes to do.*

This distinctive time scale contributes to considerable friction in interfacing education and practice. We will continue to delude ourselves with over-claims of "innovation" in education programs and "revolutions" in practice, so long as we fail to appreciate how these different time demands join to offer serious constraints on any effort to mount and sustain substantial changes in education or practice.

These five differences that promote tensions between education and practice are indicative, but by no means exhaustive. The examples cited to highlight their significant differences are similarly selective. What should be evident is that any discussion of education preparation for practice that ignores such differences can, at best, be superficial and, at worse, totally misleading. Rather than elaborate further on these differences, I will use the remainder of this paper to pursue in depth a unifying conception that I believe, if properly understood, could do much to strengthen the linkage of education to practice.

The practice science that supports the distinctive contribution of a profession is not formulated in terms of law-like generalizations. Instead, its truths are stated as principles that justify its programs and rules that justify its practices. Rules consist of two parts, directives for action and commands that authorize their use. Rules in isolation do not reveal the knowledge and value that supposedly promote them, but principles do. In principles one finds a propositional statement that one seeks to explain on the basis of theory, and a commendation to act that derives from an ethical imperative intended to operationalize a value. Thus, to understand the science of practice one must master the principles of that practice and appreciate the knowledge and values that provide their underpinning. While it would perhaps prove useful to explore principles and rules further, for our purposes this brief comment will suffice. I would rather pursue one aspect of principles in greater detail to show how an appropriate understanding in this one area can help in developing sound educational preparation in practice.

In social work education much attention is given to formal logic. Our texts, teaching aids and research reports are replete with "if . . . then" propositions, from which we infer expected causal relationships associated with such hypothetical formulations. A typical proposition of this type might be the generally accepted statement, "If the client participates in decisions that affect him or her, he or she is more likely to act on them than if he or she has no part in their formulation." This form of statement follows closely the pattern of the "hard sciences" and when we employ it, it lends a certain scholarly respectability to our knowledge claims. Now if we also believe that people have a right to self-determination, and ought to share in decisions that affect them, we generate a practice principle that might be worded as follows: "Clients *should* participate to their maximum ability in formulating decisions that they are expected to implement." Without the imperative *should* this propositional statement has more to offer a theoretical discipline than a practice-based profession. It is precisely because a value component is essential for a principle statement that we accept as fact that our practice is value-laden and intentional, and view a value-deficient practice as unprincipled.

A second form of logic, dialectic reasoning, is also used in social work education, although rarely appreciated as such. This logic generates propositions of the type "from this, in time, to that." Such propositions convey to students an appreciation of process descriptive truths, cluing them into developmental generalizations. For example, it will be generally agreed that "the infant will normally experience a period during which he or she will crawl, before beginning to walk." Such propositions are supposed to describe normal and necessary growth, which our profession values as making possible the full realization of self that is within the capacity of each individual. Principles based on such propositions usually ask the practitioner to promote opportunities for such growth, because deficits in growth-producing experiences are seen as generating needs to be met. While formal logic is often considered in some detail, as for example in research sequences focusing on the quantitative methods of science, dialectic logic is rarely explicated as a method of reasoning and brought to a similar level of awareness.

But by far the most frequently employed logic in practice is neither of these. Propositions from formal logic and dialectic, when incorporated into principles, usually provide guidance to practitioners, helping them to know where to look and what to look for. They have much less to say about the "how to do" for the particulars in each moment of practice. Where action is expected in uncertain situations, where the worker has incomplete knowledge and understanding, but dare not risk delay, lest a precious irretrievable moment for helping be forever lost, principles based on formal or dialectic type logical propositions may even prove inhibiting. Yet, as one thinks about practice, one realizes how often these moments are the most pregnant ones, with great potential for growth-producing service. The "how to" that informs such actions is based on the logic of imagination that utilizes a calculus of patterned relationships, that reasons by proportions and is most clearly intended to guide action—analogic.

In the practitioner's mind, the inner-directed query—"this seems like," "this reminds me of," "this resembles"—serves to bring from stored memories analogs that order and give meaning to incomplete and not fully understood indicators. These analogs suggest a way of responding "in the moment" that can be risked since for similar-appearing situations in the past, such responses appeared to help. Analogic reasons by association and proportion. Its propositional statements take the form, "this is to this, as that is to that." Depending on presentational rather than discursive content, utilizing imagery that summarizes complex information on the basis of relatively few variables, its very weaknesses—that is, lack of precision and prone to misleading associations—free it for use in uncertain situations.

We need not explore here the strengths and pitfalls of reasoning by analogy. They are the strengths and pitfalls of all imaginative practice. For our purposes I would simply ask you to consider how often, if at all, analogic has been identified and systematically dealt with in your education for practice. Then, as practitioners, try to imagine an instance of practice where you did not depend on analogy to guide your immediate responses in uncertain situations requiring action. The gap here between education and practice is monumental.

Failure to appreciate the significance of analogic in practice and principles for practice contributes to dysfunctional packaging of educational content for storage. For example, the popularity of the case method as a tool in teaching professional practice has long been recognized in medicine, law, business, and other professions, in addition to our own. The "case" makes possible the presentation of complex situations in a coherent, recognizable form, facilitating the encapsulated storage of considerable information in relatively brief periods of time. But using the "case" to store instances of practice for future recovery never achieves more than anecdotal value if principles of practice useful in guiding action in such cases are not concurrently associated with the case as it is being stored. It is such principles, after all, that constitute the science of practice, in contrast to the law-like generalizations that are appropriate for theoretical sciences. Yet more often than not, the case is presented as an enriching, vicarious experience providing a substitute for lacks in the students' experiences, so a common base for discussion can occur. This is true for classes where the students present their current cases as well as when canned cases are used. The anecdotal use of the case is attractive, but hardly constitutes sufficient reason for including it in the curriculum. I would make the same statement where a research "case" is taught, and the study "findings" are viewed as simply supporting or rejecting an hypothesis, with no reference to a practice principle that the hypothesis was intended to affirm or deny.

This deficiency in educational packaging has, in turn, been reflected in a recognized deficiency in practice preparation by agencies seeking to employ our graduates. While charges and countercharges have attributed the divergence of education and practice to other considerations, I would argue that no one factor or combination of factors will contribute more to distancing of education from practice than lack of attention to this serious flaw in how we impart to students what they need to know in order to act with professional competence.

A willingness to face up to this deficiency will quickly eliminate for education and practice alike, the unsystematic way in which we have developed our curricula. We have not consciously explored the relative demands—both the intellectual and emotional mastery of our practice service require. We have mechanistically organized our curricula under dysfunctional rubrics that create rather than narrow time lags between school and agency; we have extended our programs into the early college years and beyond the masters and doctoral years without sufficient attention to prerequisites; and we have done these things with very limited appreciation of the role of imagination in education and practice.

Before his death, a great philosopher is supposed to have remarked that he had come to realize that he knew very little. Responding to a disciple's protest that this was not the case, that he, his teacher, was the wisest of men, the philosopher observed: "But you do not understand. The recognition of one's ignorance is the beginning of wisdom." As a profession educating for practice, we have in recent years more openly and willingly come to recognize how much we do not know and how much of what we do is inadequately informed. A start in the direction of wisdom could be a facing up to those differences that provide the dynamics for the relationship of education and practice, and to those lacks in our understanding of the logic that informs our actions both as teachers and practitioners.

Chapter 19

Are the Traditional Curriculum Areas Relevant?

In this essay, Lewis asserts that the traditional organization of social work curricula is based more on the self-interest of those who develop and deliver it than on its educational utility. In its place, he proposes a new curriculum framework, based on common human needs, that would break down the prevailing tendency to separate the individual from the environment and provide a stronger basis to link theory and practice, ends and means.

Rubric is a section heading. The Council on Social Work Education's Curriculum Policy Statement in 1960 and again in 1970 utilized four such section headings in categorizing its curriculum content. The practice of printing early manuscript or print headings in red accounts for the color designated in the term "rubric." The maintenance of similar rubrics in these successive statements was a conservative choice, in part intended to placate those who might "see red" when they perceived the radical innovations otherwise sponsored by the later statement. Deliberately, in order to maintain continuity with the earlier Policy Statement, the 1970 revision continued the 1960 rubric in its formulation.

It happens that what we call the traditional curricula areas are synonymous with the Policy Statement rubric in name, if not in substance. In 1970, only the "Research" rubric was dropped from the 1960 statement. But none of the content that appeared under this designation was omitted from the 1970 statement. By deliberate plan, all the content subsumed under "Research" in the 1960 statement was distributed among the remaining rubrics in the 1970 statement.

It should be clear from the preceding that substance can change, while rubrics remain the same, and a rubric can be dropped while substance remains intact. In the language of the title of this essay, if we substitute curriculum areas for the terms of the Policy Statement rubric, the same will hold true. Relevance will be determined by the substantive content, not by the designation of areas, and real differences will be evident in what is taught and learned, not in altered terminology used to categorize curricula areas.

Originally published in the *Journal of Education for Social Work 17*(1), Winter 1981.

For example, no matter how entitled, a research sequence that does not promote an understanding of what is intended in accountability and evaluation, does not promote a spirit of inquiry and an urge to utilize the findings of systematic study, fails to inspire an interest in discovery as well as proof, fails to communicate even minimal skills in scientific and scholarly methods, and leaves the student in ignorance as to the structure of social work knowledge and values, is likely to be less than relevant to the practice in which the student will be expected to engage after graduating.

Should this curriculum area be categorized under the rubric term "research," as is currently common practice? Probably not. Scientific and scholarly methods might be taught more effectively under a rubric so designated: Far more than research would be included under these headings. Or the sequence can be focused on accountability and evaluation, and so designated. This would possibly promote a closer relationship of content to practice and policy. The critical factor, nevertheless, is not the designation of the area, but the content it is expected to communicate. If we agree that the relevance of curriculum content is, in turn, determined primarily by what is sought in the graduate, then the preferred educational product should influence the choice of content and the choice of rubric as well. Criteria for establishing relevance are necessary, and evidence of achievement in relation to these criteria must be provided. Only in this way can we intelligently address the question posed in the title of this essay. This assumes, of course, that the prior requirement of clarity of purpose and function, justifying the content and rubric whose relevance is to be established, has been achieved.

For this reason, I will first suggest a definition of purpose and function that meets this requirement and then consider criteria for establishing relevance. Let us assume the following to be true:

> The fundamental zone of social work is where people and their environments are in exchange with each other. Social work historically has focused on this transaction zone, where the exchange between people and the environments which impinge on them results in change in both. Social work intervention aims at the coping capabilities of people and the demands and resources of their environments so that the transactions between them are helpful to both. Social work's concern extends to both the dysfunctional or deficient conditions at the juncture between people and their environments, and to the opportunities there for producing growth and improving the environment.

Given agreement on the dual foci of the turf to which our profession lays claim, and agreement on the target of social work intervention intended to contribute to growth and improve the environment, we would need to clarify further what we expect social workers to do, if the prior requirement for clarity of function as well as purpose is to be met.

For example, in relation to problems that recipients of social work service bring with their request for help, do we expect practitioners to assume the role of problem solvers, with the intellectual arrogance that term conveys when applied to the human condition, or do we discourage the tendency to see people, groups, and communities as "problems" to be solved, focusing our function on objectives that facilitate recipient efforts to deal with their problems, and hopefully solve them? Do we prepare students to see people, alone or in combination, as sick, and charge social workers with the task of providing a cure, or do we seek to educate students to help people who are ill use what is healthy in themselves and their environments to combat their illness more effectively?

Obviously, much serious thought must be invested in clarifying functional expectations. Fur the purposes of this essay, nevertheless, let us assume that the content that would be identified as relevant to the curriculum will never be fixed, because such clarity will never be achieved fully. Hence the criteria for relevance must be applicable, whatever level of clarity has been achieved. To be consistent with this intent one must deliberately avoid an enumeration approach to the question of relevant content. Specifying things students must learn that are now taught never can lead to decisions on relevance. Every practitioner, every agency, all fields of service, in fact practically anyone, can suggest with some justification, content that should be included in the curriculum. But since the designation of such content assumes a prior agreement on relevance, the process is circular, and hence endless.

EXTERNAL CRITERIA

Given the turf on which we apply our professional efforts, the first criterion for testing relevance requires that the organizing rubric encompass both the individual and environmental conceptualization. It must inhibit any tendency to separate the two in a curriculum design.

An illustrative example of such a rubric is one based on common human needs that all people evidence in their own persons, and that generate environmental responses in all known civilized societies seeking to enhance individual and collective efforts to satisfy these needs. Thus, all people seek health, security, justice, knowledge, self-realization, intimacy, and relationships. All civilized societies, in response to these basic human needs, evolve health, economic, political, educational, and self-developmental institutions to help meet these needs.

A rubric for curriculum organization based on common human needs could meet this first criterion. It conceives of person and environment as inseparable; one without the other distorts both, directing attention away from the dual foci of our special turf.

If the first criterion is intended to inhibit the tendency to separate person and environment, the second would inhibit the tendency to separate knowing and doing. Knowledge, values, style, and action must be integrated into skill. Knowing where and when to apply such skill must be incorporated into competence. A curriculum relevant for practice necessitates a conceptualization of skill and competence that integrates thought and action. Providing information about where to look and what to look for in program, policy, and human growth and the social environment may be necessary prerequisites for a relevant curriculum, but hardly satisfies this criterion. Having accepted the aims of social work intervention, locating the targets in time and place serves an orienting function and may even help individualize the particular service encounter, but may offer no guidance at all for the "how" of the practice required.

To meet this criterion, the content in human growth and the social environment should develop skill in assessment of need-resource and in evaluating the mismatch that necessitates intervention, or else risk suffering the irrelevance that characterizes any professional educational process that focuses on theory apart from its meaning in practice. Similarly, the content concerned with the social services, programs, and policy, must prepare the student to assess alternative program designs in relation to goals and objectives, or else risk suffering the irrelevance of an inappropriate and misguided practice, devoid of any theoretical insights. Obviously, much of our current traditional curriculum in these areas is less than relevant, but not necessarily irrelevant. While a reasonable case can be made for inclusion of much that we teach in these areas as a prerequisite, a curriculum that covers material that is less than relevant hardly meets the criterion of relevance, even when it is not irrelevant.

A third criterion requires that means and ends be seen as inseparable, recognizing that the separation of purpose and practice in curriculum design conditions a practitioner mistakenly to view the perfection of skill and its application as the principle and sometimes the only measure of achievement in judging work. The concern here is not simply the incompetent nature of a skillful practice inappropriately utilized, but also the irresponsible nature of a practice conceptualized as a value-free method unrelated to a process intended to achieve a preferred purpose.

To meet this criterion, the content of the practice rubric should be taught in relation to principles, since principles incorporate both the ethical imperative and the proposition—which are the value- and the knowledge-bases for a purposeful practice. It hardly meets this criterion to teach practice as an operational expression of selected theories or as the application of certain crucial concepts as methods of influence neutral to the intentional nature of such work.

Curriculum rubrics that meet these three external criteria must necessarily be relevant to the conditions current in the community for which social work interventions are appropriate and to the objectives and goals sought both by those who use and those who support the services provided by social work programs. These criteria also will assure a curriculum sensitive to the state of skill and competence that is social work's primary resource in seeking to influence conditions that need to be altered.

INTERNAL CRITERIA

But what about the relevance of the traditional areas to the theory and practice of curriculum development in schools and departments of social work? What factors, other than those noted, determine the rubric that will prevail and survive in a school? From the internal perspective, relevance is to be viewed in relation to the inner workings of the educational enterprise, to the needs of faculty, students, administration, and field work agencies and not primarily in relation to the needs of those who are the recipients of social work services. If we raise questions about the relevance of traditional curriculum areas to the common human needs that are the concern of those we serve, we also must wonder about the needs of those directly involved in the educational effort. In my view, the persistence of irrelevance in organizing rubrics can be explained largely by the influence on curriculum of the needs of those engaged in the educational process itself.

Time and space play a crucial role in curriculum design. Time is experienced differently by faculty, students, administration, and field work agencies, and space is partitioned into territorial areas in accordance with the distinctive interests of their occupants. Without elaborating on these observations, which summarize very complex phenomena, a brief illustrative description of what they entail should provide sufficient insight to help us appreciate how history and location influence the "relevance" question.

The half-life of a faculty member is about three to four years. The crucial factor here is the time it takes to earn tenure. The half-life of the student in a two-year program is about twenty-five weeks. The crucial factor here is the time actually available for learning in the four semesters. The half-life of the administrator is about one-half year. The crucial factor here is the time it takes to initiate a change in the program, which then takes between five and seven years to implement. The half-life of the agency field instructor is about fourteen weeks, or about half the time the student is actually available for instruction during the placement year.

From these varied time perspectives, the relevance of curriculum areas will be judged differently. Great effort is required to obtain an objective measure of relevance, especially when those participating in the program are the informants whose judgments are taken as the data to be used in evaluating relevance.

Lorenz mostly aptly described the territorial imperative that undergirds traditional curriculum areas. Turfs are involved, but not the turf identified as the domain for social work practice. Changing rubric in these circumstances can be viewed as threats to jobs, promotions, tenure, standards for selecting field work placements, admission requirements, measures of student performance and achievement, and budget allocation patterns. The ability of highly educated persons to rationalize territorial claims, rally the "tribe" in their defense, and win over recruits in order to nullify threats from surrounding territories is only exceeded by the ability of a collectivity of "tribes" to rationalize the status quo when threatened by a larger force seeking to alter existing curriculum arrangements. Thus, criteria for judging relevance in this inner-directed perspective will differ from those cited previously, in which the needs served by the profession defined the purpose in relation to which content and rubric could be justified.

Obviously, the school's curriculum should employ faculty competence to good purpose, and should discourage the tendency to slot faculty into curriculum areas that do not require their special expertise. The first internal criterion requires that the school not expect to teach what the school's faculty has yet to learn. This criterion is so obvious that it is often ignored. To be relevant, the school may be tempted to meet all the educational needs of the community it serves, even when its resources make such an objective unreal. Failure to recognize this criterion tends to promote a faculty of generalists who are renaissance persons to everyone but themselves. The curriculum resulting in these circumstances will be relevant in form, and irrelevant in substance.

The second criterion is that students be selected on the basis of their interest in and ability to learn the particular content the school is able and prepared to teach. Again, this is an obvious criterion often honored in the breach.

Another criterion requires the school to recruit field work placements offering experience in that practice that the school is competent to teach. This may require considerable effort to achieve, but without such effort, the areas of curriculum will prepare students to experience an unnecessary frustration that no amount of rationalizing can justify. The flip side of this criterion requires that the school not seek to teach for a practice out of its own resources.

These three criteria simply suggest that teachers, students, and field experiences be related to program intentions and special divisions affecting work done will serve to promote rather than defeat the development of relevant rubric.

RELEVANCE OF CURRENT CURRICULUM AREAS

Now applying these six criteria—three external and three internal—let us estimate the relevance of our current curriculum areas. These estimates are not based on systematic study. To my knowledge, research in these areas is lacking, and the judgments presented here are necessarily subjective. Given the overriding framework prompted by the CSWE Curriculum Policy Statement that provides for content in Social Welfare Policy and Services, Human Behavior and the Social Environment, and Social Work Practice, schools have opted for a variety of concentrations that meet the criteria designated in the statement, suggesting the rubric that the school believes best organizes this content. It should be noted that at the time the 1970 Policy Statement was written the decision to free the curriculum for a variety of organizing rubrics reflected the fact that schools were already exhibiting these differences and guidance was needed to assure certain common standards in their development.

Currently, the prevalent rubrics that organize curricula are based on a process, problem, programmatic conceptualization, or some combination of all three. The methods are central to a process rubric. This rubric apparently remains the most prevalent formulation, if we include its various forms—that is, micro/mezzo/macro practice. The problem rubric organizes concentrations in such areas as juvenile delinquency, aging, mental health, or retardation. While prevalent in many schools, this rubric is infrequently the dominating organizational form of a school's curriculum. The programmatic rubric organizes the curriculum around fields of service, such as child welfare, medical social work, probation and parole, or military social work. In a modified form, some such concentrations are to be found in many schools, but again, as with the problem rubric, infrequently serve as the overriding pattern for organizing a school's curriculum.

These prevalent rubrics all fail to meet the first criterion, that the overriding conceptual scheme inhibits the separation of the person and environment. The programmatic rubric tips the scale in favor of the context of practice; the problematic rubric partitions the person/environment into arbitrary units that encompass a part of the unity while missing the whole of it; and the process rubric tips the scale toward the person, helping to individualize the client unit and concurrently isolating it, to use Reynolds's apt phrasing.

These rubrics meet the second criterion, in part, albeit unevenly. The programmatic rubric is stronger in its emphasis on ends than means, being heavily preoccupied with ideological justifications. The problematic rubric focuses on both means and ends, but tends to see objectives rather than goals as the ends to be sought, and the techniques of the practitioner, rather than the strengths of the client, as the means for achieving intentions. The process rubric favors the means, almost to the point of seeing them as ends in themselves. While this rubric maintains a unity of means and ends, it resembles a Roman Peace, wherein the lion of means lies down in peace with the lamb of ends, the ends inside the means.

With reference to the third criterion, that thought and action, theory and practice, not be separated by the overall organizing rubric, the state of theory and the limitations of practice largely dictate the degree to which all three rubrics meet its requirements.

The programmatic approach is far richer in social and behavioral science generalizations, and pragmatic formulations of guiding propositions than it is in principles of practice that operationalize these orienting prescriptions for practice. The problematic approach fits the situation to the state of knowledge, realizing a not unexpected byproduct, that more and more is known about less and less, to the point where the practical and theoretical are joined, but around an issue so diminished in scope as to raise question about the utility of the action, even when successfully implemented. The process rubric is rich in experientially derived formulations that serve to support different theoretically sponsored generalizations, according to the preferences of the practitioner. When sets of propositions are incorporated into practice principles, a practice science rather than a theoretical science directs the action, and for this reason more than any other, I believe this third rubric remains the most prevalent in our schools.

Thus, in relation to the three external criteria, none of the prevalent rubrics fully satisfy the requirements for establishing relevance, albeit all three provide a partial approach to these criteria. If we recognize that in different periods of political and economic activity in the community each of these rubrics has a special appeal—the programmatic in times of radical change, the problematic in times of liberalization, and the process in times of conservative politics and restricted funding—than their tactical importance rather than their strategic value can be appreciated.

CONCLUSION

In light of this admittedly cursory analysis of their merits and limitations, I would argue for a human needs rubric as a strategic overriding schemata for curriculum, because it meets the first criterion fully, and is congenial with any of the other rubrics that can serve as partializing tactical formulations for particularizing needs areas. Moreover, the human needs rubric is responsive to the uneven political-economic developments that characterize the milieu in which each of the separate needs areas is addressed.

For example, in the present time in our country, the human needs rubric—when partitioned by a process rubric—would assure continued concern for the wider intentions of practice while promoting the skill needed to protect the quality of practice from the destructive influence of reduced resources and lack of concern for human services.

Based on seven years of experience with a matrix resulting from a human needs/process rubric one can note certain of its characteristics. This rubric inhibits a tendency to try to teach everything, forces consideration of a differential use of faculty in accordance with special competencies, provides more refined criteria for selecting a student body whose profile at admissions is related to the school's intentions, and compels close attention to field work choices in light of specific concentrations dictated by the human needs overriding rubric. Without experience to go by, there is no way of knowing if similar benefits will accrue to a school's curriculum if a program or problem subcategorization of a human needs rubric were attempted.

Two principles are suggested by this initial brief effort to determine the relevance of the traditional areas based on the six criteria thought to be indicative of relevance. Initially, we assume that:

1. Relevance will depend on external and internal factors affecting the organization and substantive content of curricula.
2. Efforts to establish relevance by enumeration of what should be known and mastered are circular and should be avoided.
3. The criteria suggested, although not necessarily of equal weight or exhaustive when used to determine relevance, are nevertheless useful to testing for relevance.

Then we can state the following as first principles:

1. *Periodic review of curricula rubric based on these criteria should be part of any school's effort to determine the relevance of its program to the external and internal purposes it hopes to achieve.*
2. *Periodic review of the Council on Social Work Education Curriculum Policy Statement employed in the formulation of accreditation standards should be undertaken in order to assure the profession that the Policy Statement promotes relevant curriculum rubric, as judged by the criteria suggested.*

Chapter 20

The Continuum: Issues in Social Work Education

Lewis is critical of both the term "continuum" and its usage in this essay. As an alternative to uniform curricular structures that are externally imposed, Lewis suggests that schools be given more flexibility in adapting their programs to regional differences and in emphasizing the development of critical thinking by students. He "believe[d] we have lived with [a] variety [of curricular structures] for good and compelling reasons and that it will not serve us well to impose a single model on our enterprise."

The term continuum, as employed in social work education, was invented, not discovered. It did not evolve out of efforts to describe a practice or condition. It was borrowed as a concept thought useful to fulfill a specific function, and to promote a particular scheme for restructuring social work education. Unlike discoveries, inventions suffer from obsolescence, often become dysfunctional, and have to be replaced. Manufactured products, intellectual as well as physical, that translate an invention into tools for thought or action, can be misapplied. The wrench is used by some as a hammer, the wine-press to wring out the laundry. The term continuum has managed to evidence all the negative attributes of inventions, and it is time to retire it from our deliberations about current problems facing social work education.

The term entered our literature in the late 1950s; achieved a level of conceptual significance in the 1959 Werner Boehm study of social work education; and achieved a kind of immortality when used as a subtopic heading in the essay on "Education for Social Work" in the *Encyclopedia of Social Work*, authored by Boehm in 1971. In that essay, Boehm sought to define the term and indicate the substantive content it was intended to conceptualize.

His formulation is most instructive. He starts with the assumption that *pressure* to upgrade competence has *produced* a new *force* in social work education. This new force he asserts has led to the *suggested creation* of a DSW and PhD, the latter a higher level degree than the former and an emerging *idea* of a three-year

Invitational paper, National Conference of Deans and Directors of Schools of Social Work, November 18, 1983.

post-baccalaureate program that would do many things. He writes that *if* such thinking gains more currency, then the MSW will change its character, possibly become an MA on the way to a DSW. He hypothesizes that *if* such a development were to occur, that many difficulties would be resolved. For example, *it might be possible* to develop a clear-cut relationship between the PhD and DSW degrees. If all these "ifs" were to be realized, he concludes a "reasonable well-planned continuum from the undergraduate to the MSW-DSW-PhD level, such that each subsequent level builds on the previous ones while each level is sufficiently self-contained to enable a person to move into functions that are reasonably well-defined by practice and need to be filled" will result.

Boehm's language is revealing, for it instills the term continuum with an aura of mission, whose inevitable realization will achieve the utopian ideal, a complete rational educational structure for social work. The thrust propelling the mission is cast in Newtonian terms, such as "pressure" and "force." Following Cartesian logic, the idea is invested with the initial power of truth, while practice, the real world, serves neither as a source of truth nor an ultimate test of this truth. Boehm prophesizes that if such thinking as his essay evidences were to gain currency, emerging ideas and suggested creations will materialize. One cannot but admire the elegance of the hierarchical order his view of the continuum would bring to the chronic thought disorders that seem endemic to our professional education programs.

But faith in the rational and attachments to mental processes as the creative source do not necessarily reckon with the reasonable. Unhappily, the most reasonable is not always the most rational. In advocating for an idea, it is reasonable to consider if its time has come. It is not reasonable to ignore the reality of what is the case, in one's enthusiasm for what one wishes might become the case. The aftermaths of the Boehm study and the subsequent Bisno Report demonstrated that when reality is not congenial to one's perceptions of it, it is the idea that had best be revised, or little change is likely to be achieved. In moving from an idea to its materialization, one moves from a vision to a practice. There is always the possibility that the vision is in error and, if pursued, ceases to serve a mere intellectual function, but is converted by its advocates into an instrument for compelling reality to conform to its mistaken preferences.

As we know only too well, in social work education there are many hierarchical orderings possible and, in fact, coexisting. I believe we have lived with this variety for good and compelling reasons and that it will not serve us well to impose a single model on our enterprise. Further, we must note that during the past two decades, those in social work education who have commented on the continuum, have not confined their usage to Boehm's definition. Each discussant seems to need to improve on some aspect of Boehm's conceptualization. Thus, in addition to referring to the relationship among levels of education for social work, it is thought to: (a) describe a comprehensive integrated overall social work curriculum; (b) encompass the relevance of education to practice; (c) depict a superstructure built on a foundation; (d) delineate a generic core with its specialization offshoots; and so on. The term, in fact, has become the Lady Quicksilver in social work education jargon. With all its attractions, as Falstaff observed, the problem with Lady Quicksilver is that one does not know where to have her.

Social work scholars who have had something to say about the continuum, in alphabetical order, include Austin, Bisno, Burus, Guzzetta, Kadushin, Kendall, Lyndon, Matson, Mossman, Samoff, Stein, Witte, to name a few. As far as I can determine, the term did not appear in education for social work literature before the 1950s. It has generated more heat than light in the subsequent two decades and, for this reason I again suggest it is time to retire it from our discussions of educational issues, as no longer useful. But in retiring it, we ought not discard some lessons we can derive from the history of its use.

Our profession has always struggled with the intellectual problems that accompany any effort to integrate theory and practice, what we know and what we do. But historically, I believe it can be demonstrated that for us the source and test of truth was located first and foremost in practice, and not in ideas about it. Given the complexity of our practice reality, we are not helped to understand what we are about when mental constraints that encapsulate ideological blinders are employed to compel changes without full critical evaluation. Before we seek to create hierarchical orders in which we locate the thinkers at the pinnacle and the doers at the base, we ought to appreciate the possibility that these may be self-serving formulations. Nor does the discarding of an outworn concept require that we ignore the substantive issues that the discarded concept sought to encompass. I will devote the remainder of this brief presentation to these substantive issues.

Because of its origins in service agencies, education for social work practice has always been concerned with certain structural, substantive, and process issues. Throughout the history of education for social work, we have sought to determine where to locate education for practice; at what level of educational maturity ought preparation for skill be inserted into the training; what prior preparation in experience and education was most appropriate as prerequisite to learning social work content; and what, if any, specializations ought we to encourage. These issues have inspired debates about technical, undergraduate, and graduate education; about the place of the behavioral and social science disciplines in education for practice; and what, if any, concentrations should be fostered. I believe these areas of concern, in modern dress, are still central to our interest, having a remarkable currency in light of the newly adopted Curriculum Policy Statement. Let me take each in turn.

LEVELS OF SOCIAL WORK EDUCATION

My review of the research that has been done on undergraduate, graduate, and doctoral education for social work leads me to conclude that we know very little with any degree of certainty about what is actually happening in social work education across the country, and even less about the results being achieved. The recent reviews of practice research in medicine have concluded that overwhelmingly such studies lacked the power in design and execution to warrant certainty about most of their findings. Our own studies consistently admit to weaknesses in the nature of data collected; limitations in sample selection, coverage, and response rates; shortcomings in the statistical design and power of tests of significance utilized; etc. These weaknesses, often combined in a single study, yield an even less optimistic view of our certainties than that which is said to prevail in clinical medical research. I believe we are at the descriptive, classification stage in our knowledge in this area and ought to tailor our debates accordingly.

Clearly, what we do know warns us to give considerable weight to circumstances in which our programs operate. As deans, we are well aware of the influence of restrictions dictated by limited resources, general university policies, the level of community practice, the funding priorities of state-local public and voluntary agencies, etc., on our program structures and offerings. Not merely regional, but local demographic and political-economic differences shape the employment market and dictate service staffing patterns, which in turn influence our priorities and mission statements. Similar factors affect our competitive situation in relation to other professions and the various disciplines when seeking to attract strong faculty and students to our programs.

I believe, through most of our history, such contextual influences, more than our ideas about how our education might best be packaged, have governed the form in which our programs have developed. If this be true, and if it remains true to the present, it makes no sense at all to attempt to force a hierarchical format on the entire educational enterprise based on some internal logic dictated by a particular view of what quality education ought to be. Undergraduate, masters, and doctoral programs can be coerced into a uniform pattern only at great cost when the immediate educational environment does not support such a pattern. Moreover, because we are not sufficiently clear and do not agree among ourselves on what structure is likely to assure the quality we seek, the intraprofessional conflicts such coercion will generate are hardly justified.

It seems far more sensible to employ our resources to explore that state of educational offerings, and identify instances of workable productive formats and the contexts in which they can appropriately be applied. The new Curriculum Policy Statement (CPS) is sufficiently permissive and the revised accreditation manual sufficiently demanding in relation to minimum requirements to allow many flowers to bloom, while protecting the field from weeds and destructive parasites. In the next decade as we pursue this approach, I expect we will find more than one hierarchical order that can shape the relationship of levels of social work education while assuring qualitatively acceptable products from all our educational programs.

THE PREREQUISITES AND THE QUALITY OF SOCIAL WORK EDUCATION

Some decades back, Ralph Carr Fletcher sought to learn how differences in undergraduate preparation related to the achievements of masters students in schools of social work. He concluded that students whose undergraduate majors were in the humanities did as well or better than those who had majored in the social and behavioral sciences. Given the commitment of the field at that time to undergraduate prerequisites in the social and behavioral sciences, the shock caused by his findings can be appreciated. There was the anticipated rush to explain the probable deficiencies in the study design leading to these unwelcome findings. Recently, when I read the study by Specht et al., that reports a similar problematic outcome in relation to the BSW and non-BSW masters students, I was reminded of that period. As I noted earlier, our studies are more useful for what they describe to be the case, than in their power to explain how what they find came to be. It is nevertheless important, if our association's declared interest in quality education is to be pursued, to stay with the question: What is the best preparation a candidate might bring to the education we offer?

For example, I believe that the intellectual tools most useful for professional education, whatever the profession and at whatever level it is offered, are those that help the worker in such work-related tasks as these:

1. Make decisions affecting action in uncertain situations.
2. Engage in problem solving.
3. Utilize the case method to define a situation and formulate a plan of action with intention to influence.
4. Base moral behavioral on ethical imperatives derived from a set of relevant values.
5. Appreciate differences and understanding the importance of individualizing situations and persons.
6. Discipline the idiosyncratic in style.
7. Communicate in a manner that enhances understanding and furthers intention.
8. Engage in ongoing self-appraisal.

These preprofessional prerequisites prepare students for more demanding intellectual work, when they must learn to:

1. Identify needs and appropriate resources in the areas of their practice concerns.
2. Appreciate the ethical and theoretical foundations that inform the program of services they offer and influence their choice of objectives and methods of work.

3. Recognize the functional relevance of administrative, supervisory, and service delivery structures and roles in organizational networks that seek to implement programs.
4. Understand the processes whereby the results of practice efforts are accounted for and how additions to practice theory are incorporated into the scope of practice competence.

These additional intellectual demands, while essential content to be mastered for practice, are prerequisites to the achievement of a competent practice. Competence requires that students know how to:

1. Evaluate the relationships of need to resource and arrive at useful definitions of the imbalance to be altered.
2. Design a unit of service whose objectives are realistic and whose implementation is feasible.
3. Implement the program through appropriate administrative, supervisory, and direct practice activities judged likely to achieve program goals and objectives.
4. Develop monitoring procedures that permit an accounting of the effort expended and the purposes accomplished while assisting in systematic evaluations of results.

My formulation deliberately focuses on intellectual work, and identifies prerequisites that can be learned in undergraduate courses in the humanities, the physical and biological sciences, as well as in the behavioral and social sciences. To my knowledge, this practice-oriented stem in undergraduate education has not received the attention it deserves, and our social work students often are seriously deficient in one or more of these skills. The various formulations of foundation knowledge that have appeared in our literature focus primarily on mastery of subject areas and application technologies, assuming, I suppose, that such learning includes the prerequisite intellectual skills without which mastery would not be possible. After thirty-five years of teaching at the graduate level, I am not at all certain that this assumption is supported by experience.

The prevalent view is that one can improve the quality of social work education by transferring substantive content to earlier stages of the educational experience, and substituting more advanced substantive courses for the graduate curriculum spots thus vacated. The new Curriculum Policy Statement enshrines this approach in its formulation of the relationship of foundation and concentration. I question whether the result of the approach we have taken will be a strengthening of our students' intellectual skills, which are prerequisite to more advanced social work. I believe, we all agree that the quality of education is intimately related to the student's ability to think, as much or more than what he or she thinks about. Learning how to think, and mastery of the intellectual skills required in such learning, does not suggest the same curriculum progression that follows when we focus on what one thinks about, particularly in the preparatory stage, when prerequisite tools for advanced work have to be mastered. If we really intend to focus on quality in our educational programs, we must devote some of our more thoughtful efforts to clarifying the prerequisite issue.

CONCENTRATIONS, SPECIALTIES, AND SPECIALIZATIONS

Throughout the history of education for social work, from the formative years as training schools, through the period of affiliation with colleges and universities, to the present, schools have used problems (such as juvenile delinquency), programs (such as child welfare) and processes (such as casework, social group work, etc.) alone or in combination as overarching rubrics for organizing curricula. To the extent that special emphasis was given to the categories falling under any of these rubrics, such categories were viewed as concentrations. Thus, students could concentrate on child welfare or juvenile delinquency or casework while taking the necessary courses to meet standard requirements for the social work degree. In the 1960s, problem and program concentrations became more prevalent, reflecting the social upheavals of that decade, and processes underwent modifications to reflect the combining of methods in direct practice, with such formulations as micro, mezzo, and macro processes appearing as ongoing rubrics in some schools. The 1969 CPS, in establishing criteria for concentrations, sought to recognize what was by then a prevalent diversity, while hoping to assure minimal standards that would protect the quality of education provided by schools choosing any of such rubrics.

In social work practice, from its earliest manifestations as a distinctive arena of professional activity, the special demands of particular settings, programs, and problems have been viewed as requiring skills unique to the tasks involved. Thus, medical, hospital, public health, psychiatric and more recently pediatric, renal, etc. social work practice have been seen by those involved in specialties within the broader arena of social work practice in health-related areas. School social work, industrial social work, clinical social work, and other practices similarly have been viewed by their proponents as specialties.

Unhappily, problems are frequently redefined, processes combine, and programs disappear or merge, raising serious questions as to their utility as organizing rubrics for curricula. Similarly, practice generates continuously evolving specialties, some of which are short-lived, or so narrowly defined as to approach the level of a specific technology, rather than a practice specialty—while others are so broad—such as clinical social work—that no agreement can be reached on what practice is to be included under this umbrella term.

All these difficulties came to a head by the late 1970s when our confusions were threatening to fragment the profession into specialty interest groups, and undercut the uniform standard requirements for professional education that assured the public of a similar foundation competence for persons holding the professional social work degree. To deal with these difficulties, the professional associations of social workers and social work educators agreed to jointly sponsor a study group to recommend to schools and the field of practice how they might best proceed with the issues of "specialization."

The charge to the joint NASW-CSWE Committee on Specialization asked that the Committee develop criteria, and evidence on which to judge the criteria, but not to propose specific specializations. The wisdom that limited the charge in this way was quickly evident when we on the Committee examined the various approaches to specializations being advanced by special interest groups in the profession. We were amazed to discover how deeply these special interest groups were invested in their differences. As a Committee we unanimously agreed to put aside the variety of specialization claims, and the rationalizations that were put forward to justify them, and to only address the limited charge given to us. We thought that if we could agree upon criteria, their application would provide an empirical base for resolving many of the conflicting positions inherent in this issue.

CONCENTRATIONS

The 1969 CPS employed the word concentration in its section on practice. Criteria for a concentration incorporated into the 1969 statement were quite demanding, although experience indicates they were less than vigorously applied in the subsequent decade in the accreditation process. In seeking to allow schools to test out a range of structural rubrics through which the substantive required content of an MSW could be, and in a number of instances, were already being offered, we concurrently hoped that the criteria for a concentration would strengthen the curriculum in particular areas by deepening the learning in an area the school itself selected for special attention. At that time, as chairperson of the Committee that wrote the CPS statement, I was clear, as were the other members of the Committee, that concentration was not intended to create or denote specialization. For this reason, more recently, as a member of the joint NASW-CSWE committee, I recommended the use of the term concentration, so as to distinguish what we intended this term to denote, from the terms specialization and specialties.

The criteria we arrived at for determining a specialization ruled out the possibility that a concentration in a school could by itself designate a professional specialization. Nor could a specialty in practice alone justify the designation of a professional specialization. In our judgment the following attributes were essential to warrant the designation of a practice specialization.

1. Within an environment, a population experiencing a common condition to be altered or nurtured, must be identified in some critical number.
2. It must be demonstrated that there exists within social work, competence for work with and on behalf of this population. The skills and other elements of

this competence must be identified, related to the unique needs of the populations and the condition of their situations or environments. It must be shown that the use of this competence could be effective in altering or supporting this condition.

3. The conditions that characterize the population and the competencies required of social work specialists to deal with them must be sufficiently complex to require the guidance of a substantial body of knowledge. Such knowledge must be clearly related to the areas of transaction between people and their environments and must be translatable into effective interventions.

We also agreed that the evidence that these criteria meet be based on observable, reliable data; that the conditions addressed be consistent and persistent. We emphasized that concentrations that would fulfill the academic requirements associated with a designated specialization ought not fragment clients, losing sight of them as people. Finally, the concentration must maintain relevance to the zone of social work practice. We concluded that to achieve the educational requirements to be considered a specialist, graduate level or equivalent postgraduate education would be required.

Critical to our formulation, although not incorporated into our reports was the belief that our approach balanced the contribution of field and school to the definition of a specialization and avoided a hierarchical implication whereby the general MSW practitioner became a lesser one because of the status that might become associated with the designation of a specialist. Nor did we foreclose on the possibility of special emphases in programs at the undergraduate or doctoral levels.

So much by way of introduction. I wish here to add another dimension to the Committee's discussion of specializations.

There is, to my way of thinking, no compelling reason to develop specializations in our profession, if the criteria we proposed cannot be fulfilled. It does not follow that there are no compelling reasons for establishing concentrations in our curriculum, and specialties in our practice. Experience would suggest, in fact, that both concentrations and specialties have existed for some time, without the development of specializations. What seems probable is that until the relationship among specialties and concentrations evolve to the point that they together meet the criteria we suggested, designations of specializations would be premature.

The principal function of the discussion of specialization is to enlighten us as to our limitations in both practice and academic content, but is not likely to result in agreement on what we all would accept to be a specialization. For this reason, it is of vital importance to carefully monitor the concentration area of the Curriculum Policy Statement, and to subject to ongoing analysis the unique claims of practice specialties. From such observations and analysis, we may come to understand our profession's unique developmental pattern and determine whether it could and should evolve in the direction of specializations.

SUMMARY

1. There are a variety of hierarchical arrangements potentially useful for the structuring of education for social work. No one has demonstrated the greater utility of one arrangement for all contexts. Imposition of any one on the entire educational enterprise is not warranted. It is entirely possible to live with such variety as exists within the guidelines incorporated in the CPS, providing the statement is applied as written, and not interpreted in such a way as to impose a preferred schemata on any one program or combination of programs. Hence, we ought let many flowers flourish. In the weeding and fertilizing process of accreditation, we ought to avoid contaminating or disfiguring the blossoms.
2. Given the state of the art, we ought to depend heavily on the realities of practice as both the source and test of truths. Imagination can treat such opposed truths as hypotheses, to be tested. As Goethe observed, there is nothing wrong in entertaining incorrect hypotheses, so long as one does not believe they are true.
3. We ought to rearrange our priorities in our study and experiment with levels. Focus on the comparable merits of undergraduate-graduate programs ought to follow, not precede, a full exploration of what existing programs actually look like when implemented. We ought to describe standards of practice, seeking to cull out the best to serve as standards from practice, hoping to ultimately achieve our idealized notions of standards for practice. Only then can we design evaluations aimed to improve standards of performance based on outcome measures.
4. We need to question the prevalent assumption that attribute improvement in the quality of social work education to the number of subjects the student thinks about, and not to the student's ability to think. Stuffing the learner with content which cannot be absorbed for use is likely to achieve no more than a chronic case of mental indigestion. A careful review of the place of prerequisites in social work education is crucial in this regard.
5. We can develop educational concentrations, and practice specialties, and we have, without concurrently developing specializations. The criteria proposed to determine if a claim of specialization is warranted ought to be applied, in an ongoing effort to learn what, if any, role specializations might play in the profession.

I'll conclude with a brief note on intent. By design, the initial part of the paper sought to defuse the discussion of graduate-undergraduate issues by discarding the politically divisive term continuum. I then sought to locate the three major elements the concept continuum sought to cover—levels, prerequisites, specializations—in their appropriate time and place. My intent is to promote a useful exchange on a touchy question, one in which our common concerns bring us together, strengthening our ability to deal with the hostile environment in which all our programs find themselves.

Chapter 21

The Micro/Macro in Social Work Education

This is another example of Lewis critiquing what he regarded as the arbitrary dualism that existed in the social work field. Using a powerful illustration drawn from the headlines of the day, Lewis demonstrates how "the micro/macro formulation . . . perpetuates [the] separation of means and ends." He also provides an insightful summary of the history of this issue in the field.

Some professions are mesmerized by the brilliance of their colleagues' conceptualizations. The social work profession is more frequently polarized. If we social workers cannot divide a happening in two, placing one part in opposition to the other, we suspect its essence escapes us. During the past two decades, one such dichotomy has taken hold and, with considerable support from the academic sector of social work, has helped shape many graduate schools' curricula. This dichotomy divides all of social work into two parts, the micro and the macro. In some of its applications, it would appear that never the twain shall meet. As an instance of a prevalent tendency in the profession, the micro/macro conceptualization can be used to illustrate problems attendant on all such formulations.

I will use a thought experiment to illustrate how the micro/macro can be abstracted from a real-life happening. Let us assume you are an observer, who happens to turn around just as two youths point their guns at the President of the American University in Beirut, fire, and then flee. Not knowing the victim to be the University President, nor any particulars about the youths, other than their silhouettes, what explanation might you give to the event observed? Beyond the statement, "I saw two youths fire guns at the man, and he fell over, while they ran away," no amount of inquiry could elicit further information from you.

Now suppose you were asked to describe the setting in which the event occurred. You might recall the timing and physical location of the event and your own activity at the time. From this added information—that you were visiting the campus of American University in Beirut, a city in the midst of a civil war, you

Guest lecture at the School of Social Work, State University of New York at Buffalo, March 1984.

might link the event to the context, generating a series of hypotheses. For example, the youths may have represented one of the warring groups, and the person shot, another. Hence, this happening might have political overtones. You might even wonder if the person shot could be been just anyone, or someone of importance, to warrant so drastic an act. Pursuing this line of reasoning, you may come close to identifying the true nature of the event, a political assassination, without knowing anything about the person shot and those who did the shooting. From this example, it should be possible to draw the conclusion that knowing macro elements of the event can contribute significantly to defining it, and to one or more possible explanations of its occurrence.

Now, suppose you knew the president of the university, and you were able to judge the age of the youths to be what one could commonly expect among college students. You would obviously be able to hypothesize, tentatively, that two students or possibly friends of students or rejected applicants, shot the president in retaliation for a real or imagined wrong done them by the president or the university he represented. Without the contextual information earlier provided, it would be unlikely that you could deduce a linkage to a civil war, and associate the event with the concept: political assassination. Still, knowing the persons (the micro units), would be critical to arriving at an accurate explanation of the event.

This thought experiment would suggest that any happening is inherently macro and micro in content. Any event is thus potentially open to analysis in both dimensions. If you think about it, you'll believe as have I, that it is impossible to imagine an event that is otherwise constituted, so long as the happening is of this world, and occurs in a particular time and place. If this observation applies to all happenings, it must apply to social work happenings as well.

Thus, we are led to conclude that the partitioning of a social work event into its macro and micro components is an artifact of a mental process. No such division exists in the event itself. That the event evidences this true polarity is apparent. That it can be conceptualized in such a way as to create false dichotomies is also apparent. It is the contention of this presentation that the micro/macro formulation to guide the organization of curriculum is such a false dichotomy, resulting in considerable mischief for social work education.

How did it happen that this dichotomy surfaced in social work education when it did? After all, this micro/macro formulation was a product of intellectual work and, like all such work, is never neutral to the milieu in which it is carried out. A brief historical sketch may locate the development of this dichotomy in time and place.

During the late 1950s and 1960s, as the Civil Rights and War-on-Poverty initiatives promoted a substantial federal presence in social welfare, social work education shifted from an exclusively process curriculum framework (casework, group work, community organization, administration) to problem and programmatic organizing rubrics. It was recognized that combinations of processes were often required to deal effectively with the one problem, requiring a multiprocess skill in the practitioner. The programmatic approach in practice placed heavy emphasis on the design and evaluation phases of service delivery, often subordinating the direct service processes to a secondary role. Schools were not preparing practitioners for these demands of practice.

In that period, the battering of direct service processes was already having its effects. The study "Girls at Vocational High" helped sponsor a broadside attack on casework and group work, finding them to be ineffective. Concurrently, documentation was proffered to support the accusation that social workers were deserting the poor. Considerable press was given to the evidence that social work processes fail to solve problems and social work programs fail to serve the "cause" that justified their public support. Schools found themselves on the defensive. Some sought refuge from this attack by reorganizing their curricula using a social problems rubric and other schools switched to a field of practice framework.

Most schools chose a less disruptive compromise. They modified their process curricula, combining casework and group work into one concentration, called micro, and assigned the other processes to a concentration called macro. (At least one school assumed an ordinal rather than nominal classification, and carved out a "mezzo", located between the micro and macro.) This micro/macro formulation, while making concessions to the pressure for change, nevertheless retained the essentials of a process rubric. It was a partial response to the multiprocess requirements of a problem-oriented practice. It also accorded the macro more space in the curriculum, conceding to the demand for added preparation in administration, policy, and evaluation.

No sooner had the micro/macro conceptualization taken hold, than it began to make friends and influence people. New meanings were attached to the terms, as they took on the coloration of their surroundings. The initial process focus had assigned small units, persons, and small groups to the micro, and larger units—neighborhoods, communities, organizations, legislative bodies—to the macro. But soon efforts intended to deal with personal or familial problems were seen as micro, and those directed toward dysfunctional societal conditions, as macro. Thus, piecemeal social changes on an individual unit basis (retail changes) were viewed as micro, and broader social changes affecting large, population cohorts (wholesale changes) as macro. It became evident that in purchasing a relatively facile solution to difficult practice issues, the schools had bought in to a formulation that would lead to a further denigration of the masters' curriculum.

For example, pushing this dichotomy to its logical conclusion, undergraduate and some graduate programs proposed to merge processes further, projecting a generic practitioner model, a "generalist" social worker. This "Jack of all trades" would, it was argued, best serve the changing demands of problem-oriented agencies. For these agencies, coverage needs were of greater concern than their lack of ability to deliver a service that required an in-depth mastery of any one process. The unresolved differences that had historically separated casework, group work, and community organization were to be largely ignored. In relation to each of these distinctive processes, such basic questions as—Who controls the process? Whose goals are worked on? What roles are to be carried by participants in the service?

How much weight ought to be assigned to nurture and nature in targeting areas for change?—had always solicited different answers in the past. Rather than attend to the unique qualities of these processes, the fact that they utilized many techniques in common sufficed to justify their being merged and viewed as a single entity.

The trivialization of methods that followed the ignoring of differences in processes, in turn, encouraged the idea that came to be known as the continuum. Divested of its verbal mystifications, the continuum proposed that the undergraduate professional degree prepare for generalist practice, now a "code word" for the direct service processes (the micro), reserving for graduate education (the macro) and "specializations." Not surprisingly, it was proposed by some to eliminate the Masters' degree entirely and substitute a three-year doctorate to follow on the BSW. What started out as a modest modification in curriculum in response to changes in practice, ended with a plan for the demise of the very program the modifications were intended to protect.

By the 1970s, "accountability" replaced "innovation," the flow of monies to solve problems began to dry up. Jobs in the macro practice arena became scarcer than long-term counseling relationships in a public welfare agency. Studies began to find casework helpful and the continuum founded on the rocks of reality. The mischief done by the imposition of this false dichotomy on curriculum development, nevertheless, exacted a heavy price. Could there have been a more viable response to the pressures of the 1960s and the contractions of the 1970s, one that utilized the dynamic possibilities inherent in a true polarity? I think so, and will present this alternative later. But first, I will present a further discussion of the lacks in the micro/macro, the social problems, and the fields of practice rubrics for organizing curricula.

The social problems and fields of service approaches to curriculum organization have been tried at various times in the history of social work education. The problems approach suffers the limitations inherent in all problem formulations: there is limited agreement on the nature and scope of a problem; there is no end to the number of problems that can be identified and that call for solutions; and there are always many possible processes that can be employed to deal with the problem. These characteristics play havoc with a curriculum and make efficient use of resources almost impossible. Moreover, students graduating with social problem expertise quickly discover how transient is the interest in their particular social problem, and how scarce are jobs that promise career progression if one depends on expertise in one particular problem area.

Fields of service have a tendency to proliferate. When this rubric last dominated curricula in graduate schools of social work, some nine fields were identified, each contending for a place in the specialization sun. When the 1949 Curriculum Policy Statement was prepared under the leadership of Marion Hathway, the shift to processes—casework, group work, community organization, with minor attention to administration and research—was seen as progress, in that it reduced nine sequences to five, offering some bases for a more generic view of social work skills, and a more manageable and efficient use of faculty competencies.

The shift to a processes rubric, with its heavy focus on methods, revealed a significant gap in social work curricula. The processes focus directed the students' and faculty's attention to means, not ends. The knowledge component became central and the value component peripheral. What the graduate would know and could do, was perceived as critical; what he or she would be, was treated as incidental. The micro/macro formulation of the processes rubric perpetuates this separation of means and ends.

The ends/means polarity in social work has been a source of much conflict in the profession. It has always been an issue in practice as well as in policy debates. One facet of this debate gets played out in efforts to locate the target for change in the helping process. Richmond focused on the "individual and wider self;" the Milford Conference focused on "person in situation;" Gordon targets in on the person–environment interface; systems advocates focus in on the eco space. But all share in common an intention to include the context as well as the client in the unit of attention. Bertha Reynolds captured the essence of the "target-for-change" issue in two of her typically insightful comments.

She once observed that social workers do not mind helping people in trouble, but they do mind when these same people make trouble about their trouble. The occasion for the remark was a client protest action at a public welfare center, where a supervisor called in the police to make an arrest. Her comment suggests the probability that the worker will more readily accept that part of a client's behavior that carries recognition of the client's contribution to the troubles evidenced, than client's behavior that attributes their troubles to the agency program and the wider community.

There is more than nature/nurture difference in these two views of the source of the trouble. As often happens in practice, where the clients concede that their own negligence contributed to their troubles, they are likely to be viewed as "motivated" for help. Where the clients attribute their troubles to the social conditions that impinge upon them, they are likely to be viewed as abusive toward those close to them and toward the social institutions in their immediate life space.

Reynolds, at another time, observed that psychoanalytic theory helped our profession to individualize its clients, but in the process isolated them. The insight here focused on the tendency to downplay the milieu or in modern terminology, ignore the ecosystem, when attending to the psychological dimensions of a client's problems. Unlike the earlier remark, the stress here is not on the personal societal influences in generating troubles, but on the immediate environment that provides the context in which the client's situation can be best understood and worked on.

Bertha Reynolds was especially sensitive to the difficulties facing the practitioner who must constantly seek a balanced appreciation of the individual and social contribution to the client's troubles. She was mindful of the difficulties encountered by the worker who must concentrate on the individual's problems, yet concurrently try to maintain a linkage between the client's unique self and the environment that contributes to the client's character. She was not alone in these concerns. It is no accident that they have challenged the profession throughout its history.

By seeking to encompass the social in every assessment, these conceptualizations of the targets for intervention move the focus from individual failure to include societal failure as well. This shift in focus inevitably highlights a social change purpose in each service transaction. The social change intentions of the worker, guided as they must be by goals and objectives, direct attention to ends as well as means. Perhaps the clearest expression of this means–ends polarity was first formulated by Porter Lee in his paper, "Social Work as Cause and Function," in which he separated "cause" and "function" by sequencing them over time—i.e., "from cause to function." Lee's failure to appreciate the ends in means, the cause in function has been perpetuated since by most discussants of this polarity.[1]

For our purposes, it is sufficient to note that function is central to the micro/macro formulation, and that cause—i.e., social purpose—is peripheral. The challenge is to so construct our curricula as to make the mechanistic separation of cause and function impossible, while allowing for a process, problem, or field of service emphasis, whichever seems most appropriate.

I will now suggest a curriculum structure that responds to this challenge, to incorporate "cause" as well as "function" in the curriculum while avoiding the type of false dichotomy typified by the micro/macro formulation. We start with certain common human needs, which constitute a viable set of "goods" for which all people aspire. Everyone seeks well-being, security, justice, knowledge, self-actualization, and aesthetic satisfaction. These "goods" are universally valued, and much effort is expended to obtain them.

Civilized societies provide resources intended to meet these common human needs, through health, economic, political, educational, religious, and aesthetic institutions. The society and the individual both value these "goods," both view them as critical moral rights that a civilized community contracts to help its members realize. These ends are sought by organizations that employ social workers, constituting the underlying "cause" that justifies their function. In this view, it is a semantic fallacy to separate cause and function, and equally fallacious to view the individual and social as inherently conflictual.

In a curriculum, organized on the basis of a human needs rubric, courses would have to attend to the intentional nature of method. For example, no psychosocial assessment would be complete without an appreciation of social resource as it impacts on the client's situation and condition. In the health area, the assessment would require the student to evaluate the relevance of the health network—its economics, politics, range of services—for the particular client in the particular situation. How the agency and its program limits the availability of its services, thus affecting the recipient's behavior, attitudes, and motivation, could not be subordinate, and the client's limitations dominant, without doing less than justice to the ends sought by community and client alike in seeking the service. Viewing the client as a social participant, in effect, brings the individual/social together, and implements a cause in every exercise of function.

If the needs rubric instills a value component throughout the curriculum, a process rubric organizes the curriculum around knowledge—the former justifying what should be done, and the latter focusing on how it should be done. For this reason, I would concurrently organize courses in accordance with the major processes sequences—casework, group work, community work, administration, policy planning, and research. These processes have developed methods for achieving their purposes that reflect their unique histories, and ought not be prematurely merged or compressed in response to transient events in practice. When supported by orienting courses such as Human Growth and the Social Environment, Social Welfare History and Structure, and by well designed field work instruction and faculty advisement, these sequences can help prepare graduates who are informed in the work they are expected to perform. I believe that ends and means are inseparable in practice, and will be inseparable in such a curriculum matrix. Nevertheless, ends justify means, not the other way around. For this reason I locate processes sequences within the concentrations as defined by the human needs rubric.

We have applied this schemata for about thirteen years at Hunter. This matrix achieves a number of very useful objectives, in addition to the concurrent focus on means and ends. The needs rubric is quite sensitive to changes in the political economy of social work, allowing responses to changing societal conditions on a differential basis, not requiring a total revision of the school's program. Thus, in a period when health-related programs were expanding, emphasis in recruitment and student assignment to the health area was possible, while maintaining other concentrations, and reducing those for which demand declined. At the same time, a deliberate decision to develop an entirely new area of curriculum—the World of Work—was taken with a significant allocation of resources, in anticipation that this concentration would expand in response to a need that was likely to grow. Similarly, processes important to work in the health area could be made available for students in that concentration, while processes deemed more useful in the World of Work could be offered to their students. Orienting knowledge courses, to the degree we could manage the logistics, were dovetailed to substantive content required by each of the concentrations, including development of selected electives.

It is important to note that we assumed transferability in learning. Just as in the past students graduating with skills in one process of social work practice frequently accepted employment that required skill in other processes and were able to use their expertise in one to quickly attain acceptable skill in the other, so we expected students who learned "how to think about" the substantive content in one concentration, to transfer such a way of "how to think about" to another. A number of students transfer in their second year to a new concentration. Many students also add courses in a second process during their two-year program, thus deepening their mastery of the one originally selected on entry into the school, while gaining skill in other.

Field work opportunities necessarily play a role in shaping the size and scope of concentrations and processes. In the New York City metropolitan area, the large number of placements available allows for considerable flexibility in this regard.

Finally, it must be noted that all faculty have both a concentration and sequence assignment—a "cause" as it were, and a "function." Thus, in each concentration practice (including administration and research), Human Behavior and the Social Environment, Social Policy, and Field Work faculty constitute a cohort, who work together on the major concerns of their concentration. In a sense, this creates minischools within the curriculum. But the requirements of the processes also draw those faculty together across concentration boundaries. The end result of this duality of interest is a faculty that has to work together, and a turf that must be shared in common. As Dean, I can testify to the remarkable way in which this matrix utilizes efficiently a multifaceted faculty talent pool.

The loneliest thing I know is a new idea, one whose time has not come. Understood by no one but its author, it can mark him as a clairvoyant or a fool. But let one other mind grasp its meaning, there is no limit to the influence it can generate. The curriculum alternative I have described was a new idea that took hold in one school, and has proved useful in fair weather and foul, in periods of stable budgets and drastic cutbacks. If one other school should happen to grasp this idea and explore its potential, who knows what changes may be wrought in graduate education for social work?

What I have sought to illustrate in this example is an alternative to the micro/macro conceptualization of the curriculum. Returning to the micro/macro formulation, I'll conclude with a more detailed discussion of its implications for practice.

The principal processes utilized in social work practice, such as casework, group work, community organization, administration, and policy/planning are shaped by various methods, often used in combination. No one method is exclusively employed in one process, nor does any one process consistently employ the same combination of methods. The attributes that these processes share in common are the most obvious characteristics of any process—a beginning, a middle, and an end. Since these are human-initiated processes, not surprisingly they all involve the worker and some other individual or combination of individuals in a relationship. For most of social work practice, these processes are sponsored by an organization, but there are exceptions. The processes differ in most other attributes significant for practice.

Casework usually involves the worker in relationships with individuals, families, and small therapeutically-oriented groups. In the main, the individual alone, or as a member of a family or group is the recipient of the service, and the client and his or her environment is the target for change. Social group work usually involves the worker in relationships with groups. These may include therapeutic groups, but also a variety of groups with definite enrollments, such as clubs, teams, interest groups, committees, classes, and organized groups without definite enrollments, such as recitals, dances, forums, drop-in socials, etc. The recipient of service is usually a group and a target of intervention is the group and its environment. But this does not exclude work with individuals who are associated with such groups.

Community organization usually involves work with intergroups, whose members are representative of various groups. The recipient of services usually is some functionally defined community whose various constituencies are represented in the intergroup. The target for change is usually the "community" and the wider societal context in which it is located. This does not exclude work with special task-oriented groups and individuals, as such work is deemed useful to the functioning of the intergroup. I will not pursue this further, but a similar formulation can be made for administration and policy/planning.

I would like to make two points about the attributes of these processes. Whether one uses psychotherapy, problem-solving, behavioral, educational, or other methods, the processes, not the methods, add coherence to the practice. The processes provide the major historically significant linkages to our past. The fact that one person may master more than one method, and use such mastery to affect different processes, does not in any way justify the view that methods, which may share techniques in common, are similar. Nor does it justify the view that processes can be combined without distorting their essence, that which makes them significantly unique. These points may be more sharply defined through the use of an analog.

The grain of sand, two sand dunes, and a desert all have sand in common. As with sand, so with persons, in the aggregate they undergo qualitative changes. But whereas sand remains sand, in isolation or in the aggregate, the individual self undergoes change in association with other selves. One way to appreciate the significance of these attributes of aggregation is to study their impact.

A grain of sand can irritate the eye, a sand dune can stop a tank, and a desert can defeat an army. An individual can refuse to buy a product, a group can threaten to boycott it, a community can ban its production. True, it is possible to ignore the levels of differentiation characterized by qualitative difference in aggregates. By combining levels on the basis of their shared characteristics—the unit they have in common—a generic whole is created, at great cost to the lost qualities attributable to their differentiation.

For the practitioner seeking to work with people, the unit of attention can be the individual, alone or in aggregates; the group, alone or in aggregates; or the intergroup, alone or in aggregates. Depending on which level is selected, the process that evolves can be assigned to casework, group work, or community work. Any one practitioner can elect to focus on one or more units of attention and can change focus over time. It is the unit of attention that determines the process that will evolve, not the various methodological skills that are applied to help shape the process.

In practice, allocating two or more units of attention to categories, such as micro and macro, obfuscates unique qualitative characteristics of different levels. The concept of the "generalist practitioner" and the "generic method," while supposedly intended to produce a practitioner competent to shape all processes with a set of skills applicable across the board, is more a wish than a reality. Recognizing this to be the case, the micro/macro formulation modifies this expectation somewhat by encompassing fewer units, in each category. The logic of this solution initiates a regress that should culminate in practitioners whose skill in-depth prepares them for one particular unit of attention, promoting a division of labor by levels based on what needs to be done, not who does it. It is to be expected then, that the more competent the expected practice, the more concentrated will be the practitioner skills best utilized for a particular unit of attention.

On the other hand, agencies whose programs suffer constriction in resources, and who are compelled by their mandate to provide coverage beyond their resource capacity, will opt for a more generic mode of intervention and a generalist-type practitioner. Quantitative demands on limited resources are bound to produce qualitative differences in the nature of the services offered. When the contraction of resources for fiscal reasons results in the exercise of this option it represents a depletion of service. It is unreal to pretend from such contractions that new services are created. It may appear more economical to have in one practitioner a combination of skills, even if this requires some sacrifice in expertise. Client problems, however, may not be cooperative and may evidence complexities for which a lesser skill is hardly sufficient. Thus, the goals of service may be modified to meet the limits of resource and the ends may be sacrificed to the means. As in education for practice, so in practice, the resulting emphasis on processes relegates purpose to a peripheral role—and weakens the cause in function.

In summary, I have sought to explore a major conceptual tool employed in the social work profession to organize its educational curriculum and to bring its practice into focus. The micro/macro formulation, I have argued, represents a false dichotomy that effectively splits a true-polarity—"cause in function"—in two. This split has had a deadening effect on the dynamics that could result from the quantitative potential inherent in the tension between knowledge and values, means and ends, present in each service transaction. I have suggested an alternative conceptual rubric that has avoided the micro/macro fallacy and exploited this dynamic.

It was Goethe, I believe, who observed that there was nothing wrong in entertaining a false hypothesis, so long as one does not believe it to be true. In contrast, I would note that there is much that is wrong in entertaining a false dichotomy, particularly when one believes it to be true.

Chapter Note

1. See the second essay in this volume for a more detailed discussion of these issues.

Chapter 22

The Teacher's Style and the Use of Professional Self in Social Work Education

In this self-effacing reflection, Lewis applies the well-known practice concept—conscious use of self—to assess his own development as a teacher. With humor and insight, including those of other colleagues, he discusses the role of style in teaching and the different perspectives teacher and students bring to the educational experience.

What follows is the saga of one teacher's search for a more effective use of professional self. His goal was to help students learn how to learn, and to do so making good use of their own learning styles. Over forty years of teaching (ten at the masters degree level and the last thirty years at the doctoral level), were involved in this quest. Despite the orderly way the story unravels in this text, the actual experience often resembled organized chaos, full of mistaken leads, false starts, and perpetual doses of self-doubt.

In 1961, after ten years of teaching masters level research, I persuaded a colleague, Dr. Harry Moore, to join me in an informal, conscious, although not systematic study of the MSW level student's approach to the formulation of a research question. Responding to an initial assignment in our introductory research courses asking students to formulate a research question, I suggested a close relationship between categories of questions submitted and distinctive styles of learning and problem solving. The published article resulting from this study (Lewis, 1961) concluded that the research course could provide an opportunity for enriching the total professional education for the social work student. What I did not realize was the degree to which the intellectual environment of the times served to support or detract from the student's success in utilizing distinctive learning styles (Ackerman, 1969).

At about the same period, "time" and its significance for student learning confronted the school's faculty with serious management problems. Specifically, students were complaining about the inordinate amount of time they had to de-

Originally published in the *Journal of Teaching in Social Work 5 (1)*, 1991.

vote to their required research theses. Nonresearch faculty believed this demand diverted students from their concentration on papers required in other courses, and thus detracted from, rather than added to the students' overall learning opportunities. In order to think more clearly about the issues involved, I initiated an informal inquiry with a class of second-year students who were to complete their research projects in the first semester (Lewis, 1959). They kept logs, submitted weekly, which asked them to note time spent on their project; what was worked on (specified by phase of research process); where and when this work occurred. The students were told not to keep a separate record of these reports, but simply to submit them each week in our research class session.

Three weeks into the second semester after the completed projects were submitted, the students in all research project courses (five sections) completed a simple questionnaire asking them to indicate, in relation to what they thought other students had experienced, whether they spent more, about the same, or less time on each of the phases of the research process. They were also asked whether they thought, in relation to what they thought other students had experienced, whether they thought, in relation to their own use of time, that they had spent too much or too little time on the project. Finally, in the closing weeks of the second year, faculty advisors were asked to rank their second year advisees as falling into the lower third, middle third, or upper third of the graduating class in overall performance and to identify any outstanding students.

This informal study put an end to the faculty debate about time spent on research projects (Lewis, 1960). It found that students' recall of time spent on the thesis had no relationship to actual monitored time spent. This held for all three categories of students. One tantalizing finding was the discovery that all students listed by faculty as outstanding believed they had spent too much time on the thesis, regardless of how much time they actually spent.

Eileen Younghusband, in a conversation with me, offered a hypothesis to explain this finding. She believed that good students could think of many other things to do with their time, and hence viewed any time spent on the thesis as too much time. The weaker or average student rarely faced this self-initiated pressure. What I did not appreciate at that time was the style of students' relationships in time—some fought it, some submitted to it, and others used it. Nor had I a conscious awareness of my own use of time as a teacher. Yet, these relationships to time were crucial elements in my learning style. These informal empirical inquiries prompted me to re-examine a number of assumptions I had made in my teaching.

Starting where students were not, Philip Lichtenberg defined the purpose of his teaching to be ". . . to reach learners in their actual beliefs, understandings and commitments; and, at the same time be concerned to encourage those learners to adapt their personal growth and changing to the productive tides of history. . . ." He went on to observe, "Yet if they learn only what they already know and we pose no alternatives for them, then we are not engaging them in an educational process" (Lichtenberg, 1983). It would have saved me much effort had he published his cogent essay some twenty years earlier. The two studies had clearly raised for me the critical question: Given the learning styles of students are not likely to change, even if enriched, and given the habituated responses of students reflected in how they related to time, what could I hope to do to shake students up sufficiently to help them to go beyond what they already knew by offering them another way of knowing? Fritz Machlup (1979) argues that:

> Every "good" teacher can become a really "effective" teacher if, to his fine qualities as a lecturer, expositor, discussion leader, advisor, and sympathetic friend of students, he adds the simple technique prescribed: to make reading and other homework indispensable for students attempting to pass his course. It is especially important that his lectures be not repetitive of assigned reading materials, not substitutes for reading, but truly complementary with reading; that many classroom discussions be based on assigned reading or exercises but in a way that the student who had skimped on his homework feels that he is at a serious disadvantage; that examinations during the end of the term test the successful comprehension of the materials read by, or problems assigned to the students—a comprehension, of course, that does not depend on memorizing.

He notes as a possible explanation as to why students of bad teachers report more inside reading and homework, that "the bad teachers'" students spend much more time reading and studying for the course than they would if they comprehended what their instructor taught.

By no means secure in the belief that I could ever achieve the virtues of the good teacher as Machlup notes them, nor systematically utilize the techniques he proposed, I arrived at an hypothesis similar to the one he proposed. My hypothesis, however, made a virtue of student noncomprehension, rather than treat it as a failure in pedagogy. I entertained a hunch that offering students alternative ways of knowing (a la Lichtenberg) and confronting them with the incomprehensible (a problem not amenable to their problem-solving skills), in short, starting where the students were not and deliberately using what they did not know, I could open them up to risking uncertainty in order to know more and differently. And I accepted as inevitable that by my own participation in class and conferences, I would also have to model such risk-taking for my students. In short, I would have to use myself in a self-conscious, self-critical way to model what I wanted from them. This brings me to the central theme of this discussion: The use of professional self as teacher in helping students to learn.

THE PROFESSIONAL SELF

Building on the work of Virginia Robinson, Bertha Reynolds, John Dewey, Carl Rogers, and Gordon Hamilton, William Rosenthal hypothesizes four action levels of use of self in the development of the social work practitioner (Rosenthal, n.d.).

The first two levels are represented by the practical actor and the theoretic actor. The former is the actor "learning by doing," where the actor does not know or learn very much about the doing itself. At this level the actor engages in tasks that are relatively uncomplicated and repetitive. The theoretic actor, the second level, is "held to be an agent of his or her own behavior." The actor at this level knows the rules that underlie certain kinds of activity and acts according to them and, therefore, is the agent of his or her own behavior, without being aware of his or her agency. The third level involves action in which the person is a self-conscious or aware agent of his or her own behavior. At this level, self-awareness is a product of the "acceptance and use" of professional criticism. Finally, the fourth level is achieved when the actor is aware of him- or herself as agent, aware of self as personally involved, aware of the need to discipline the personal involvement, and is able to own and maintain awareness of self and professional self, making conscious use of the latter.

Rosenthal's conceptualization suggests a pattern of maturation in the engagement of self in action, but provides no explanation of motivation for attaining and sustaining the action that is seen as appropriate use of professional self. Bandura (1978) cautioning against unidirectional causal models that emphasize other environmental or internal determinants of behavior, proposes a reciprocal determinism that includes behavior itself as a causal factor. He argues with those who show little enthusiasm for the notion that people can exercise some influence over their own behavior and change their environment, or who would explain behavior without postulating any self-generated influences. He questions the use of the concept of self-awareness, which he believes minimizes self-directed change through personally arranged incentives.

In Bandura's social learning theory the observation that professional self-criticism is required to achieve the conscious actor level, can be viewed as an oversimplification. He argues that recognition of self-motivation based on internalized standards as well as external standards actively monitors the self-system, rewarding and punishing in accordance with the quality of behavior achieved. For example, he notes that ". . . after ethical and moral standards of conduct are adopted, anticipatory self reactions for violating personal standards ordinarily serve as self-deterrents against reprehensible acts" (Bandura, 1978). This is so despite the various means by which self-evaluative consequences can be disassociated from reprehensible behavior. Thus, Bandura offers a plausible explanation of internally motivated sources of behavior change granting a significant role as change agent to the individual (Rokeach, 1973)—an explanation quite congenial to Rosenthal's view of the role of the professional self in any practice.

Using Rosenthal's and Bandura's formulations, I felt comfortable in identifying my proposed approach to enhancing student learning, or an exercise of my "professional self" sustained and promoted by self-evaluation and acquired standards that I was motivated to achieve. By inclination, I am a self-starter. I generate my own agendas and then organize my time and energies to fulfill these self-imposed expectations. Having decided to "not start where the student is," I had to follow suit and not start where my natural inclination led me. My classroom teaching, I decided, had to start with an unfamiliar form of reasoning not congenial to the analytic style and process orientation I had always used. Enter center stage, analogic, reasoning by analogy.

ANALOGIC

Fortuitously, at this point in my saga, I was invited to spend a year as a fellow at the Center for Advanced Study in the Behavioral Sciences. It provided me with ideal physical surroundings, freedom from work assignments, and exposure to a cohort of outstanding scholars. I decided to use the year to pursue a question that had bothered me since high school days: "How does the brain know it is being asked a question?" (Lewis, 1982). One unanticipated happening at the Center was my introduction to issues in meta-ethics and normative ethics that were beginning to surface among philosophers. These issues had significant implications for the professions.

For months my mind was occupied with qualitative methods, germane to philosophical discourse, and my "analytical self' was put on the backburner. Without my conscious awareness, I drifted into the minefield of short-term, long-term memory; mental storage and recovery problems and, finally, the importance of reasoning by analogy and its role in imagination. My usual reliance on the certainties of formal logic (if . . . then) and the explanations of dialectic logic (from this in time to that), was subordinated to a concern to use analogic.

The most prevalent logic utilized in practice is analogic or reasoning by proportions. (This is to this, as that is to that.) In a calculus of analogic one does not add, one associates; one does not divide, one partitions; one does not multiply, one overlays; one does not subtract, one discards. If the unit of attention in analogic is an image, than analogic calculus is a calculus of imagination. By the time I reached this formulation, I had already opened myself to an alternate way of knowing, and enriched my way of learning. This byproduct of the Center year, it occurred to me, provided a key to a more effective use of my professional self in teaching. Concurrently, it directed me to reexamine the role of style, which gives practice its attractions.

STYLE

Of all the attributes of skill, style alone asserts the individualities of the practitioner in a fashion that is both unmistakable and not easily compromised. In teaching, innovations are to be encouraged, as should the widest range of distinctive styles. But as with excesses in behavior and attributes, excesses of individual style that can destroy goals and objectives need to be curtailed. Style transmits the warmth and color of the human involvement in the teaching process. Still, the idiosyncratic elements of a teacher's styles need to be disciplined. Having to contend with student styles, administrative and institutional styles, professional styles, the prevalent cultural styles, the teacher must scrupulously control his or her personal style without sacrificing its unique and enhancing attributes.

Learning styles are of particular interest to the teacher. If, as in my case, the intent is to teach the student how to learn, the appreciation of distinctive styles is more than of particular interest. The task requires the student to identify and appreciate the potentials of his or her learning style. While operating in their individual styles, many graduate and doctoral students are not aware of the limitations of their learning style, and even less aware of how one comes to know it. Further, the teacher's style of learning necessarily exercises a major influence on behavior and attributes of students, and can be inhibiting for students whose styles are not similar to the teacher's.

As an initial step in describing my effort to help students know and appreciate their personal styles, style needs to be defined, so that its attributes can be appreciated. I defined style as a consistent arrangement and sequence of elements in a process that imparts to an action or product an unmistakable identity. Where styles are manifest more in action than in a product (as is true of teaching), the opportunity to hear or observe the style is curtailed. The same holds for student's learning styles. As Michael Polanyi (1958) observed, in the performance of a task, the worker focuses his or her attention on the application of prescribed guidelines to appropriate, timely, consistent, and uniform behavior. For example, a student may be peripherally aware of the seemingly irrelevant accompaniments of his or her task; but when these irrelevancies begin to command more of the student's attention, they often begin to distract his or her so much that his or her learning falters or stops entirely. When the student rearranges these distractions into some new order, they may compete for his or her attention with the prescribed guidelines and paralyze his or her learning. In positive circumstances, when the arrangement can be integrated with the associated prescribed behavior, an innovative learning results in learning that reflects a distinctive style (Goffman, 1961).

A student's efforts to mimic his or her teacher's style and the teacher's encouragement of students to enrich their individual styles both suggest assumptions about the nature and origin of styles that deserve more attention. Students behave as though styles can be acquired; teachers as though styles are given, perhaps at birth. Obviously, these are not either/or possibilities (Lomax, 1972). Whether styles have genetic or cultural origins is debatable, but it is sufficient to this discussion to note the influence of style on the formulation of a question and how time and analogical reasoning contribute to each learner's style.

THE USE OF PROFESSIONAL SELF

When I realized the relevance of style to the achievement of my educational goal—helping students to learn—I attempted a systematic explication of my style, for critical review by my doctoral seminar students. The students, of course, were hardly typical of all social work graduate students. Screening for doctoral study was severe, with self-selection reducing eligible applicants to a small cohort, and then selecting less than a third of these for admission. All were already experienced professionals. They included agency executives, faculty of schools of social work, program supervisors and in-service staff training managers among others. I shared with them my intent to start where they "were not," my deliberate use of analogies from the sciences, art, and humanities, and the likelihood that I would go off on tangents if I thought it useful, or if a student's interest suggested such side trips. I suggested they keep in mind that while what I say may at times seem crazy, the question is: Is it crazy enough to be true? Given my tendency to let my enthusiasm take over, and my unhappy tendency to talk too much, I encouraged students to interrupt my presentations at any time they had something they felt should be considered.

I quickly learned how limited was the utility of this approach, to the purposes I had in mind. These experienced students were, with occasional exceptions, unwilling to interrupt, unwilling to be critical and with rare exception, most concerned about their difficulty in following course material. They started from where they were, even if I didn't, and they quickly arrived at the point of asking each other—what is "he" talking about?

For example, in the first session in a course in epistemology, I might ask some upsetting questions and conclude with a written assignment for next session. The questions could not be answered with a "yes" or "no" response. Examples of such questions are illustrative: Is there a distinct body of social work knowledge, or is social work the application of knowledge derived from the academic disciplines and the human service professions? If the answer was the former, how would you recognize such knowledge? If the latter, then how should one select such borrowed knowledge? Finally, how would one justify a doctorate in social work, if there was no distinct body of social work knowledge? Of course, the class would split on these questions allowing me to ask, "If there were such a thing as social work knowledge, analogous to psychological, psychiatric, anthropological knowledge, what form would it take?"

Thus, at the outset, I tried to establish the character of the seminar. Questions posed would not be readily answered and, if confronted, would require classifications that utilized analogs. They were not answerable by logical and dialect reasoning alone, nor by appeals to experience or history. The written assignment might ask them to read a chapter in the text on the nature of work, and attempt their own original conceptualization of the characteristics of intellectual work. Not unexpectedly, my proposal for alternative analogs to conceptualize a "body of knowledge" and "work" further complicated what could be accepted as answers to the original question and assignment.

After three class sessions along these lines, one could sense the revolt brewing in the class. Students were arranging appointments to see me individually to discuss the difficulty they were having in doing assignments, in following class discussions, and in understanding sections of assigned readings. Concurrently, students were forming small support groups, going over class notes, and debating issues posed by class discussion and reading. As Machlup hypothesized in the passage quoted earlier, since the students did not comprehend what the instructor taught, they spent more time on reading and homework assignments.

But the real test of this style of instruction was the nature of the students' request for help. They were willing to risk expressing their confusions and frustrations, and they were open to consider alternate ways of looking at and thinking about the course content. This process, in time, challenged the teacher to respond constructively to their requests. The teacher's style and use of self had to model the behavior expected of the students. With rare exception, this involved the teacher in risking alternatives that encapsulated the student's interest, while respecting the strengths in knowledge of subject and experience in practice that they brought with their request for help. Without exception, these one-to-one sessions would broaden the scope of the student's declared interest, while concurrently sustaining the tension that accompanies doubt.

With student permission, I would bring the substance of such private sessions to class for discussion. The class would readily identify with the student's difficulties, and with my own inability to resolve them. The wider context on which this illustrative class session was located—that is, the full caseload of the doctoral student—also entered into the plan for this way of beginning my course. To "do," one maximizes certainty and minimizes doubt. To "know," one maximizes doubt and minimizes certainty. Most of these students were oriented to the doing in practice—that is, not oriented to knowing and living with uncertainty and doubt. In this respect, starting where the student was not, readily instilled the doubt, with its initial paralyzing effect, that all scholars learn to live with when pursuing a subject to the edge of its certainties.

THE ROLE OF THE ILLUSTRATIVE CASES

Three decades of teaching have taught me to be aware of the cutting edge issues confronting the practitioner in order to be helpful to my students. I would never want to teach at the doctoral level in a subject area in which I was not concurrently a practitioner, involved in research and scholarly work. But from the perspective of my teaching style, and my use of professional self, this requirement is a minimal one. In addition, I rely heavily on illustrative material in the sciences, arts, and humanities for the analogs I cite in class. Given my goals in teaching, having in reserve analogs that serve a heuristic function, not directly drawn from social work practice, enriches the imagery that provides the content for analogic calculus. Moreover, drawing on the disciplines and allied professions for analogs increases the probabilities of connecting with the subsidiary interests of students, and their analogs.

CONCLUSION

My key points are as follows:

1. The use-of-self in teaching can be graded by levels. The professional use of self is the most demanding of the four levels.
2. The unique self of the teacher is most clearly manifest in his or her style.
3. Analogical reasoning, with its reliance on imagery, enhances the richness of the unique style of the teacher.
4. How the teacher formulates questions, solves problems, and uses time, contributes significantly to the unique message his or her style conveys.
5. There is a process, by no means straightforward, whereby the teacher's distinctive style, promoted by a disciplined use of professional self, is revealed to students.
6. The teacher's style conveys the attractions of his or her skill. These include such elements as principled behavior, commitments, empathy, tolerance, etc.—elements that are often viewed as what is "caught" in a rich learning experience.

It is worth noting that despite the consistency of course title and outline, like most teachers, I have never taught the same course twice. Responding to variables in student characteristics, in their interests, in the environment of practice and the profession, as well as in my own understanding, the content necessarily must change. What remains relatively stable is my style, and it is to the style as much as the content that students make reference when they say, with some trepidation, "I'm taking the Dean's seminar."

BIBLIOGRAPHY

Ackerman, J. E. (1969). Two styles: A challenge to higher education. *Daedalus 98*(3), 855–869.

Bandura, A. (1978, April). The self system in reciprocal determinism. *American Psychologist*, 344–354.

Goffman, E. (1961). *Encounters*. Indianapolis: Bobbs-Merrill.

Lewis, H. (1959). The place of the research project in the master's curriculum, in Selected papers in methods of teaching research in the social work curriculum. *Journal of Social Work Education*, 10–18.

Lewis, H. (1960). Students' use of time in completing master's degree research projects. Unpublished paper, Philadelphia, PA.

Lewis, H. (1961). The significance for social work education of the student's approach to the formulation of a research question. *CSWE Bi-Monthly News*, special supplement 9(2).

Lichtenberg, P. (1983). Alternative strategies for a critical pedagogy, paper presented at the Annual Program Meeting of the Council on Social Work Education, Fort Worth, Texas.

Lomax, A. (1972). The evolution of culture and expressive style: A comparative approach

to social change. In G. V. Coelho and E. A. Rubenstein (Ed.), *Social change and human behavior*. Bethesda, MD: National Institutie of Mental Health, 41–67.
Machlup, F. (1979). Poor learning from good teachers. *ACADEME 65*.
Polanyi, M. (1958). *Personal knowledge*. Chicago: University of Chicago Press.
Rokeach, M. (1973). *The nature of human values*. New York: Free Press.
Rosenthal, W. (n.d.). Awareness, conscious use of self, professional self-identities: Implications for education. Unpublished paper, New York, NY.

The references used by Rosenthal include:
Dewey, J. (1958). *Art as experience*. New York: Capricorn Books, G.P. Putnam & Sons.
Hamilton, G. (1954). Self-awareness in professional education, in *Developing self-awareness*. New York: Family Service Association.
Reynolds, B. C. (1937, April). The development of a professional self. *The Family 18*, 61–66.
Robinson, V. P. (1949). *The dynamics of supervision under functional controls*. Philadelphia: University of Pennsylvania Press.
Rogers, C. R. (1958, April). A process conception of psychotherapy. *The American Psychologist*, 141–149.

Chapter 23

A Framework for Forecasting in Social Work Education

Toward the end of his career, Lewis looked to the past to seek clues as to the possible futures of social work practice and education. In this essay, he critiques the usual methods of forecasting, which are based on linear projections of current problems and trends. He proposes in their place a more dynamic and dialectical approach that takes into account the uneven development of forces in society and the profession.

Theory has the power to explain and predict. Its strengths are greatest when it can do both. Between the two, I would judge the ability to explain more significant in evaluating a theory than the accuracy of its predictions. Most efforts to anticipate the future do not rely on predictions. There is general recognition that, at their best, predictions are more useful in helping us to anticipate a future we may want to avoid. They rarely provide guidance in the choice of actions to be followed in order to achieve a future we would prefer. Relying on predicting is a risky business, even if accurate anticipation of a fact previously unknown can be intellectually gratifying. Forecasting the future on the basis of theory that successfully accounts for facts already known may be more demanding, but also more fruitful. Projecting from known facts the nature of which can be explained is most useful for action. This is particularly true when the theory accounts for the processes that are likely to influence our opportunities and abilities to create the future we would prefer.

In this presentation, trends affecting professional education and practice, known to be true, will provide the substantive basis on which projections will rest. This process of forecasting has been described as the process of predicting a variable from itself. It differs from prediction that seeks to anticipate an unknown fact, preferring to extend the current curve into the future. An illustrative case will be cited. It offers explanations that derive from existing trends. It focuses on problems addressed, programs implemented, and interventions developed. The influence of these trends in social work education and practice will be noted. Finally,

Presented at the annual doctoral convocation, Wurzweiler School of Social Work, New York, May 4, 1990.

I will suggest propositions that can guide the process whereby large-scale, slow changes in professional education and practice can be achieved.

In 1978, NASW established a Commission on Professional Futures, chaired by Bertram Beck. The Commission employed a set of four scenarios to explore uncertainties, including what the profession and professionals would do if events described in the scenarios were actually to occur. In the decade since the Commission reported its findings, the profession has had an opportunity to check the scenarios against the real-life drama, including the profession's responses to the actual happenings. Granted the nonpredictive nature of this forecasting method, and the tendency toward extremes in scenario expectations that accompany this method, certain cautions expressed by participants in the Commission should be noted.

First, regardless of which scenario evolved, the profession's responses should avoid self-serving actions that divert the profession from its social mission. Second, the profession should avoid a narrow perspective, one that blinds it to the broader societal developments influencing its ability to fulfill its mission. Despite its disclaimer, the Commission's method directed it to evaluate predictions of professional responses, and was most helpful in suggesting futures to be avoided. To the best of my knowledge, no systematic review of the Commission's findings in light of actual developments in the decade since they were reported, has appeared in our literature. On the other hand, during this decade efforts to forecast the profession's future—in relation to problems, programs, and processes, have proliferated.

Most efforts to forecast the social problems to be addressed by the profession for a decade or more ahead assume current problems as the basis for projections into the future. An inventory of chronic conditions likely to generate a demand for social work interventions typically include deficiencies in health care, housing, education, income, personal services, and the justice system. The need for preventive as well as corrective interventions are noted and demographic data are employed to anticipate the likely scope and intensity of the problems these conditions generate. With rare exceptions, these forecasts foresee a shortage of professionally educated social workers, assuming that qualified personnel are expected to meet the demands for skills needed to solve the problems identified.

Priorities proposed for the allocation of resources to deal with these problems vary, reflecting the peculiar history of each problem and demography of the communities and constituencies affected. Most often, it is assumed that current relationships among community power groups will be sustained into the future. Deviations from this assumption may be anticipated, but such changes are likely to be the result of a major breakthrough in effective interventions, a radical change in population characteristics, a natural or manufactured disaster, etc.—in short, an overwhelming nonsystemic intrusion that alters the relationship of forces within the system.

The problem-based forecast tends to be cautious in nature, minimizing risky assumptions and maximizing the influence of relative certainties in the trends projected. It invites a problem-solving approach to intervention, but does not give sufficient weight to the fact that such interventions deal with problems, but rarely, if ever, solve them. Nor does this problem-based forecast overcome the reductionist tendencies in this approach—i.e., viewing trends separately, seeking to assemble a whole from the sum of these parts. As we know too well, people and organizations have a variety of problems, but are more than the sum of such parts. A forecasting approach that rests on our ability to identify the critical problems to be addressed must assume a basis for identifying such problems, and a basis for measuring the variables central to the development of these problems. Unhappily, most such forecasts lack the information needed to make such measurements, and all lack a theoretical grounding that is capable of explaining the process whereby the anticipation of the future will be realized.

Most efforts at forecasting social work's future assume a homeostatic equilibrium, with current patterns representing a fairly steady state; deviations are accounted for by wider systems intrusions. Thus, it is assumed that existing problems, interventions, and programs will persist. These often unstated assumptions are frequently accompanied by a heavy dosage of change rhetoric. Anticipations are presented as to what should or ought to be, not what will be. There is little expectation that it will be possible to alter the existing balance of forces. It is generally assumed that our nation will continue to develop as a private enterprise, highly industrialized, individualistic, and commercialized economy. It will also continue as a pluralistic, democratic state. Most problem-oriented forecasts anticipate the persistence of a modified welfare state, with voluntary, commercial as well as state-provided social services. Social conditions are expected to generate an excess of problems and demand for services. These are fairly safe assumptions for short-range forecasts. They do not require a theoretical frame. They are strong on descriptions and weak on explanations.

A frame that builds on a theoretical base and aims to utilize existing facts to explain must also assume a relationship between broader societal conditions, the problems they generate and concurrent developments in the profession. In the approach to be presented in this essay, an uneven development in different spheres of our society (economic, political, personal, scientific, and aesthetic) is also assumed. It does not assume a linear, gradualistic perspective, with changes in different spheres simply serving to maintain an existing homeostatic balance. Within the profession, it assumes interpenetration of cause and function. The tension between the two, societal reforms and service delivery, generates a change process that accounts for changes in the profession itself, and in its interaction with wider societal forces. It hypothesizes a major role for the profession in shaping its own future. This theoretical frame poses the following explanatory propositions:

1. *In periods of reaction (unraveling social reforms) the profession retreats from reform, focusing its energies on function and process. In periods of conservatism or liberalism, the profession focuses on problems while expanding or sustaining modes of intervention. In periods of radicalism, the profession focuses on program innovations linked to efforts at social reform and prevention.*

This proposition recognizes the presence of three foci at any one time: process, problem, and program. Moreover, it assumes that reactionary, conservative, liberal, and radical developments in the wider societal context do not impact on all five spheres of a civilized society concurrently.

2. *It is rare for all spheres of a society (i.e., economic, political, aesthetic, personal, scientific) to concurrently experience similar changes.*

This proposition suggests an uneven development in spheres of civilization in any society. Thus it implies that no one characterization is sufficient to cover all developments in a society at any one period, or for all fields of social work practice.

3. *Forecasting is likely to be more useful when it distinguishes developments on the basis of factors specifically relevant to each sphere of civilization. Anticipation should normally yield a changing pattern over time, rather than a linear extension into the future.*

This proposition assumes a changing mosaic in social development, resulting from the uneven developments in each sphere of civilization. It expects at any one time, that focus on process, problems and programs will vary by sphere, and that the tension of cause and function will vary accordingly in each field of service.

4. *In any society one or more spheres will dominate the decision-making processes, influencing the developments of the others. It accepts an isomorphic relationship between spheres. This tendency, in turn, will shape the developments of the profession as well.*

This proposition, for example, recognizes the dominance of the economic and political in our nation. The developments in the scientific, aesthetic, and personal spheres reflect in their development the dominance of these two spheres. Within the profession, emphasis on cost and responses to political pressures have a dominating influence on problem definition, program innovation, and method of intervention. In the profession these influences affect the personal interests of provider and recipient of service, the style of work, and the research/scholarly activities and products—the knowledge base of professional work.

These propositions, taken together, provide a theoretical frame. They guide forecasting efforts by suggesting evaluations of each concentration (societal spheres) as distinctive units. It directs attention to the dialectic of cause and function in each sector, and how social reform and service provision interact to fuel changes that can be anticipated. It also promotes a more significant role for the profession in determining its own future, indicating priorities in resource allocation in light of the dominance of spheres in the wider context. It also considers the dominance of process or problem or program in the social services.

It is apparent from the preceding that retrodicting—that is, anticipating the past (causation) links explanations based on current facts to plausible origins. The variable time is readily rearranged, as are the wider societal influences. The limitation of such explanations is obvious: It is difficult to disprove such explanations because manipulation of variables can readily modify the causal chain to fit the explanation within the theoretical frame. It is also apparent that anticipating the present—i.e., classification—is likewise based on current fact, but produces descriptions rather than explanations. Meanings are largely dependent on analogical formulations, and suffer the risks attendant on the use of analogies.

Both anticipations of past and present vary in their power to explain, dependent upon which of the three foci (programs, problems, and process) provide the fact base for the explanation. Programs are most readily specified and documented; problems are more difficult to differentiate and involve arbitrary assignment of boundaries; process (i.e., methods of intervention) are least likely to provide specifiable time lines, are more dependent on knowledge innovations than self-evolving development. These same limitations are present in forecasting—i.e., anticipation of future facts—particularly those predictions that do not depend on explanations of current known facts. For this reason, focusing on programs, then problems, and lastly processes is most likely to produce forecasts that also include explanations.

The propositions proposed are intended to provide a minimal statement of a theoretical frame for forecasting developments in social work practice and education in the next decade. In assigning a major role to internal driving forces that are more amenable to the profession's own pressures for change, the theory rejects the homeostatic perspective. The influence of external forces, well beyond the reach of professional control, is recognized and appreciated, but is assigned a minor role in the change process, controlled by the actors and agency in the practice drama. Based on the guidance offered by the propositions, a plan of action that can achieve desired changes in professional practice should include the following:

1. The parties affected by professional actions and attitudes should be included in developing a plan for action and a specification of purpose.
2. In the field, programs engaged in implementing the delivery of social work services should play a central role in developing plans for future programs. These should include innovative approaches as well as suggestions for terminating existing, no longer functional, programs.
3. Community as well as professional interest groups should play a major role in identifying target problems and populations to be addressed in plans for future developments. These plans should include problems in the delivery of services.
4. Professionals, including those in allied professions, should have a major role in planning for the modification, enrichment, and innovation of methods of intervention.
5. 1 to 4 in the preceding above should be applied in each of the spheres of societal needs encompassing fields of social work practice—e.g., the justice system; the world of work and income support; personal services (family, children, adult); the arts; education (formal and informal); and community development. The field of social health concerned with survival needs including physical and mental health, safety and shelter, is to be governed by the same guidelines (1–5).

Within each practice arena, the tension of cause and function will provide the dynamic for change. Priorities will be negotiated and, if imposed, are likely to be unenforceable in practice. Uneven emphasis on cause and function can be anticipated, given the uneven development of each sphere in the society as a whole, and in the history of the profession. The overall "plan," which will in effect be a coordination of the plans of each field of practice, evolves from this planning process. The "plan" will specify expectations for the decade ahead, with the expectation that its utility will depend on the participant's motivations, capacities, and opportunities to carry out the work necessary to make it a reality. Given the process—a participatory democratic effort—it can be anticipated that subplans will change in time, thus altering the overall plan as goals are realized or fail to be achieved; thus, in this view, forecasting ceases to be a one-time effort. It requires periodic inputs from all participants, to remain a relevant depiction of the future directions of professional developments.

This somewhat detailed presentation of the broad outlines of a forecasting process, utilizing a theoretical frame, provides the rationale that served as justification for a forecasting process of one school of social work. The results of this process are contained in a report entitled "A Partnership in Caring." While the report serves as a benchmark for the initiating phase of the forecasting process, and offers considerable material for analysis, it remains a single illustration, with the limitations such illustrations normally evidence. The analytical part of the presentation, while more abstract, is more likely to serve the profession if subject to monitored application and critical review. A summary description of the illustrative case follows.

A BRIEF REVIEW OF THE ILLUSTRATIVE CASE PROCESS

Responding to the report of the Mayor's Commission on the Year 2000, "New York Ascendant," the Council of Advisors of the Hunter College School of Social Work proposed a convocation to examine how the school might assist in implementing the recommendation of the report. The Commission's Report was published at the same time the School was celebrating a substantial new addition to its physical plan. The Council invited representatives from the private sector, the public sector, and the nonprofit voluntary sector to discuss the report's implications for social service programs in social work education. Robert F. Wagner, Jr., Chairman of the Mayor's Commission, was invited to present the highlights of the report. The audience attending the Convocation included executives and lay leaders of social service programs, key public officials, leading professional social workers, social work educators, and representatives of important funding agencies.

Very early in planning for the Convocation it was decided to involve the School's faculty, Professional Advisory Committees, and social service agency representatives to assist in developing responses to the report for each field of social work practice. A senior faculty member, Professor Charles Guzzetta, accepted to oversee the processes whereby recommendations would be formulated. He monitored the preparation of the separate responses and prepared a coherent statement highlighting findings and recommendations. Funding to support this effort was, in part, provided by a grant from the New York Community Trust.

In addition to the diligent efforts of faculty and Advisory Committees, one hundred agencies were solicited by mail for their reactions to the report and for suggestions and recommendations. A series of breakfast meetings also sought agency views on the document. Each meeting focused on one field of practice, and each sought to involve agency lay leaders and executives. One breakfast meeting was directed toward middle management personnel and executives and included agencies in all fields of practice.

The final report resulting from the study process appeared in an attractive publication and one thousand copies were initially distributed to targeted populations. It quickly became obvious that the demand for the report would exceed our supply and five hundred additional copies had to be printed.

This brief summary of the activities involved in the Council of Advisors' effort to connect with the Commission's report presents the bare bones, not the substance, of what has transpired thus far. What follows is a listing of key aspects of the process, raising a number of questions about how a public School of Social Work can contribute to a broad community effort to improve the quality of life of its citizens.

1. The school's curricula structure organizes its programs using a value-based rubric: The common needs for health, security, justice, personal services, and knowledge justify fields of practice. Each field designates a concentration in the school's curriculum. Designed to respond to common human needs, there are concentrations in social health; world of work; protection and social justice; family, children, youth and adult development; and educational community development. The existence of the concentrations, each with its own professional advisory committee, consisting of social workers and allied professionals, facilitated a readily adaptable channel through which to pursue the "problems" that the Commission's report identified.
2. The existence of the Council of Advisors, consisting of lay participants with long experience on social service agency boards and representatives of different constituencies in the city, assured an interest in the work of the Wagner Commission and initiated the process of involvement in planning the convocation.
3. The close relationship of the school with some four hundred agencies in which its students are placed for field work practice provided access to a wide spectrum of community groups having a deep interest in the issues posed by the report and their implications for social work education.
4. With the Commission's report providing detailed data on major social problems and their likely development over the next decade, the Convocation was free of the need to assemble relevant facts. The intention of the Convocation

was to evolve a set of guidelines for action by the school, which would result in educational programs response to the problems identified.

5. The undergirding principle followed in the work involved was one familiar to social workers in practice and consistent with the philosophy of the social survey movement since the first Pittsburgh Survey conducted under auspices of the Russell Sage Foundation in 1907. The people/organization/communities likely to be affected by the recommendations of the Convocation should be actively engaged in the process whereby recommendations are arrived at.
6. The process followed, having been tested in this one instance, provides a model for periodic replication. Thus, ongoing evaluation of the implementation of recommendations, and periodic opportunities to update recommendations to reflect changes in fields of practice, are not only feasible, but such periodic efforts are to be viewed as a major recommendation of the Convocation.

The next phase of the forecasting process will include the formation of a Committee on Priorities to monitor the implementation of the objective noted in the blueprint. Provision for each concentration to select one or two projects to be pursued over a one- to two-year period will be made, as part of the priority choice effort.

Chapter 24

Some Thoughts on My 40 Years in Social Work Education

There are three striking things about this retrospective essay. One is the strength of Lewis's convictions about the role of social welfare in society—convictions he maintained for his entire professional career, regardless of the personal and professional consequences. Another is how Lewis was able to incorporate new ideas and new developments—in social work, society, and the world—into his conceptual frameworks without sacrificing his principles or core beliefs. Finally, the essay also reflects his measured optimism about the future because of, rather than in spite of, the harsh lessons of history.

Some forty years back, when I joined the full-time faculty, the Connecticut School of Social Work was still in its formative stage. My responsibility was to introduce a research sequence and community organization content into the curriculum. In that capacity, I served as a teacher and thesis advisor for research students in their second year. The thesis required the student to choose a research topic in September; prepare a proposal for faculty approval in October; conduct a trial run in December; and collect data after the Christmas break in January.

One student studied the program preference of senior citizens who were members of the Springfield, Massachusetts Jewish Community Center. In September, he chose his topic; in October, he received project approval; in November, he constructed his interviewing schedule, and, in December, he conducted his trial run on a selected group of elderly not included in his sample.

In January, he arrived in my office in tears. He was in shock and could hardly speak. It seems that most of his sample had left for Florida for the winter. The student had anticipated sample loss as a result of illness or death, given the ages of the population he was studying. But neither he nor I anticipated sample loss because of geographic mobility. Unhappily, the trial run, which should have enlightened us to this possibility, was conducted on a population matched for age, sex, and physical status, but not matched for cultural patterns, lifestyles, and economic status.

Speech given at the fortieth anniversary celebration of the University of Connecticut School of Social Work, November 11, 1989. Originally published in the *Journal of Progressive Human Services 3*(1), 1992.

I cite this happening to alert this audience to the fact that the history and perspective I will present is circumscribed by my own forty plus years in social work, and my own ideological bias. It could happen that these attributes, which I assume to be strengths, in fact may serve as blinders, causing me to miss the obvious. For this reason, I ask you to be critical of what I have to say, if only to identify where, in my wish to present certainties, I am guilty of selective oversight.

The following practice principle captures the essence of my presentation:

When one cannot control a social process, and decisions made by others determine its agendas and shape its development, one is most likely to achieve one's objectives by attending to the avoidable while managing the inevitable.

Put differently, our profession will achieve more by anticipating the future it wants to avoid than one it would prefer. In looking toward the future, projections rather than predictions are more likely to yield useful anticipations.

For those of us who have lived through more than two generations in social work, for whom the past is too long, the present too full, and the future too brief, such anticipations provide hindsight, insight, and foresight. Necessarily, we come to respect history, and the way we have used time, not always to good advantage. For the analysis that follows, I'll draw on the recent history of our profession, covering a period of time in which I have been actively involved in its policy making councils

THE IMPACT OF CONTEXT: THE COLD WAR

The principle I cited earlier suggests that forces outside professions influence their development. This is certainly true for social work.

Great hopes were short lived at the end of World War II, just when the Connecticut School of Social Work got underway. The United Nations came into being, based on the assumption that we had to choose between having one world, or none. At the same time, in a major shift in national policies and priorities, our country declared an end to peaceful cooperation with emerging socialist states. Instead, we began a prolonged Cold War with countries that chose to reject a free market economy. Lasting for over two score years, this Cold War has only recently showed signs of abating. The Cold War also managed to generate increased militarization of the economies of the major combatants. While the major combatants in this war also became the major producers of armaments, both sides learned the hard way that no economic system can long assure to all its citizens both guns and butter. The Third World countries, many just emerging from colony status, choose sides in this war of economies, but as the Cold War decades have shown, they suffered most.

During the Cold War period, forces well beyond the reach and control of our profession set the tone and direction of national policy and limited the options of the profession and its schools. Nevertheless, the need for social services increased, creating a demand for more social work schools to staff the growing number of service programs with trained practitioners. As they developed new programs, they provided and organized services that the constraints of the wider scene allowed. These were not necessarily the programs that the profession, in another context, would have chosen. One of the most disturbing features of the Cold War at home was its confirmation of the negative attributes of a free-market economy. Unhappily, under market controlled distribution mechanisms, the disadvantaged were further disadvantaged during the post-World War II years. Even now, as we move, however reluctantly, to end the Cold War and to demilitarize our economy, the gap between rich and poor continues to widen. Likewise, the collective and centrally planned economy of the Soviet Union also found that it could not sustain both guns and butter without exacting a terrible price from its own people.

One of the profession's first casualties in the Cold War period was social group work. This was a serious loss, since this method of social work was the most democratic in the profession. The core concept of group work and the goal of its major proponents was participatory democracy. Not unexpectedly, as the agencies that employed group workers found their resources increasingly in short supply, this part of the method was an early victim of cut-back management. What survived was the method's narrower function, therapeutic aid. In many schools the social group work method was submerged within casework curricula, becoming part of the clinical or micro method sequence.

MORAL RIGHTS AND PATERNALISM

In the Cold War period the ideologists who shaped social policy rejected the view that government has a moral responsibility to meet people's basic sustenance needs. Instead, these policy makers decided that the private sector, operating in a "free market," was the best provider. Interference in the lives of citizens by government could only be justified on paternalistic grounds, and such paternalism was the proper province of nongovernment services. But only the deserving should be assisted by these individuals and organizations. Those whose incomes fell below a minimum standard should be judged undeserving, unless it could be demonstrated that their plight was the result of market inefficiencies. In such cases government should step in when all other means prove insufficient. This retreat to Victorian paternalism justified reactionary social policies. During most of this period the profession struggled to expose manipulations of information, the false claims, distortions of fact, and outright lies that characterized the rationale for these policies.

Manipulation became an issue within the profession as well. Some practitioners, reacting to the unfair outcomes they perceived as emanating from inadequate resource provision, supported the use of manipulation in professional practice. It was argued that withholding information, exaggerating, distorting, or outright lying could be acceptable when the results advanced a client's, an agency's, or the profession's interests, or a social cause in which the manipulator believed. In effect manipulations" used to justify cuts in services for the "country's own good" prompted some to advocate manipulations for the "client's own good." And so the wider scene achieved an ideological coup by generating in those opposed to its destructive practices, the mimicking of its unethical methods. Manipulations are usually successful where the manipulators have power over those being manipulated. In advocating manipulation by social workers who lacked real power, short-term gains sacrificed the client's long-term interests and the client's long-term trust of the worker. Those who rejected manipulation under any circumstance did so based on the ethical principle that people should be treated as ends, not means. Nevertheless, the issue of manipulation remains a contentious issue in our profession.

HUMANE ALTERNATIVES

The Cold War period contained the constant threat of nuclear annihilation. It seemed very real for the generation that lived through the Korean and Vietnam Wars. But threats to life often generate counter forces seeking more humane alternatives. In our country, the threat of nuclear destruction was countered by the struggles against poverty, racism, sexism, homophobia, and war, and for a more just and secure society. The welfare rights, civil rights, women's liberation, gay-lesbian rights, and the antiwar movements, all sought a more caring, less threatening future, one that could not be achieved so long as the Cold War and a militarized economy dominated national social policy.

The profession and its schools responded to these counter movements in many ways—in direct political action, curriculum innovations, and seeking to overcome within their own organizations the conditions these movements sought to correct. But the profession also turned inward for self-preservation. Protecting its turf became a dominant concern, as challenges to its claims of effectiveness, from within and without, threatened its standards and community sponsorship.

At the time the Connecticut School came into being the national struggle to end discrimination based on race and ethnicity was already underway. In my experience in Nebraska, just prior to joining the Connecticut faculty, we, the professional association of social workers, helped open up access to social services for Black families. We helped to integrate public pools, the symphony, and recreational facilities; and provided opportunity for Blacks to teach in the university. At the Connecticut School the curriculum on the origins of social service programs was changed to include the history of self-help movements among our country's racial and ethnic groups as well as the more typical white, Protestant, North European programs. Yet, my own personal experience in Nebraska and in Connecticut shows that the introduction of such content was often challenged by those who considered the issues it raised to be divisive and irrelevant.

LEARNING FROM THE PAST

The future is often telegraphed to us in subliminal tendencies adorning the present. Hindsight now confirms that the movements of the 1950s and 1960s and the reactions to them in the late 1970s and 1980s were foretold for those who could understand the hints provided in the late 1940s and early 1950s. For example, in the late 1940s, Henry Wallace's proposition that full employment be a national social policy priority was roundly rejected by the electorate as utopian. This should have prepared us for the continued acceptance of poverty as an attribute of our national economy. The decision, in this period, not to pursue the Ewing Report, which called for a National Health Service program, should have prepared us for the rising cost of health care and the uncovered, uninsured millions. The Korean War should have alerted us to the further expansion of military expenditures. After all, they had fueled the recovery from the depression of the 1930s and apparently would continue to absorb federal tax monies to stabilize a "free market" economy. The postwar expansion of psychiatric services, enriched by World War II experience with trauma and mental breakdown under stress, should have prepared us for an emphasis on the troubled individual psyche, focusing on illness and treatment in professional interventions. The migration of Southern Blacks into northern and western urban areas, the large scale entry of women into the labor market, the role of geographic mobility in undermining family and community support networks, and the dramatic increase in the elderly, all should and did alert us to the emergence of new social needs. But we did not calculate correctly what resources, including skilled personnel, would be needed to serve them.

THE PROFESSIONAL CADRE

The period witnessed a dramatic growth in the number of BSW, MSW, and DSW programs. But this expansion did not always generate more agency-based social workers. Not only were the resources needed to pay for skilled workers and support services unavailable, but professionally trained personnel found agency-based work demands overwhelming, offering limited opportunity to utilize skills stressed in their training, and many constraints on autonomous work. The growing interest in private entrepreneurship, and the competition for government contracts by newly organized for-profit programs, forced many non-profits to enter the for-profit arena. This entrepreneurial atmosphere favors the private marketing of professional skills and directs some of our most talented graduates into private practice. Thus, the current complaint of non-profit and public agencies: that schools are gearing their curricula to the needs of autonomous practitioners and, in so doing, are directing graduates away from agency-based practice.

LOOKING AHEAD

This brings me to the present. What hints are evident in current developments that provide foresight and guidance for future planning? One school, looking to the future of social work and social work education, noted the following recurring themes in current budget and policy decisions (Sarri, Vinter, & Steker, 1988):

1. Resolve the problems of poverty.
2. Strengthen family life.
3. Reduce welfare dependency.
4. Increase access to health care by the poor.
5. Promote full employment and higher wages.
6. Meet the needs of children, especially those in poverty.
7. Increase the capacity of states, local governments, and the private sector to provide for the welfare needs of the poor with corresponding reduction in federal responsibility (to which we must add provide housing for low-income families and caring services for persons with AIDS-HIV).

Other schools, contemplating the year 2000, cite similar themes as likely to set their future agendas. Unhappily, there is far less agreement on how the profession should respond to these themes. Differences reflect the peculiar histories, professional philosophies, surrounding environment, available resources, and candidate pools, all of which influence what the profession can do to affect the issues raised by these themes.

Taking a different tack, a social work scholar trying to forecast the future focused on other themes and their manifestations (Meyer, 1988): professional values, the role of organizations, funding sources, social work education, research, and the development of practice theory. These themes focus on social work as an institution rather than on the social problems the profession addresses in its practice. They force us to consider the lack of a coherent and comprehensible practice; the pull of private practice; and the need for skilled agency-based practitioners to serve the most disadvantaged. They also raise questions about differences between BSW, MSW, DSW degrees "in the professional scheme of things;" the tendency of professionals to see their employing agencies as enemies that batter them with impossible caseloads; inadequate pay; lack of professional autonomy leading to emotional, physical, and intellectual burnout; funding difficulties; and demands for accountability. Other issues relevant to social work include the gatekeeper function of social work education; the role of schools in shaping practice; the limits of current research question and methods; and the eclectic repertoire of practice theories in any scenario of social work's future.

THE PRACTICE DRAMA

Both the social problems and the social work institution approach anticipate concerns of the profession by projecting from the present. But neither offers a rationale for understanding the changes they anticipate. For myself, I prefer to use a model of change over time taken from the performing arts (Burke, 1945). I conceive of the future as a result of enacting an impromptu drama. This drama creates its own script as it is enacted. The actors include professional workers, service recipients, and those who provide needed resources. The action occurs as these actors relate to one another over time. The scene of this drama is the cultural, political, economic and societal context. The agency serves as the stage setting. The purpose of the drama assures a value base and ethical component in whatever actions evolve.

This artistic analog allows for the creative and anticipates the unexpected. Moreover, it offers the opportunity to consider issues from a variety of philosophical perspectives. The actors bring the perspective of idealism; the action realism; the agency pragmatism; the scene materialism; the purpose mysticism; and the unraveling present phenomenalism. It allows "many flowers to bloom," many views of the future to be embedded in each moment of the present. Necessarily, the themes suggested by this model do not differ from those noted earlier. They are responses to the same contextual and practice issues.

The actors seek a future that is ideal. The worker would like competent practice to be supported by ample financial and community resource. The clientele would like an effective service targeted to meet their needs. The resource providers would like a proficient and well-managed operation assuring maximum return for minimal investment. This utopian perception is best viewed in poetic terms: "man's (sic) reach should exceeded his grasp, or what is a heaven for?"

Given the choice, the actors would elect a standard for practice that represented the best of what our present knowledge and resource permits. Action seeks to achieve the best of what is possible, that is standards from practice. The action perspective draws attention to the possible, given the resource constraints that govern practice. Realistic appraisals may dampen the expectations of the actors, but they also make action more likely. The agency concerns itself with what works, given the limits of its resources. Pragmatic evaluation shape its preferences: it opts for standards of practice—only occasionally managing standards from practice, and almost never standards for practice.

The initial part of this talk dealt with the scene and the mission. Now, I'll focus on the actors, action, and agency, and see what futures their present states portend. In short, I'll guess at what their script will look like after they have enacted this drama.

The major theme of the service drama during the past decade has been distributive justice. During this period ethics has dominated the value component of our profession, in no small measure because of the lack of ethics that characterized our nation's political and economic scene. As the militarized priority demands resulted in cuts in social programs, aggravating social problems, ethics has served as a code word for social responsibility. In the ethics frame, equity became the reformist focus taking precedence over equality. In this debate, treating equals equally and unequals unequally, served to identify the progressive forces favoring the affirmative action advocated by the welfare rights, civil rights, women's, and gay–lesbian movements. But—concern for distributive justice—always in the background of this debate, could not be attained in a militarized or free-market economy. These inequities are most dramatically present in health care, with multimillions having no health coverage; and in housing, with multithousands homeless, unable to afford to rent space. Although the effects of these inequities have been intolerable, it appears that they will not be modified by appeals to rational self-interest or responsible social concern. As the past forty years have shown, under current policies the rich get richer and the poor pay more. What is needed is more radical changes in the allocation of resources, including tax-supported government intervention at all levels, to compensate for the flaws in our political economy. National health programs and national housing programs are likely to occupy the agendas of all future efforts to achieve distributive justice. Without distributive justice, the caring role of our profession will continue to be sabotaged by overwhelming deprivations; our methods will be further focused on the narrower interventive interactions seeking remedies rather than prevention. Given this scene, the actors in the service drama will have to join various coalitions whose self-interest in equity press them to struggle for political and economic reform. Working to empower clients and as advocates for client needs, although necessary, will not suffice, if the goal of distributive justice is to be realized.

In the current scene, not-for-profit agencies operating on the basis of philanthropic motivation, find themselves increasing dependent on publicly funded contracts to assure their own survival. Moreover, as for-profit corporations have entered the market to compete for such contracts, the not-for-profits have moved to initiate subsidiary for-profit programs under agency sponsorship. The more forward profit-based practice has furthered the tendency to cream the eligible population and to shift the difficult, expensive cases—usually the poverty-stricken—to public programs. If this development is not resisted in the decade ahead, it can only result in a two-class system of service, with the poor receiving the poorest or no services at all.

The motivation to provide social services on grounds of common decency and concern for our fellow human beings, has long been the special pride of our American way of life. In this perspective, people are ends in themselves and equity is an entitlement that gives our society its special claim as an example of a caring people. When profit is the end and people's needs the means for achieving this end, serious problems result when those who need service can't pay for it. Our philanthropic tradition has always served to provide some corrective support for those who are the inevitable victims of the market. Thus, the survival of the non-profit agency, and its continued functioning as a vital part of our general welfare structure, is a matter of great concern. In alliance with progressively oriented political and economic groups, this sector of our economy needs our support. It must be sustained, and not driven out of the welfare scene by for-profits, whose resources are such as to enable them to exercise increasing influence over the public sector.

Having considered the scene, actors, agency, and mission, I'll conclude with some observation about the action, necessarily focusing on the future of methods in the coming decade. Should the Cold War actually come to an end and allocation of resources shift to favor butter over guns, the theme that will dominate the next half century will be respect—respect for the dignity of persons and the differences among peoples. The current demand for recognition of difference is apparent internationally in the upsurge of nationalism and, at home, in the increased promotion of cultural pluralism among our minority populations. The action of these groups make it clear that distributive justice is a necessary part, but not the whole of social justice. In addition, there is an increasing demand for an appreciation of the unique components of different cultures, in all aspects of communal life. Inherent in this development is the expectation of service recipients that those who provide help will respect and appreciate these cultural differences in the manner in which service is rendered. In both theory and practice methods of helping will inevitably have to reflect the enriching effects of this perspective. Doing to, having yielded its authoritarian stance to doing for, the paternalistic alternative, will hopefully move to doing with, in a client-centered practice.

Should it occur, this change would result in a more holistic, broad-based approach to method, with social cause embedded in function. It would emphasize the positive elements in ethnic and cultural diversity. It would also highlight the ethical component in each practice encounter, bringing to a conscious level the value preference inherent in a helping relationship. Skill will come to include sensitivity to ethical choices and dilemmas, and ability to assess the needs of recipients in light of values as well as knowledge.

The last forty years for the Connecticut School, the profession, and myself, have been prologue. Despite some bright spots, these years have been darkened by clouds of threatened war and nuclear extinction. They also have been years in which the struggle to achieve distributive justice witnessed major breakthroughs. I anticipate a future that is far more promising, in which conflicts will be resolved without the threat of war, with considerable rivalry between the so-called free market and relatively planned economies, with increased recognition that issues of distributive justice can only be resolved within the wider framework of social justice. While my anticipations are few indeed, regarding our profession's development, I do expect our interventions will become increasingly client-centered, culturally enriched, and ethically relevant and, for these reasons, more effective.

BIBLIOGRAPHY

Burke, K. (1945). *A grammar of motives*. Berkeley: University of California Press.

Meyer, C. (1988). Trends and issues in direct social work practice, in *Social Work Futures*, M. Dinerman, ed. New Brunswick, NJ: Rutgers University School of Social Work, 225–236.

Sarri, R. C., Vinter, R., and Steker, M. (1988, March). *The future of social work and social work education*. Ann Arbor: University of Michigan School of Social Work.

Permissions

The following articles were previously published. Every effort has been made to contact copyright holders of the articles reproduced in this book. If any have been inadvertently overlooked, the publishers will be pleased to make restitution at the earliest opportunity.

"The Cause in Function," Winter 1977, *Journal of the Otto Rank Association* (12). Published by the Otto Rank Society in Doylestown, PA.

"Reasoning in Practice," November 1975, *Smith College Studies in Social Work 46*(1): 3–15. Reprinted by special permission of Gerald Schamess, Editor, *Smith College Studies in Social Work.*

"The Battered Helper," April 1980, *Child Welfare 59*(4): 195–201. Reprinted by special permission of the Child Welfare League of America, Washington, DC. http://www.cwla.org

"Management in the Nonprofit Social Service Organization," 1975, *Child Welfare 54*(9): 615–623. Reprinted by special permission of the Child Welfare League of America, Washington, DC. http://www.cwla.org

"Ethical Assessment," April 1984, *Social Casework* 65(4): 203–211. © *Families in Society: The Journal of Contemporary Human Services.* Reprinted by permission of Family Service of America, Milwaukee, WI.

"The Whistleblower and the Whistleblowing Profession," Winter 1985, *Journal of Clinical Social Work with Children.*

"Teaching Ethics Through Ethical Teaching," 1987, *Journal of Teaching in Social Work* 1(1): 3-14. Reprinted by permission of The Haworth Press, Binghamton, NY.

"Ethics and the Private, Nonprofit Human Services Organization," 1989, *Administration in Social Work 13*(2): 1–14. Reprinted by permission of The Haworth Press, Binghamton, NY.

"Morality and the Politics of Practice," July 1972, *Social Casework 53*(7): 404–417. © *Families in Society: The Journal of Contemporary Human Services.* Reprinted by permission of Family Service of America, Milwaukee, WI.

"Are the Traditional Curriculum Areas Relevant?" 1981, *Journal of Education for Social Work 17*(1): 73–80. © Council on Social Work Education. Reprinted by permission of the Council on Social Work Education, Alexandria, VA.

"Teacher's Style and the Use of Professional Self in Social Work Education," 1991, *Journal of Teaching in Social Work 5*(2): 17–29. Reprinted by permission of The Haworth Press, Binghamton, NY.

"Some Thoughts on My Forty Years in Social Work Education," 1992, *Journal of Progressive Human Services 3*(1): 39–51. Reprinted by permission of The Haworth Press, Binghamton, NY.

Index

For Product Safety Concerns and Information please contact our EU
representative GPSR@taylorandfrancis.com
Taylor & Francis Verlag GmbH, Kaufingerstraße 24, 80331 München, Germany

www.ingramcontent.com/pod-product-compliance
Ingram Content Group UK Ltd.
Pitfield, Milton Keynes, MK11 3LW, UK
UKHW022000180926
475701UK00003B/117
* 9 7 8 0 4 1 5 8 6 0 9 7 0 *